Palgrave Macmillan's Postcolonial Studies in Education

Studies utilizing the perspectives of postcolonial theory have become established and increasingly widespread in the last few decades. This series embraces and broadly employs the postcolonial approach. As a site of struggle, education has constituted a key vehicle for the "colonization of the mind." The "post" in postcolonialism is both temporal, in the sense of emphasizing the processes of decolonization, and analytical in the sense of probing and contesting the aftermath of colonialism and the imperialism which succeeded it, utilising materialist and discourse analysis. Postcolonial theory is particularly apt for exploring the implications of educational colonialism, decolonization, experimentation, revisioning, contradiction, and ambiguity not only for the former colonies, but also for the former colonial powers. This series views education as an important vehicle for both the inculcation and unlearning of colonial ideologies. It complements the diversity that exists in postcolonial studies of political economy, literature, sociology, and the interdisciplinary domain of cultural studies. Education is here being viewed in its broadest contexts, and is not confined to institutionalized learning. The aim of this series is to identify and help establish new areas of educational inquiry in postcolonial studies.

Series Editors:

Antonia Darder holds the Leavey Presidential Endowed Chair in Ethics and Moral Leadership at Loyola Marymount University, Los Angeles, and is professor emerita at the University of Illinois, Urbana-Champaign.

Anne Hickling-Hudson is associate professor of Education at Australia's Queensland University of Technology (QUT) where she specializes in cross-cultural and international education.

Peter Mayo is professor and head of the Department of Education Studies at the University of Malta where he teaches in the areas of Sociology of Education and Adult Continuing Education, as well as in Comparative and International Education and Sociology more generally.

Editorial Advisory Board

Carmel Borg (University of Malta)
John Baldacchino (Teachers College, Columbia University)
Jennifer Chan (University of British Columbia)
Christine Fox (University of Wollongong, Australia)
Zelia Gregoriou (University of Cyprus)
Leon Tikly (University of Bristol, UK)
Birgit Brock-Utne (Emeritus, University of Oslo, Norway)

Titles:

A New Social Contract in a Latin American Education Context
Danilo R. Streck; Foreword by Vítor Westhelle

Education and Gendered Citizenship in Pakistan
M. Ayaz Naseem

Critical Race, Feminism, and Education: A Social Justice Model
Menah A. E. Pratt-Clarke

Actionable Postcolonial Theory in Education
Vanessa Andreotti

The Capacity to Share: A Study of Cuba's International Cooperation in Educational Development
Anne Hickling-Hudson, Jorge Corona Gonzalez, and Rosemary Preston

A Critical Pedagogy of Embodied Education: Learning to Become an Activist
Tracey Ollis

Culture, Education, and Community: Expressions of the Postcolonial Imagination
Edited by Jennifer Lavia and Sechaba Mahlomaholo

A Critical Pedagogy of Embodied Education

Learning to Become an Activist

Tracey Ollis

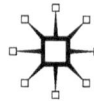

A CRITICAL PEDAGOGY OF EMBODIED EDUCATION
Copyright © Tracey Ollis, 2012.

All rights reserved.

First published in 2012 by
PALGRAVE MACMILLAN®
in the United States—a division of St. Martin's Press LLC,
175 Fifth Avenue, New York, NY 10010.

Where this book is distributed in the UK, Europe and the rest of the world, this is by Palgrave Macmillan, a division of Macmillan Publishers Limited, registered in England, company number 785998, of Houndmills, Basingstoke, Hampshire RG21 6XS.

Palgrave Macmillan is the global academic imprint of the above companies and has companies and representatives throughout the world.

Palgrave® and Macmillan® are registered trademarks in the United States, the United Kingdom, Europe and other countries.

ISBN: 978–0–230–34051–0

Library of Congress Cataloging-in-Publication Data

Ollis, Tracey.
   A critical pedagogy of embodied education : learning to become an activist / Tracey Ollis.
     p. cm.—(Postcolonial studies in education)
    ISBN 978–0–230–34051–0 (hardback)
   1. Critical pedagogy. 2. Social action—Study and teaching. 3. Teaching—Social aspects. I. Title.

LC196.O55 2012
370.11′5—dc23   2011040103

A catalogue record of the book is available from the British Library.

Design by Newgen Imaging Systems (P) Ltd., Chennai, India.

First edition: May 2012

10 9 8 7 6 5 4 3 2 1

Transferred to Digital Printing in 2013

Contents

Series Editors' Preface	vii
Preface	xiii
Acknowledgments	xvii
List of Acronyms	xix
1 A Critical Pedagogy of Activism	1
2 Case Study Research	21
3 The Politics of Adult Education	37
4 The Lifelong Activists	57
5 The Circumstantial Activists	109
6 Embodied Learning	163
7 Informal and Social Learning	187
8 A Critical Pedagogy of Embodied Education	209
Notes	227
Bibliography	231
Index	241

Series Editors' Preface

In 2011 and 2012, we witnessed major social actions that have resulted in a variety of social movements worldwide. Protestors in Tunisia sent President Zine El Abidine Ben Ali fleeing to Saudi Arabia; an estimated 1 million Egyptian protesters in Tahrir Square were the downfall of President Hosni Mubarak; in Libya, protestors eventually ended the 42-year presidency of Muammar Gaddafi; in Spain, more than 100 activist groups protested the expense of the World Youth celebrations in honor of Pope Benedict XVI's visit; and in London over 400,000 took to the streets to protest the toughest spending cuts since WWII. In addition, we have witnessed student protests in Vienna, Italy, Hungary, and London, among others, and also indignant protestors in Athens inveighing against the "debtocracy" in their respective countries.

The preface for this book was written just as 700 *Occupy Wall Street* activists were being arrested in New York City. Protests are erupting daily across the nation, as a "US autumn" emerges to push against neoliberal policies that have brought about an intensification of economic inequality in the United States—policies that have resulted in a mortgage debacle that caused massive numbers of homeowners to lose their homes, while a collapsing economy has ushered in a double digit unemployment rate, as millions of workers have lost their livelihood. All the while, the affluent 1 percent of the population continues to reap heavily the benefits of neoliberal "shock doctrine" practices, as Naomi Klein (2007) asserts, where the wealthy capitalize on times of economic downturn or natural disaster to appropriate resources from those of modest means. Hence, while the wealthy benefited from the hardships of the financially downtrodden, they also gained from an unprecedented government stimulus package, which corporate moguls spent irresponsibly, in the absence of clear and rigorous federal accountability measures. Such examples of corporate corruption among the affluent, in conjunction with major government cutbacks to social programs for those of modest means, has become today the central focus of a growing activism, which loudly declares, *We are the 99 percent.*

With an abundance of current examples of activism, whether on the streets, through social networks, or over independent air waves, there can be no better time for the release of Tracey Ollis's book, *A Critical Pedagogy of Embodied Education: Learning to Become an Activist*. This timely volume offers a much needed critical examination, which not only seeks to make meaning of the practices of activists within these neoliberal times (see also Foley, 1999) , but also considers thoughtfully and with specificity just what a critical pedagogy of activism looks like and what it can offer to those who find themselves in the midst of intense postcolonial shifts and a fury of social actions geared toward catapulting our societies toward an emancipatory politics of decolonization and a lived ethos of participatory democracy.

Although we often acknowledge activism as an important dimension of the postcolonial tradition—particularly when we speak of breaking the silence of subaltern voices or constructing a third space for those who have been historically disempowered and left voiceless at the margins of mainstream political life—seldom do we speak of a pedagogy of activism in ways that critically complicate the phenomenon, while systematically examining efforts to support its evolution. As a consequence, it is not surprising to find, as Paulo Freire (1971, 1985) often warned, that activism can easily become split from theory, therefore being devoid of praxis. This can happen because of a tendency to dwell on the urgency of action, without sufficient critical engagement of the deeper philosophical and ideological dimensions that inform political action beyond questions of the immediacy of strategy or tactics. Gramsci wrote of the need for spontaneity to be tempered by conscious direction. It remains to be seen whether this has been occurring in the several "springs" and "autumns" occurring in the North and South and on both sides of the Atlantic. This issue was repeatedly raised in reference to the UK riots.

It is this longstanding absence in our critical understanding of activism as a political necessity of democratic life and its processes of political formation and pedagogical development that Ollis carefully seeks to unveil, through a grounded empirical case study approach that highlights the similarities and differences in learning practices of activists in her native Australia. Her passionate belief in the rich and meaningful knowledge embedded in the everyday life of activists across the trajectories of their formation, along with the thoughtful inclusion of activist voices in her study, is what ultimately brings a vitality and power to her articulations of what she terms *lifelong activists* and *circumstantial activists*.

Utilizing the narratives of activists within a variety of settings and different life experiences, Ollis teases out the distinctions that exist in the identity formation of lifelong activists who develop through an extended period of involvement in movement work, as compared to circumstantial activists who find themselves suddenly thrust into the arena of activism. For the latter, a sudden and unexpected event emotionally catapults them into action, often fueled by an emotional agency that is far more disruptive and explosive than their counterparts, and can, without any careful direction, take a much different trajectory than that augured by observers on the Left. This important distinction serves as a significant breakthrough and philosophical departure in conceptualizing the different ways in which activists in these two camps embody knowledge, in order to make sense of their role as agents of change in the world.

Moreover, Ollis's notion of embodied learning is key to the manner in which she effectively utilizes experiences gleaned from activists, in order to "expand on existing knowledge of cognitive ways of knowing to include non-rational ways of knowing." This is, of course, of vital importance to the postcolonial educator who recognizes only too well that, within the Western tradition, embodied knowledge of the disempowered or disenfranchised has, for too long, been deemed suspect, illegitimate, or of little value to the process of knowing, even within some radical political circles. In contrast, Ollis rightly argues that it is impossible to truly understand the development and identity formation of activists without careful attention to the manner in which the whole body is implicated in their learning practices and in the evolution of their participation within social movements.

Also worthy of highlighting here is the manner in which Ollis grounds her analysis of activist learning in the literature of adult popular education. Scholarship on popular education and social movements has, over the years, documented and advanced consistently the vital role of adult education in social movement activism (O'Cadiz et al. 1998; Allman 1999; Mayo 1999; Kane 2001; Holst 2002; Kapoor 2004, 2009; Hall & Clover 2006; Borg & Mayo 2007). Through her critical engagement with the history and practice of radical adult education, popular education, communities of practice, and embodied learning, the volume provides a powerfully argued perspective on the role of activism in the process of social change.

More importantly, Ollis disrupts with insight and passion the one-dimensionality so typically associated with discourses on activism. By so doing, this groundbreaking study supports students, scholars, and activists within the postcolonial tradition to examine with both greater complexity and humanity the contemporary landscape of activist practices, as part of an important critical pedagogical tradition—a tradition that historically has worked to challenge hegemonic constraints of capitalism and its imperative formations tied to the violence of cultural invasion, social exclusions, and deep structures of economic inequality. In the face of these political and economic conditions of everyday life that function to thwart a pedagogy of activism, *A Critical Pedagogy of Embodied Education: Learning to Become an Activist* inspires and renews critical hope in the power of activism and social movements, in the midst of our current struggles for social justice, human rights, and economic democracy, around the globe.

References

Allman, P. 1999. *Revolutionary Social Transformation: Democratic Hopes, Political Possibilities and Critical Education*. Westport, CT: Bergin and Garvey.

Borg, C & Mayo, P. 2007. *Public Intellectuals, Radical Democracy and Social Movements: A Book of Interviews*. New York: Peter Lang.

Foley, G. 1999. *Learning in Social Action: A Contribution to Understanding Informal Education*. London and New York: Zed books

Freire, P. 1985. *The Politics of Education: Culture, Power and Liberation*. South Hadley, MA: Bergin and Garvey.

Freire, P. 1971. *Pedagogy of the Oppressed*. New York: Continuum.

Hall, B. L. & Clover, D. 2006. "Social Movement Learning," in R. Veira de Castro, A. V. Sancho, & P. Guimarães (eds.), *Adult Education: New Routes in a New Landscape*. Braga: University of Minho.

Holst, J. 2002. *Social Movements, Civil Society and Radical Adult Education*. Westport, CT: Bergin and Garvey.

Kane, L. 2001. *Popular Education and Social Change in Latin America*. London: Latin American Bureau.

Kapoor, D. 2004. "Popular Education and Social Movement in India," *Convergence*, Vol. 37, No. 2 (55–63).

Kapoor, D. 2009. "Globalization, Dispossession and Subaltern Social Movement (SSM) Learning in the South" in A. Abdi and D. Kapoor (eds.),

Global Perspectives on Adult Education. London and New York: Palgrave Macmillan.

Klein, N. 2007. *The Shock Doctrine: The Rise of Disaster Capitalism.* London, UK: Picador.

Mayo, P. 1999. *Gramsci, Freire and Adult Education: Possibilities for Transformation Action.* London, UK: Zed Books.

O'Cadiz, M. d' P., Lindquist Wong, P., & Torres, C. A. 1998. *Education and Democracy. Paulo Freire, Social Movements and Educational Reform in São Paulo.* Boulder, CO: Westview Press.

Preface

Personal Reflection on the children out of detention protest, Melbourne, Australia, 2011

On April 3, 2011, I attended a protest rally organized by the Refugee Action Collective (RAC). The rally brought together a diverse group of people concerned about current government policy in Australia regarding the detention of children and young people who are asylum seekers. At the time of the protest the Australian government detained more than 140 young asylum seekers from the ages of 13–17 in this center. More than a 1,000 young people are in detention in Australia overall. These young people, who originate from Iraq, Iran, and Afghanistan, have minimal contact with the outside world and limited opportunity to live the life afforded to most teenagers in Australia. They are unaccompanied by parents or relatives and many have fled war-torn countries. They are stateless young people; not only do they live where they are physically detained, they live in an "emotional prison" as well. They spend their days waiting for news about family, visas, security clearances, immigration, and citizenship. A large number of these young people are depressed and are on antidepressants, many have self-harmed, or have had thoughts of suicide.

This largely peaceful protest in Broadmeadows, at the Melbourne Immigration Transit Accommodation is a holding center for young refugees. Let there be no doubt that this is a detention center, although not expressed as such by the Federal Government of Australia. The center is surrounded by a large wire fence, with barbed wire on top and the facility is locked and guarded. As with most protests, there were a broad coalition of groups with an interest in social justice issues present at the rally. Activists from the Socialist Alliance (SA) Marxist groups, women's groups, groups concerned with the environment, and the organizers of the protest, The Refugee Action Collection (RAC).

Two performance artists wearing orange overalls, a representation of the prisoner detainees in Guantanamo Bay in Cuba and a symbol of the Global War on Terror, performed music. There were also many people who seemed new to protest. They appeared to be nonaligned with the usual array of protesters on refugee action. Many families, teenagers, and young children were present on this day. They were concerned about the issue of asylum seekers and refugee policy and about the detention of children and young people in the centre.

We marched for about a kilometer from Sydney to Camp roads, protesters carried balloons and protest signs with slogans such as "Human Rights Now," "No One is Illegal," "End Mandatory Detention," "Welcome Refugees," "Refugees are not Illegal," "No Off Shore Processing," and "Close the camps down." The red flags of the Marxist group were flown in the air. The protest had the atmosphere of a carnival, with so many children and parents there—it had the atmosphere of a family fun day. We arrived at the detention center, where there were many police present. There were a number of speakers, coordinated by RAC, including refugees, asylum seekers, and Australian migrants. One teenage boy spoke about how he had met some of the young refugees in the center and how his life differed so much from the lives of these young boys who were detained. It was a poignant and emotional speech. People chanted "shame" to the government's policy of determent of refugees; they chanted "shame" again to the policy of sending boats of refugees offshore to have their claims for asylum processed. Toward the end of the protest, three young refugees broke away from their minders, quickly scaled the barbed wire fence and joined the protesters. They were extremely anxious, in shock, and clearly traumatized from the experience of being detained, but they had wanted to join the protesters. Suddenly, the environment of the protest changed as the organizers and activists tried to grapple with the potential legalities of these young people having escaped from the detention centre. The refugees were injured from scaling the fence and the barbed wire, they needed medical attention, and they were anxious, distressed, and needed support. The organizers needed to regroup and make some quick decisions about this unplanned crisis. People crowded around the refugees, someone gave them water, wiped the young men's brows with wet towels, others organized medical attention and called an ambulance.

Suddenly one of the performance artists in a wheelchair chained himself to the locked gates in solidarity with the refugees who were detained. Protesters started shaking the gates, it was an aggressive act, with the potential for violent confrontation with the police. One of the organizers tried to stop this action pleading with the activists "Don't do this we want to build a broader movement, we don't want violence, we don't want to provoke the police." Suddenly, the disabled protester was sprayed with capsicum spray by the police, he fell out of his chair and lay on the ground in pain, he was angry and distressed, the protesters were moved back from the fence.

It was a protest filled with crisis and drama. The emotions displayed in this protest ranged from solidarity, passion, empathy, anger, and rage. The young refugees were shown a canvas of artwork that protesters had written on—they were messages of support to these young people, letting them know that many Australians welcomed them into their country. After some time, the organizers of the protest negotiated with the police and the Center staff to allow the refugees to return to detention peacefully and without reprisal for joining the protest.

An enormous array of skill had been used to pull together networks of hundreds of people for this event. It required knowledge, skill, and strategy. It also required the desire to be there on the day, it required agency and the desire to act, the desire to protest. What drove hundreds of activists on to the streets of Melbourne on that day, and what knowledge and skills were needed to successfully and skillfully manage a protest of this proportion? What drove people who had never been a part of a protest to be activists on that day? Who were these newcomers to protest? My experiences of this protest on asylum seekers and of others, and the skill and knowledge I have developed informally during my years as an activist, no doubt inform this book.

Acknowledgments

No book is ever written alone, it is always a reflection of conversations, ideas, experiences that have formed the whole of a life. I would like to acknowledge those people who have been on this journey with me.

Firstly, my partner Graeme McDonald who, over a long conversation over dinner one night, encouraged my interest in the "accidental activist" and my desire to make some sense of the activism that occurs outside of social movements. You have always been my greatest support, your sharp intellect and sense of humor has brought me through this journey.

There are many conversations that I have had with colleagues, mentors, and friends over the years of this research that I would like to acknowledge. I would like to thank Tony Kruger, Tarquam McKenna, Colleen Vale, Michelle Grossman, Lesley Birch, Jo Williams, Julie Stephens, Russell Wright, Deb Ollis, Charles Mphande, Elaine Swan, Robyn Broadbent, Donna Rooney, Jacques Boulet, Vicki McConville, Namgyal Dorjee, Rosie Finn, Colleen Hall, Nicole Pepperill, Jenny Macaffer, Des Cahill, Christine O'Callaghan, and David Hayward. Rachel Chamberlain, Kate Driscol, Russell Solomon, Jennifer Brooker, and Di Sisley kept me sane throughout the final stages of writing.

To my supervisors: Michael Hamel-Green, who first taught me as an undergraduate in community development many years ago and who has been an intellectual and activist mentor over many years. And to Merryn Davies, who has encouraged me to really think about the writing of the French philosopher Pierre Bourdieu and who equally shares a passion about education for social change. Together, you have inspired a research journey that is everything it should be—collegial, critical, intellectual, robust, and inquiry-based. I am extremely grateful to you both.

To Rob Townsend and Jen Couch, my dear friends and colleagues, you are, and continue to be, inspiring.

To my colleagues from Popular Education Network Australia (PENA), Jo Williams, Jorge Jorquera, Anne Harris, Rob Townsend, Liz Branigan, Rob Miller and Lea Campbell—your conversations, support, and solidarity have kept me passionate about social justice education.

I would like to thank the series editors Antonia Darder, Peter Mayo, and Anne Hickling-Hudson for believing in the importance of this research.

There are several academics whose writing I have long admired, David Beckett, Dianne Celia Hodges, and Antonia Darder—their writing helped me to find my voice—they taught me to be brave, they taught me to be bold and critical, most importantly, they taught me about the importance of education for social change.

To the activists who gave their time, energy, and insight into their important work, Cam Walker, Felicity Marlow, Jean McLean, Garry Rothman, Jorge Jorquera, Terry Hicks, Tricia Malowney, Tim Forcey, Bahar, Eva, Grace, Rose, Jonathan, Catherine, Max, Kerry and Andrew, I am in complete awe of your knowledge, agency, and skill. To progressive social change activists past and present around the world at this time and moment in the Occupy Movements, the Middle East Protests and others. I acknowledge your commitment, agency and action on some of the most important human rights and social justice issues of our time.

Finally, this book is dedicated to my children, Marcus, Oliver, Nilla, and my godson Rinchen; no doubt you will continue our custodial role of sustaining and nurturing this planet for the future.

Acronyms

ACE	Adult and Community Education
ABS	Australian Bureau of Statistics
ALP	Australian Labor Party
ASIO	Australian Security Intelligence Organisation
BLF	Builders Laborers Federation
CPA	Communist Party of Australia
DLP	Democratic Labor Party
DSP	Democratic Socialist Party
FAR	Fertility Access Rights
FCRC	Financial and Consumer Rights Council
FOE	Friends of the Earth
FP	Federal Police
GLBTI	Gay, Lesbian, Bisexual, Transgender, and Intersex
HEC	Higher Education Certificate
HSC	Higher School Certificate
HREC	Human Research Ethics Committee
LP	Liberal Party
MASA	Men Against Sexual Assault
NUS	National Union of Students
RCADC	Royal Commission in to Aboriginal Deaths in Custody
SA	Socialist Alliance
SOS	Save Our Sons
TAFE	Tertiary and Further Education
USA	United States of America
VCE	Victorian Certificate of Education
WETF	World Economic Trade Forum
WST	Worker Student Alliance
VACCA	Victorian Aboriginal Child Care Agency
YCL	Young Communist League

1
A Critical Pedagogy of Activism

Introduction

Why is there a need for a book on the pedagogy of activism at this time and epoch in history and, in particular, a book that examines the learning dimensions of social justice activists as they go about their important work? I write this book in the present international environment of nation-states' responding to a global financial crisis; there are riots in the United Kingdom and a global financial crisis affecting the economies of most of the countries of the world. The world appears to be in a time of great transition and upheaval. It is a time of immense social, economic, political, and environmental turmoil across the planet. In addition, in what some have called the "Arab Spring," revolutions have taken place in Egypt and Tunisia, largely spearheaded through prodemocracy protestors, pushing for an end to the power of oppressive regimes. Similarly, in Libya, a civil war is raging and it has seen the inevitable fall of the Gaddafi regime. At the same time, students protest in Chile for a more equal education system, and again in the United Kingdom against increased tuition fees. Moreover, the protest of the "occupy movements" are echoing around the world, as protestors challenge the dominance of neoliberal economic policy and the present global financial crisis. In this time of massive global change there are movements, all over the world, of people who are stateless and homeless due to flood, drought, fire, and war. In response to this, Western democracies such as Australia have largely tried to inhibit the entry of asylum seekers and refugees with a harsh policy of determent. There is a resurgence of concern about "the other", based on race, religion, and cultural difference. In response to these events, and others, many social justice activists around the world are engaged in protests of some kind about issues of inequality, discrimination, human rights, and injustice. Their important work, largely unpaid, is driven by desire and agency to make the planet a better place. As Margaret Meade has claimed: "Never doubt that a small group of thoughtful committed, citizens can change the world, indeed, it is the only thing that ever has."

No doubt, there is an enormous amount of skill that is developed as activists go about their important work, mainly informally and "on the job." This book gives recognition to the knowledge and skill development of these activists as they go about their social justice work. This book outlines the pedagogy of activism and the process of learning to become an activist. Based on empirical research conducted in Australia, it explores the embodied learning of activists as they learn to be and become activists. This book, in contrast to other writing on social purpose education, explores the differences and similarities between two groups of activists: Lifelong activists who have been engaged in campaigns and socials movements over many years, often a life time; and the learning of circumstantial activists—those protestors who come to activism due to a series of life events. I uncover, through multiple case studies, the embodied pedagogy of activists who gain knowledge through the practical experience of being in the world of activism. Their learning is often driven by emotional agency, is social, informal, and critically cognitive. Using critical pedagogy as a lens, the book not only expands our understanding of the epistemology of activism, but also provides insight into adult education as an embodied practice.

This chapter introduces the book topic and provides an overview of the journey of research. It outlines the epistemological framework of critical pedagogy and reveals its relevance to the learning practices of activists. My own positioning as a researcher and activist is introduced, and the chapter examines the emerging concept of the "circumstantial activist" by exploring the typology of lifelong and circumstantial activists used in the study. The contribution to knowledge that this book makes to the epistemology of adult learning lies in its exploration of the similarities and differences in activists' learning. A chapter-by-chapter outline of the book is provided so that the reader has a guide to comprehending and understanding the case study methodology used in the research revealing the narratives of activists' pedagogy. The activists' stories give insight into the ontology of activism and the learning practices that occur as activists go about their social justice work.

Defining Activism

This research demonstrates that the learning of activists is educationally rich and historically situated in the post-Enlightenment tradition of humanism (Kenny 2006, pp. 94, 95). Community development and activism "is a part of the project of modernity, [and] draws attention to the state in its creation of disadvantage." Kenny (2006) argues that activism is a strand of community development whereby people "strive continually to understand where the strategic opportunities for action lie" (p. 385). Resistance toward state apparatus in Australian society is not new as Australia is a Western democracy with a long history of trade unionism (Burgmann 2003). Social movements and social change in Australia have long been an important part of the political and social landscape (Maddison & Scalmer 2006). However, even as Australia was being colonized by Britain in the eighteenth century, there was resistance to invasion by Australian Aborigines, the Indigenous Australians (Burgmann 2003). Since the nineteenth century, activism in Australia has been connected to social movements encompassing issues such as women's suffrage, women's liberation, Indigenous land rights, civil rights, and reconciliation. Activism has also been associated with the peace and antinuclear movements, the antiwar protests of Vietnam and Iraq, the environmental movement in its various forms, and the anticorporate globalization movements. As Couch (2009) argues:

> From the salt mines to Seattle, throughout history, movements such as these have challenged and deposed dictators, stopped armies, undermined corporations, established basic human rights and halted entire industries, all without the use of violence (2009, p. 4).

Maddison and Scalmer (2006) argue there is a great deal to learn from the practical wisdom of activists (p. 7). For the purposes of this research, the scope of activism is shaped by the broad theories of community development that take into account practices such as policy development, community campaigning, community building, neighborhood development, popular education, and active involvement in social movements (Kenny 2006). However, there are different spaces and places of activism that are not always connected to social and political movements (Brown & Pickerill 2009; Jasper 2009). For example, circumstantial activists protest but do not always participate actively in social movements. Theorists such as Kenny (2006) have argued that the "activist model" of community development in Australia has its roots in "left" movements for social change such as feminism, socialism and environmentalism (pp. 202–3). Community development includes resistance toward the state and often includes direct action (Kenny 1999, 2006). However the broad ontology[1] of community development is always a project of progressive social change. This can occur through small acts of resistance to government policy to large public protests organized by established social movements (Kenny 2006). Kenny argues that activists such as Alinsky were informed by the theory of community development (Kenny 2006). Alinsky's (1971) activism brought people together in order to mobilize for social change, a primary project of community development theory and practice. Alinsky's (1971) activism was always a project of education. Many community workers are involved in social movements and campaign groups for social change—they are activists in nature because their everyday work in communities is focused around resistance of some kind (Ife & Tesoriero 2006). Mayo (2001) argues that social movements can learn a great deal from the theory and practice of community development: issues such as how to build a group and how to maintain a network of people. Activists need to have outstanding communication skills. They need to know how to resist change within the system as well as outside the system. It is argued that these skills are all informed by community development theory and practice:

> Whatever the difference in their perspectives…community development workers and activists need to share an increasingly sophisticated common core of knowledge and skills. To build community groups and develop community-based alliances, they need to be skilled in using participatory action research to analyse issues, alongside their communities, identifying potential allies and opponents and developing effective strategies accordingly (Mayo 2005, p. 101).

This book demonstrates how progressive activism and community development are inextricably connected. Resistance occurs in many ways through the mobilization of mass social movements and in the work of local and small community campaigns of resistance toward the state. My own positioning as an activist reflects my history of paid and unpaid work as a community development worker in the early 1980s, which always included an activist's approach of working toward broader political and social change in communities. I have continued to be involved in a range of social and political movements, sometimes as an activist in smaller campaigns and, at other times, by participating in protest as a part of wider social movements. Community development was often practiced alongside and together with social movements and campaign groups. I argue that activism that is informed by even the smallest acts of resistance in the everyday work of community workers is just as significant and important as the mass mobilization of thousands of people in direct protest.

Less well-understood is the notion of circumstantial activism, which is not included in present social movement theory and study. It is recognized that there are many activists who protest, but who do not necessarily relate to or have connections to formal political organizations or social movements (Brown & Pickerill 2009; Jasper 2009). This is a significant gap in the theory and practice of social movements. If we can understand the motivation and learning practices of circumstantial activists, social movements would be better placed to encourage and nurture participation of this distinct group of activists, building movement members and the capacity for greater resistance. In Australia, for example, an extended period of drought recently caused many individuals to become more committed and interested in climate change. These activists were not generally members of established social movements seeking broader structural responses to environmental issues. Instead, they were often working with small groups in their own communities. This is primarily because their activism was still emerging. Like other circumstantial activists, they were motivated by personal circumstances or a particular social issue, or by their transition to a time in life when they were more able to be actively involved in protests. Because these activists are not generally aligned with political parties or social movements, their learning is significantly underrepresented in the literature relating to radical adult education and social movement learning. This present research does not differentiate between activism that occurs locally in the everyday work of community workers and organizers, and the social and policy activism that happens within political systems of government, nor the activism of social movements and solidarity groups and networks. These practices of activism are all a call for social change of varying kinds.

The "Accidental Activist"

The concept of the "accidental activist" is central to this research. Circumstantial or accidental activists are those activists who have come to activism due to a series of life circumstances. In contrast to "lifelong activists," they have not usually been involved in social or political activism prior to their initial engagement in activism, nor have they obtained formal education in the arts, politics, law, or humanities—areas of education that have been traditionally associated with the formal education of activists (McAdam 1986). In conceiving this study, my starting point was to think about the differences and similarities for circumstantial activists in comparison to lifelong activists who had been involved in activism over an extensive period of time. More particularly, how did the learning experiences of these individuals differ from those of their more politically savvy peers?

In 2005, there were several campaigns that fascinated me and gained the attention of the Australian community. The "Friends of Van Nguyen,"[2] for example, was a campaign organized by two close friends of a young Australian under arrest in Singapore. Van Nguyen had been charged with trafficking drugs in Singapore and was eventually executed by the Singapore government. Another campaign was run by Terry Hicks in support of his son, David, who had been charged with aiding terrorism by the US government and was detained in the US detention centre at Guantanamo Bay. Terry's activism was pivotal in spearheading a local campaign that soon became national and then international in scale in response to concerns for the welfare of David Hicks and the other detainees (Ollis 2008a). Another campaign was run by Heather Osland,[3] imprisoned for more than nine years for murdering her husband, even though she did not strike the blow that killed him. Heather and her family had been exposed to domestic violence, sexual assault, and torture for more than fifteen years. These protestors and some of the people behind their powerful campaigns had not taken a traditional route to activism through student politics, nor were they people who appeared "ideologically aligned" with the "left" of politics, as is frequently the case with those activists who engage in progressive social change. Instead, a series of life circumstances had contributed to their becoming emotionally engaged and involved in campaigns of national importance and, in the case of David Hicks, of international concern. These specific campaigns were the initial catalyst for this research and the development of a typology of activism that explores the differences in learning for "circumstantial activists" and "lifelong activists" (Ollis 2008a).

Prelude to the Research

The final year of my master's of education degree focused on the broad epistemology of informal learning, workplace learning, and social learning, theories that have dominated the liberal education landscape both the Australian and the international context, for some time (Lave & Wenger 1991; Wenger 1998; Goud & Garrick 1999; Eraut 2000; Beckett & Hager 2002; Engeström 2007). I resolved that much of my own learning had been social and informal and that the same could be applied to my own work as an activist. The central idea that was developing even in the late days of my master's degree was that a social and informal learning epistemology could be applied to the learning of activists. Dewey (1937) believed that all learning begins with a state of confusion and that this confusion leads to a search for answers. Freire (1972b) claimed that learning occurs through critical questioning. As I questioned, explored, mused, and analyzed the weaknesses and strengths of these various theories of learning, I did not realize at the time that these ideas were developing into the foundation for a dissertation.

The main focus for this enquiry was to highlight and hold up to view activists' learning as a legitimate way of knowing or as "really useful knowledge"(Johnson 1988).[4] Little research had been completed on the pedagogy of activism in Australia. This was of concern, particularly because learning experiences in social action are educationally so rich. Branagan and Boughton (2003) argue that, in Australia, "the study of learning in activism continues to be in its formative years and has only recently been recognized as 'real' adult education" (p. 347). Yet, as outlined in chapter 2 of this book, the history of radical adult education is more than a century old with origins in the Marxist schools of the Communist Party of Australia (CPA) (Boughton 2005) and the activities of other social movements (Foley 1999, 2001; Burgmann 2003; Boughton, Taksa, & Welton 2004). Yet, in spite of this history, the universal focus on behaviorism in education policy and practice has continued throughout the twentieth century and still remains the dominant epistemology in Australia and in Western European education (Beckett & Morris 2004). I argue that the dominance of behaviorism in educational pedagogy has privileged some epistemologies of learning at the cost of others, including learning in radical adult education. Therefore, this research is, in itself, a process of activism in that it gives voice to the pedagogy of activists and demands that their knowledge and skill be recognized in the mainstream epistemology of adult learning in Australia.

Activist as Researcher

I have always been an activist, even before I knew what the term meant. The values of post-Enlightenment humanism really made an impression on me. Growing up in the 1970s as a teenager, a post Vietnam War adolescent, I encountered a world that was changing rapidly. Youth counter-culture and feminism are key examples of the social movements that were influential during my adolescence. I was growing up on the wave of new social movements (Crossley 2002; Burgmann 2003; Mayo 2005).[5] I understood that the second wave of the women's movement, the peace movement, the environmental movements and the antinuclear movements were changing Australian society and the rest of the world. Then on November 11, 1975, the prime minister of Australia, Gough Whitlam, was sacked by the then governor general Sir William Kerr. This event created a crisis for Australia's "constitutional monarchy."[6] I remember wondering how a political event could have such an impact, not only on an individual but on the whole of society. I remember, at the age of 14, arguing with people around me about the dismissal, and there was a stirring of political consciousness within myself and others. These events realize Dewey's observation that all inquiry starts with a state of confusion, precipitating a naive questioning that could lead to a solution. As Dewey writes: "to see that a situation requires inquiry is the initial step in the inquiry"(Price 2000). All activism, in fact all politicization, is an invitation to learning. To be politicized is to learn. This event of 1975 sparked an awakening. I started to realize that the nation's economy, politics, and society were intrinsically connected in some way. This naïve structuralism, combined with the development of my early feminist and Marxist politics, was pivotal during my early learning as an undergraduate student and young adult (Althusser 1969).

Theory has always been important to me. It has allowed me to build meaning and to develop my own criticality, to explore ideas, to understand systems, to understand the role of civil society in developing a more humane world, and, more importantly, to understand the concept of resistance. bell hooks (1994) argues that theory helped her to make sense of her own life: "I saw in theory then a location for healing" (p.59). As a woman growing up black and working class, hooks turned to theory to help her understand the world. As the daughter of a working class migrant, I also saw in theory a way to understand difference in society. In effect, theory can help you find your voice; it can help you understand inequality and hegemony (Gramsci 1971). Theory can also provide insight into what needs to be challenged and changed. Like many of the lifelong activists interviewed for this study, I was involved in student politics in the early 1980s. One of the first campaigns that I was involved with was a campaign to get tenure for the academics in the performing arts course in which I was enrolled. I also campaigned for more women's roles to be performed at the performing arts school at James Cook University in North Queensland. These early days of activism later broadened to my involvement in campaigns connected to the women's movement (focusing on issues including access to abortion and domestic violence), union issues and, later on, a lifelong commitment to housing rights activism. Most of my paid and unpaid work has entailed working in community development or as an unpaid activist to instigate change for women, public housing tenants, and the homeless. As an activist educator for the last 17 years, I have learned a great deal from the students that I have taught in various community development courses, both at Tertiary and Further Education (TAFE) and at other higher education institutions. Many of these students have been migrants and refugees who have fled civil war in their own country. Many are now employed as community development workers and are engaged in issues of social justice, human rights and activism in their own communities. I see in their learning the powerful and transformative practices of activism as they work for social change. My own experience of teaching and practicing community development, and those early and continuing experiences of being involved in social movements as an activist inform and influence this book.

The Importance of a Book on Activists' Pedagogy

This research makes a contribution to the epistemology of adult education. It contributes to the field of radical adult education, a much neglected tradition of adult education that views education as an emancipatory process (Newman 1994, 2006; Foley 1999). In Australia, much of the theorizing in radical adult education to date has afforded attention to critical learning or critical thinking (Foley 1999, 2001), acknowledging, for example, that activists gain structural knowledge about systems and structures, and that they learn to reframe discourses about the world around them (Branagan & Boughton 2003; Jesson & Newman 2004). Analysis of learning in social action gives prominence to the informal nature of the pedagogical practices of activists (Foley 1999). This knowledge is often viewed as tacit and implied and not always identified or articulated as knowledge or as a learning process (Foley 1999). Even present statistics on adult education in Australia collected by the Australian Bureau of Statistics (ABS) largely exclude the informal learning that occurs in popular education movements, local campaigns, and social movements, focusing instead on self learning and informal learning practices (Pink 2007). Thus, Australian research to date does not include the "really useful pedagogy" of these activists. The purpose of this study is to highlight the rich learning of activists as they work informally and socially through the practices of activism. The empirical research presented here, collected through in-depth interviews with 17 activists, introduces a typology of activism that contrasts learning between lifelong activists and circumstantial activists and explores the differences and similarities in their learning (Ollis 2008a).

Whilst there is research in Australia that focuses on the learning practices of activists in social movements, the emphasis is mainly on the critical learning of activists (Foley 1999; Whelan 2002, 2005b; Boughton, Taksa, & Welton 2004; Boughton 2005). More recently, scholarship on activism in social movements has focused on the practical wisdom of activists, which they regard as largely informal (Maddison & Scalmer 2006). Such approaches, however, have emphasized a sociopolitical analysis of activism rather than offer a detailed exposition of activists' learning experiences (Foley 1999). This research examines and expands on the existing knowledge of radical adult education by introducing two groups of activists.

The first group has a lifelong history of engagement in activism characterized by involvement in student politics, political parties and social movements. In comparison, the second group of activists are circumstantial activists, those like Terry Hicks, who, through a series of life circumstances, come to activism having not generally been involved with social movements or campaigning previously (Jasper 2009). As Jasper reminds us, there are many people who protest, but who are not necessarily engaged in social movements. Thus, their learning practices are often excluded from mainstream theorizing on learning in social movements (Jasper 2009). This research seeks to make a contribution to adult education, and education in general, by examining the learning practices of these activists who are often outside formal social movements, in comparison to their seemingly more politically savvy peers. There is limited evidence to date in Australia or overseas that explores the learning of circumstantial activists, or those who protest and participate in activism but do not necessarily identify with or participate in social movements (Brown & Pickerill 2009). Social movement theorists have argued for research to be conducted that looks at the motivations of activists who protest outside of social movements (Jasper 2009). We need to understand why they are participating and, more importantly from the perspective of this study, to understand their pedagogical practices (Jasper 1998, 2009; Crossley 2002; Eyerman 2005; Brown & Peckerill 2009).

This empirical research explores ways in which activists' learning is embodied, and how the use of the whole person informs how they "make meaning" and their "ways of knowing." This learning can be embedded in significant identity change as they learn to be and become activists. Activists use emotions, reason, cognition, and the physical body to make meaning (Ollis 2008a, 2008b). They develop instrumental knowledge about world systems of government and politics (Jesson & Newman 2004) and, significantly, their learning is rooted in the "junk" category of knowledge (Schön 1983). The junk category of knowledge is learning associated with activists' concrete material experiences of the world that they inhabit. Learning is both informal, situated, and social (Lave & Wenger 1991). Activists learn from one another on the job of activism. Through situating themselves in the practices of activism and through socialization with one another, they develop a habitus of practice and, through time, space, and the opportunity to practice they become experts at what they do (Bourdieu 1977).

Apprenticeship learning in activism, particularly in the environment of student unions and social movements, is a significant finding of the research as activists often use the support, assistance, and guidance of mentors (Lave 1996). In the tradition of apprenticeship, newcomer activists are mentored by activists who are more experienced and masterful. For the lifelong activists in this study, the role of apprenticeship learning is evident from their early practice, before they become master practitioners themselves. This happens through the development of a "community of practice" such as student political environments (student unions) at university, or political organizations and social movements (Lave & Wenger 1991).

This research has confirmed that circumstantial activists' learning is both informal and social. They learn about the world of activism, they learn about state, national, and international systems of government, and they learn to use the media (Foley 1999; Branagan & Boughton 2003; Jesson & Newman 2004). While many of them may have an apprenticeship-like relationship with a mentor who assists in the development of their skills, for many circumstantial activists this occurs outside of the usual learning spaces of social movements and student politics. A different trajectory of learning takes place for these activists, in comparison to the lifelong activists in this study. Circumstantial activists are frequently taken out of their comfort zones as learners. They need to develop knowledge and skill very quickly to be able to practice effectively as activists. This is rapid learning on the job of activism or what is sometimes referred to as "the hot action" of practice (Beckett & Hager 2002). Some of the circumstantial activists remain on the periphery of activism and never fully merge into a similar practice with the other activists with whom they work (Wenger 1998). Their involvement in protests stems from life circumstances that may have changed them in some way but not led them to fully identify as activists. Nonetheless, their skill and knowledge, like that of the lifelong activists in this study, is significant.

This research establishes that the holistic learning practices of both groups of activists are sophisticated, intelligent, and skillful, and that there is much to learn from their intelligent use of their bodies. This research, therefore, makes a contribution to understanding of radical adult education, and to adult education and education in general. The research emphasizes the importance of moving from rationalist approaches to pedagogy to an embodied way of knowing (Crossley 2008). It challenges behaviorist constructions of knowledge associated with the current paradigms of learning in Australia and in Western education. It is hoped that this book highlights the significant learning practices of these activists and gives their learning the prominence it deserves.

Central Research Questions

What Are the Stages and Processes of Learning and Identity Formation for Activists Engaged in Social Action?

This question is central to understanding the learning practices of activists. The research is guided by the assumption that activists' learning processes are very rich and embedded in their daily practices (Newman 1994; Foley 1999). To understand their learning practices, the study explores how they came to activism and what knowledge they developed through practicing activism. Using a broad epistemological lens of critical pedagogy (Freire, 1972; Darder 2003; Brookfield 2005) and philosophy (Merleau-Ponty 1962; Bourdieu, 1977) this research seeks to understand the learning that occurs while activists learn to change the world (Branagan & Boughton 2003). What are the differences and similarities in learning for circumstantial (newcomer) activists and more experienced lifelong (old timer) activists? What knowledge and skill do they need to be effective in their practices? What are the necessary conditions for activists to learn effectively? The sub-questions below seek to expand upon these issues by exploring the stages and phases of learning in activism. They include questions relating to informal and formal learning processes, explore the development of identity formation, and the role that circumstances play in becoming an activist. If learning to become an activist is a process of identity work, do circumstantial and lifelong activists experience this identity change in the same way?

Subsidiary Questions

What Is the Role of Formal and Informal Learning in the Learning of Activists?

This research is not focused on formal transmission models of knowledge that dominate the liberal education landscape in Australia and overseas, because activists rarely learn this way. In chapter 3 of this book, the existing literature is examined, revealing that adult activists' learning is largely informal (Newman 1994; Chase 2000; Whelan 2002, 2005b; Branagan & Boughton 2003; Jasper & Goodwin 2004; Maddison & Scalmer 2006; Goodwin & Jasper 2009). This research seeks to understand the learning that occurs for activists in their everyday practices in communities and social movements, and what motivates and sustains their participation in activism. Drawing on

Lave and Wenger's (1991) theory of situated learning or "communities of practice" and Bourdieu's (1977) theory of habitus, this subquestion seeks to examine the situated learning of activists as they commune and socialize with one another on the job of activism. This is explored in detail in the discussion presented in chapter 7.

How Does an "Activist Identity" Develop in the Course of Activism and Activists' Learning?
A great deal of research into the informal and social learning tradition has focused on the role of identity and identity formation in learning to become a worker or learner (Chappell et al. 2003; Soloman 2003). The postmodern notion of the "self" as a project of identity development–that we learn to become who we are in the daily business of being in the world–is explored (Merleau-Ponty 1962). Research has shown that if activists are educated and middle class they are more likely to participate in social movements (McAdam 1986). In addition, there is some indication that religion has a role to play in whether or not individuals are more likely to be activists. The research examines the processes of identity formation that occurs for adult activists and considers if there are any significant differences in identity formation between the lifelong and circumstantial activists in this study.

What Part Do Circumstances Play in "Becoming an Activist"?
As previously stated, there is evidence that some people who participate in protest often do so outside of social movements and political organizations (Jasper & Goodwin 2004). It is important to examine the learning of both groups in detail to understand the differences and similarities in their learning practices. I also wanted to explore the important contribution that these activists make to progressive social change. Many of these activists come to activism because of a series of events or life circumstances, and for some of these protestors, deeply personal circumstances have contributed to their taking action. These activists come to protest, initially with very little understanding of the political practices and processes of social change, and they generally have limited knowledge of social movements. But they engage in campaigning nonetheless. Some activists are said to "play" at being an activist before they actually identify and become one (McAdam 1986). Will they continue to be involved in activism over the longer term?

What Are the Facilitating Conditions for Improving and Supporting Activists' Learning?
This subquestion seeks to explore the conditions necessary for learning to occur through activism. How can we facilitate, improve, and support activists' learning? Providing the necessary conditions for activists' pedagogy is an important focus of this inquiry and is discussed in detail in chapter 8, A Critical Pedagogy of Embodied Education. By understanding how and what activists learn, it is hoped that this study will assist social movements and community groups to understand what they can do to offer and improve the conditions necessary within their organization for learning to take place.

Book Structure

The book commences by outlining the context for the contribution that this empirical research makes to the learning tradition of adult education. The book is constructed around the use of multiple case studies (Stake 2006) primarily to give an in-depth understanding of the complexity and richness of activists' learning. The case studies are complemented by chapters that first contextualize, and then provide a thematic analysis of the data. The order of the chapters and the research data is presented below.

Chapter 2—Case Study Research—examines the epistemological framework for this empirical research. Using the theory of phenomenology in a qualitative research paradigm (Denzin & Lincoln 2000), this qualitative research is a process of social change in itself (Kincheloe & McLaren 2000). The method of case study research and multiple case study research is discussed (Stake 1995, 2003, 2006). It examines the initial and early stages of a developing inquiry into activists' pedagogy and the desire to explore activists' social and informal learning. The chapter unpacks the research process from the early stirrings of initial inquiry, to the development of a research proposal. It goes on to examine the data collection phase where seventeen in-depth interviews were conducted with activists including nine lifelong activists and eight circumstantial activists. Informed consent processes and confidentiality processes for the use of data are described. The ethical considerations of the research are also examined. The chapter concludes by covering the critical attention given to the research data in the research supervision process.

Chapter 3—The Politics of Adult Education—gives an overview of the literature that underpins this study. It focuses, in particular, on the literature relating to the learning traditions of radical adult education (Jesson & Newman 2004), popular education (Freire 1972b), informal learning (Foley 1999), social learning in communities of practice, (Lave 1991; Lave & Wenger 1991) and embodied learning (Beckett & Hager 2002; Beckett & Morris 2004; Hunter 2004; O'Loughlin 2006; Beckett 2008). These traditions of adult learning set the framework and context for this study. The literature reveals the problem associated with activists' pedagogy being viewed through a prism of rationalism or the critical intelligence of activists, with little reference to the agency the emotions provide in activists' desire to act on issues of social injustice.

Chapter 4—The Lifelong Activists—draws on the data from interviews to outline the early stages and phases of their learning. It examines the importance of early involvement in student politics, or politics in general, at university and highlights the significance of socialization into political ways of knowing that families, teachers, and mentors play in the lives of these lifelong activists. The research reveals that the identity formation of the lifelong activists occurs incrementally over an extended period of time. Their learning practices are largely informal, social, and embodied. These activists have developed an extensive repertoire of practices, and have had significant exposure to mentors, social movements, and political organizations. More experienced activists develop expertise in event management and planning. There is a spiritual and emotional dimension to the development of activists' knowledge. These activists are committed to the post-Enlightenment ethos of utilitarianism and humanism and have a profound commitment to making the world a better place. There is also a spiritual dimension to their learning: they view their activism as a calling. These activists believe they are meant to be there.

The case studies provide an opportunity for the stories of the activists to be a central part of this book. The case studies highlight the narratives of Jorge Jorquera, Felicity Marlowe, Cam Walker, and Kerry, activists who have been engaged in social and political movements for many years. The important role that student politics plays as a socializing space for novice activists is highlighted in all of the case studies apart from one. The importance of activists' socialization with other activists and the informal learning that occurs through socializing is a significant finding of this research. Similarly, the role that mentors play in assisting the skill and knowledge development of activists is uncovered in this chapter.

Chapter 5—The Circumstantial Activists—provides an overview of the data for this emerging group of activists, those who come to activism due to a series of life circumstances. Like lifelong activists, circumstantial activists are shown to learn mainly informally and through socialization with one another. The data reveals the embodied nature of learning associated with emotional agency in circumstantial activists, for their passion and anger are frequently reported as accounting for their initial impetus to take action. This emotional agency can be disruptive and explosive. However, activists also report a spiritual dimension to their way of knowing. It is argued that circumstantial activists are rapid learners and that they often learn a great deal of new knowledge about political systems of government and social issues in a very short period of time. They are not always connected to social movements and often protest outside of these formal structures. The shift in the self occurs very quickly and is, at times, in contradiction to previously held political beliefs and values. Rapid identity work on the self occurs as they learn to be, and become, activists.

The case studies of Terry Hicks, Catherine, Tim Forcey, and Grace, presented here, reveal the unique role that circumstances played in these activists' decisions to protest, and looks at their rapid knowledge and skill development that occurred along the way. The chapter explores issues of identity for circumstantial activists. Some hesitate to identify themselves as activists because of a perceived radical connotation to activism. They are often out of their "comfort zone" and need to learn skills quickly in order to be effective in their practice as activists.

Chapter 6—Embodied Learning—uses theory to synthesize the data and illuminate the findings of the research. It is argued that activists' learning is embedded in their being-in-the-world of activism (Merleau-Ponty 1962). Activists use the whole body in their development of knowledge; they use reason, emotions, and the physical body in their learning practices (Ollis 2008a). A critique of the historical dominance of behaviorism in adult education in Australia is provided with its focus on performance, behavior change, exams, and benchmarking learners' performance against one another. Rather than giving importance to practical knowledge often learned through experience (Beckett & Morris 2004). I argue that the focus on cognition and rationalism in the understanding of activists' pedagogy and radical adult education should be expanded to include embodied ways of knowing (Jesson & Newman 2004). There is a need to expand on the existing knowledge of cognitive ways of knowing to include non-rational ways of knowing. This chapter argues that activists' learning is firmly positioned in the "junk category" of knowledge, which stems from their concrete material experiences of the world (Schön, D 1983). The emotions are central to how they make meaning and, as they develop greater expertise, they learn to practice emotional management (Hochschild 1979). Communicative learning, focusing on the skills activists develop through community education and interacting with the media, is explored as well as the influence of spirituality on developing activists' agency.

Chapter 7—Informal and Social Learning—builds on the existing knowledge of the informal nature of learning in radical adult education. Using the theory of "communities of practice" (Lave & Wenger 1991) the chapter explores the social and informal nature of activists' pedagogy. Bourdieu's (1977) "habitus" is used to expand on Lave and Wenger's theory of situated learning in communities of practice. Bourdieu's theory of habitus and Merleau-Ponty's existential phenomenology is applied in order to understand the importance of activists' somatic learning in the spaces and places of activism (Merleau-Ponty 1962). The formal learning of activists is described as well as the autodidactic knowledge development of organizers (Bourdieu 1984). Finally, this chapter explores the skills developed by activists whilst they are engaged in the "hot action" of practice, and asks: how do circumstantial activists develop greater expertise (Beckett & Hager 2002)? The central argument presented in this chapter is that circumstantial activists develop knowledge and skill over a very short period of time. There is an important role that significant mentors play in passing on their knowledge and skills to novice activists.

Chapter 8—A Critical Pedagogy of Activism—provides a summary of the research findings and outlines the significant learning of activists that has been demonstrated in this empirical research. Recommendations are made for facilitating the learning practices of activists, which emphasize the importance of providing opportunities for social and informal learning through developing communities of practice. The chapter concludes imagining how a critical pedagogy of embodied education could be shaped in the spaces and places of teaching and learning in general, and in activists' communities in particular. Here, I explore some of the pedagogical practices that move beyond transition models of education associated with rationalism, behaviorism, individuals, and objectivity. To develop a critical pedagogy that engages explicitly with relations of power, and gives prominence to the collective learning in popular education and social movements for progressive social change. I argue for a dialectical and reflexive view of theory and practice (praxis) and a dialogical engagement in teaching and learning.

2

Case Study Research

Introduction

This chapter outlines the methodological design of the research, the research questions, the aims of the research, and the methods chosen. Using a postpositivist framework of inquiry, this qualitative study uses the theory of phenomenology to inform the research process (Denzin & Lincoln 2000). The research crosses the boundaries of two disciplines, one represented by the theoretical tradition of social sciences and the other by the education tradition of adult learning. The research is inductive and framed by the activists' stories. By using a multiple case study approach to the research (Stake 1995, 2003, 2006), the stories of activists are held up to view and their learning is identified, while still enabling the readers to construct their own interpretation of the narratives embedded in the case studies. My own experiences as an activist are positioned within the methodology so that they serve as a guide for the research and, in doing so, enable this study to explore the complexity of conducting research where the researcher is positioned as both outsider and insider. Finally, an outline of the research methods is given and the scope and limitations of the research are discussed.

Qualitative Research

The primary methodological approach for this study is the qualitative research paradigm (Denzin & Lincoln 2000; Merriam 1998), which, in this instance, draws on an interpretive epistemology (Liamputtong &

Ezzy 2005). The research is constructivist (Merriam 1998; Denzin & Lincoln 2000; Kincheloe & McLaren 2000; Stage & Manning 2003) and therefore develops knowledge according to its construction by the researcher based on an interpretation of the data and the literature (Liamputtong & Ezzy 2005). It is also a "critically hermeneutic" research, which acknowledges that in "knowledge work" there is only interpretation of the research, as opposed to factual findings (McLaren & Kincheloe 2007, p. 24). The researcher is immersed in the process of research as an active participant (Merriam 1998; Stage & Manning 2003).

Much consideration was given to the research design of the study. This was important in setting the boundaries required for the collection and analysis of the personally revealing narratives. The framework of the research has been revised, adapted and changed over the course of the study to accommodate participants' needs. Research is not a static process but one that is fluid, and changing (Clough & Nutbrown 2002). The complexity of the choices a researcher makes in terms of methodology and overall research design are well described by Clough and Nutbrown (2002) who state:

> At the heart of these interwoven research activities are endless processes of selection; and in constantly justifying this selection, a "good" methodology is more a critical design attitude to be found always at work throughout a study, rather than confined within a brief chapter called "methodology" (p. 31).

The constructivist (Denzin & Lincoln 2000) nature of this inquiry allows the researcher to delve more deeply into the learning practices of activists. From the outset, the research processes sought to gain in-depth information from the participants and the design and the methods were chosen with the purpose of uncovering rich data. The nature of constructivist research is "inductive and interpretative" (Stage & Manning 2003, pp. 20–21). In this instance, there is a focus on the individuals' experiences of learning in activism rather than on the collective experience of group or social movements, because learning is often a deeply personal journey. While there may be a shared context for the journey, or similarities in activists' stories, no two learning experiences will be the same. The constructivist nature of this research allows these experiences to be explored, unpacked and analyzed to uncover or construct an interpretation of the nature of the learning that takes place.

Phenomenology

This research is influenced by the philosophy of phenomenology. As Price (2000) argues, "Phenomenology is the philosophy of experience. It attempts to understand how meaning is made in human experience, and it sees experiences of the world as the foundation of meaning" (p. 436). The empiricist nature of phenomenological research situates people's individual and collective experiences in the "life world." Therefore, the individual's experience is influenced by the world and his/her interaction in it. Phenomenology's premise of "being-in-the-world" (Price 2000, p. 447), and a rejection of objectivism in research, allows the researcher and the activists interviewed in this study to participate in a way that values and legitimates their experiences, their learning practices and, more importantly, activists' own perceptions of their learning. By analyzing their experiences, this book will provide a comprehensive understanding of what promoted or impeded activists' learning.

Research as Social Change

Being an activist myself, I have long admired the ability of other activists to develop extensive knowledge very quickly and to develop, with great efficiency, an often specialized area of expertise. I had been introduced to a body of knowledge called "critical pedagogy" while studying for my master's degree at the University of Melbourne, which uses a broad critical theoretical lens (Freire & Shor 1987; hooks 1994, 2003b; Kincheloe & McLaren 2000; Darder, Baltadano, & Torres 2003; Brookfield 2005; Freire, Freire, & Freire 2005). Critical pedagogy places issues of inequality, race, class, gender, ability, and social change at the center of educational theorizing. This paradigm is sometimes referred to as social purpose education or education for democracy (Armstrong & Miller 2006). I identified with the social change aspect to this pedagogical approach to education, which draws on the critical theoretical tradition of the Frankfurt School in Germany (Marcuse 1964; Adorno 1969; Horkheimer 1974; Habermas 1984), the writings of Paulo Freire (Freire 1972b, 1974), as well as the work of the French philosopher Michel Foucault (1980, 1983, 1988). A critical pedagogical framework requires that education should be seen as a process of social change; critical pedagogy also highlights inequality and differences in education (Brookfield 2005). Darder,

Baltadano, & Torres (2003) eloquently outline the broad social justice agenda of critical pedagogy, stating:

> Critical Pedagogy loosely evolved out of a yearning to give some shape and coherence to the theoretical landscape of radical principles, beliefs and practices that contributed to an emancipatory ideal of democratic schooling in the United States in the twentieth century. In many ways it constituted a significant attempt to bringing an array of divergent views and perspectives to the table, in order to reinvigorate the capacity of radical educators to engage critically with the impact of capitalism and gendered, radicalized relations upon the lives of students of historically disenfranchised populations (p. 2).

Why Are You Doing "Objectivist" Research?

I was recently asked by a friend, a colleague and a fellow activist, why I was "doing objectivist research." This observation was made because I had refused to interview her for my research. I thought that as a friend and activist she would be "too close" and interviewing her would potentially make my analysis "too subjective." In her own PhD thesis, she had positioned herself as a researcher/activist and had interviewed many people with whom she had engaged in activism over a long period. This enabled me to reflect on the "discourses of objectivism and subjectivism" and on my own position as a researcher in relation to these discourses. I deliberately did not choose the research methodology generally associated with social change research—Participatory Action Research (Wadsworth 1997). I wanted to have a level of distance between myself, the participants in the research, and the data. I wanted to tell activists' stories because not all activists' experiences are generic; they are heterogeneous. Being someone concerned with power and power relations, I believed my role as researcher invariably gave me greater control over the research process and the research findings. However, this research was connected with my own empirical positioning as an activist. Whelan (2002) explored the complexity of insider/outsider research in his PhD thesis. Whelan, also an activist engaged in the environment movement, argues in relation to insider/outsider positioning that:

> Insider research presents strengths and weaknesses, opportunities and risks. One potentially negative consequence of complete participation or immersion which is identified by Seale (1998: 226) is that researcher's risk "going native" or developing "over rapport." Seale encourages

participant researchers to develop "marginality" by balancing familiarity and distance or "strangeness" in order to understand the perspectives of informants (Whelan 2002, p. 192).

While Whelan went on to position himself, like my colleague, as an activist/researcher, I have chosen to maintain a position of distance between myself and the data in the manner suggested by Seale, who refers to "balancing familiarity and distance or strangeness" (Seale cited in Whelan 2002, p. 192). While my own experiences as an activist resonate with many of the experiences of the lifelong activists in this study, many experiences of circumstantial activists do not. To presume that my own learning is similar in any way to that of someone like Terry Hicks[1] is preposterous, at best. It is arguable, therefore, that this research is subjective research but with a level of distance between myself as the researcher and the research participants.

The research aims evolved from the central premise that there were differences and similarities in circumstantial and lifelong activists' learning. They also developed based on the assumption that activists' learning practices do not just focus on cognitive ways of knowing. Most research to date has focused on cognition, reason, and the intellectual capacity of activists' learning (Newman 1994, 2006; Foley 1999; Branagan & Boughton 2003; Boughton, Taksa, & Welton 2004). Limited attention has been paid to embodied or emotional ways of knowing. Adult learning is often a journey associated with a change in the "self" so the research also sought to uncover the identity change that occurs as activists "learn to become an activist" (Chappell et al. 2003). The social change focus is intended to enable this research to explore ways in which civil society groups can facilitate the learning practices of activists.

Case Study Research

The case study method has been used for the purpose of providing rich data about individual activist's learning, or what are sometimes described as thick descriptions of the actual phenomenon being studied (Merriam 1998). The use of case studies illuminates activists' learning through their autobiographical accounts by producing an account of their being, becoming, and learning as activists. As Stake (2003) argues,

> Case studies need accurate description and subjective, yet disciplined interpretation; a respect and curiosity for culturally different perceptions

of phenomena and emphatic representation of local settings—all blending (perhaps clumped) within a constructivist epistemology (p. 149).

These case studies present activists' experiences as a primary source of data, using biographical material obtained from the semistructured interviews to inform the overall picture of activists' learning. Secondary data sources such as artifacts, documents and records have occasionally been used (Silverman 2001). These qualitative case studies are heuristic as well as particularistic; they are focused on the particular phenomenon of activists' learning practices (Merriam 1998, p. 29). The purpose of heuristic case study research is to focus on the experiences of participants within a social context (Stage & Manning 2003). In this instance, the interview findings are used to highlight the minor and major themes in the research. Some interviews have been developed into case studies with the inclusion of other biographical and documentary material to illustrate specific stories or narratives that emerge from the research (Stake 1995, 2006).

> More commonly than not, case study research in education is conducted so that specific issues and problems of practice can be identified and explained; researchers in education often draw upon other disciplines such as anthropology, history, sociology and psychology both for theoretical orientation and for techniques of data collection and analysis (Merriam 1998, p. 34).

Multiple Case Study Research

This research uses multiple case studies to illuminate participants' experiences of being and becoming activists. The multiple case study approach analyses individual case studies with reference to the whole or multiple case studies, which Stake (2006) defines as the "quintain" (p. vi). The case researcher becomes a biographer, writing and interpreting the "life histories" of the in-depth cases chosen to highlight particular themes that arise in the study (Stake 1995, pp. 96–97). The case studies are biographical accounts of the participants' experiences of activism, written and interpreted by the researcher. Authorship is retained by the researcher; the resultant case study is the researcher's understanding of the case. This is highlighted by Stake (2003) who writes:

> What results may be the case's own story, but the report will be the researcher's dressing of the case's own story. This is not to dismiss the

aim of finding the story that best represents the case, but to remind the reader that, usually the researcher ultimately decides criteria of representation (p. 144).

Nevertheless, the contexts of case studies have been checked with research participants for validity and correctness when the in-depth case studies were in draft form.

The Method

Purposive Selection

The activists interviewed for this research were contacted via a number of formal and informal networks including those of NGOs, community-based organizations and local activist groups, and through the networks of those involved in environment, women's, peace and anticorporate globalization movements. The call for participants was advertised through a number of more formal processes. In the early stages of participant selection, I presented my research at a Masters in Public Advocacy course at Victoria University and the request for participants was promoted on the university's courses website. I made contact with activists through the NGO Friends of the Earth (FOE), the Community Development Teachers Network, through other activist educators and activists based in Melbourne. The promotion of the research was successful, with most of the interviews being completed during the first eighteen months of the research. Circumstantial activists were contacted personally by mail and email, or through contact with lawyers, advocates or public relations officers acting on their behalf. This was necessary because most of the circumstantial activists who were interviewed were not usually involved with social movements and formal activist groups. Purposive sampling was used to select participants for the two groups of "lifelong" and "circumstantial" activists. As Merriam (1998) states:

> Purposive sampling is based on the assumption that the investigator wants to discover, understand, and gain insight and therefore must select a sample from which the most can be learned (p. 61).

Purposive selection was used in order to ensure that the sample included activists engaged in a broad range of current social issues and campaigns in Australia. In addition, gender, age, and ethnicity balance were sought to ensure that the research was representative of activists' communities. The research has a national focus and has broken new ground because there are no studies to date in Australia for which extensive interviews have been conducted to investigate activists' pedagogy. The activists who were interviewed were engaged with issues such as women's equality and domestic violence, Latin American politics and international solidarity, climate change and the environment, poverty, disability rights, refugee rights, and urban development and gentrification, while others were involved in the David Hicks campaign, the anticonscription campaigns of the 1960s, movements for peace, and the anticorporate globalization movement.

Scope and Research Limitations

Many of the issues and social movements described above are not unique to Australia, but are of global importance in terms of their links to human rights, social justice, and the environment (Ife & Fiske 2006; Ife & Tesoriero 2006). Some of the causes activists were supporting at the time of this research are among the most important social, political, and economic issues of our era. It is hoped that by analyzing the pedagogy of activism this research will draw attention to both the learning practices of activists and to the array of social justice issues with which they are involved. The scope of the research has been limited due to funding constraints. There were many activists I would have liked to interview who could not be reached due to limited resources. Therefore, while the research is national in scope, there is a particular focus on individuals in the state of Victoria, some of whom have nevertheless worked on issues of social change in other states or overseas.

Seventeen in-depth interviews were conducted with activists in order to consider and comprehend the complexity of learning that takes place through their activism. There is little qualitative research conducting in-depth interviews with activists in Australia that have a particular focus on their pedagogical practices. While there have been studies conducted on activism and its connection to social movements and social movement learning (Newman 1994; Foley 1999, 2001, 2004; Branagan & Boughton 2003; Kovan & Dorkx 2003; Jasper & Goodwin 2004; Boughton, Taksa, & Welton 2004; Boughton 2005), there have been few studies that reflect on individual activists' biographies through telling stories of activism using a case study methodology. One published study is Maddison and Scalmer's (2006) *Activist Wisdom*, which focuses on activism and the practical knowledge of activists; another is Foley's (1999) study of activism in a environmental campaign at Terania Creek. However, what is really unique about this study is that it examines the practices of activists who protest outside of social movements. The typology of circumstantial and lifelong activists contributes to the knowledge of adult education and social movement learning.

It was encouraging to find that right from the initial call for participants, people wanted to tell their stories. As one activist stated, it gave him the opportunity to reflect on his own practices of activism at a time when he was disillusioned with the "left" of politics. Gender balance was sought in the study, although there were certainly greater numbers of male activists wanting to be interviewed than women. There were many activists whom I could have interviewed but did not because it was important to maintain gender balance in the study. There were also many more lifelong activists who were happy to participate than circumstantial activists. "Purposive selection" was consequently crucial for being able to encourage circumstantial activists to be engaged in the research. Some activists were unwilling to be involved in the research, and were quite frank in telling me this. The initial confidentiality clause that had been required by the university's Human Research Ethics Committee (HREC) was discouraging to these activists, who believed that their identity should be acknowledged. They had invested many years of hard work and emotional commitment to their work as activists and they wanted ownership of their stories and wanted to be named in the thesis or any published work. Because of this, another application was made to the HREC for the option to disclose identity for some interviewees. A number of participants availed themselves of this option.

The three years during which the research was conducted saw some significant political changes in Australian society, the most important of which was a change at the federal level from the Conservative coalition government to a Labor government under the leadership of Kevin Rudd and now Julia Gillard. Prior to this, the Conservative Howard government had been in power for almost 11 years. The dominance of neo-liberalism and conservative economic policy, therefore, provides a potent context for these activists' practices. The research was conducted at a time when Australia, like Britain and the United States, was engaged in the war on terrorism and the subsequent invasion of Iraq. As such, many of the causes with which activists were involved were reactive to the legislative and policy agendas of the former Howard government.

In-Depth Interviews

Semistructured in-depth interviews were chosen as a method to elicit "rich" data. Liamputtong and Ezzy (2005) argue that "a good interview is like a good conversation" (p. 55). Lists of indicative questions were established and framed around the key research questions in the candidature proposal. A pilot interview was held initially to gauge whether the indicative questions produced enough information related to the key research questions or whether they needed to be adapted and changed. The interviews started with the participants providing an autobiographical account of their family life, experience of politics or any special circumstances that led them to take action for social change. The autobiographical data provided a broad picture of the person, his/her activism, politics, and ideology, and confirmed his/her involvement in civil society groups and social movements. More specific questions related to activists' learning practices were included later. But the point initially was to obtain a biographical account of their activism. The first transcript was examined with my supervisors. Together, we analyzed the semistructured interview process and checked whether or not the indicative questions had been able to obtain sufficiently rich data. Some minor adaptations were made after evaluating the pilot.

During the in-depth interviews, activists entrusted me with quite detailed information about their lives and I felt very privileged to be given access to often deeply personal accounts of their learning and emotional agency, and the passion and commitment behind their desire for struggle and resistance. Liamputtong & Ezzy (2005) observe that

> the in depth interview is a privilege. There is something deeply rewarding and satisfying about talking to another person for an hour or more in such a way that you come to understand a particular part of their life "in-depth." (p. 55)

As I became more experienced as an interviewer, the discussion seemed to flow smoothly in the interview process and I rarely looked at my sheet of questions. I was engaged in the research process and the interviews were like a good conversation about learning practices, social interactions, historical events, and the people who had encouraged the learning practices of the interviewee activists.

Some accounts of activists' learning were deeply moving, particularly when issues of personal significance to the person were raised. There were times when I was emotionally moved by the accounts of activists' practices, and engaged in dialogue about their stories. This is sometimes referred to as a "coconstruction" of biography that occurs as the researcher and the interviewee become immersed in the interview and there is a mutual construction of the biographical account of learning as participants try to make sense of their own histories (Liamputtong & Ezzy 2005). As the interviewer and listener to these stories, I was transported to places such as Cuba, Venezuela and Brazil, Afghanistan, Pakistan, Turkey, Palestine, the United States, and rural and urban Australia as the activists recounted and situated their learning in significant moments and places. What was surprising from the interview process was the emotional agency of their activism. Words expressed included being "angry," "enraged," "passionate," and "upset." Activists often spoke about a "sense of betrayal" as a motivation for taking action. A broad range of emotions were referred to frequently throughout the interviews. The use of humor was also frequently a part of the interviews. Many of the activists used humor as way of dealing with adversity. There were occasions when an interview would be filled with laughter as activists succumbed to "gallows humor" and laughed at their own circumstances of difficulty or adversity as a way of coping with the remembered events. These interviews still resonate with me. I was changed in some way by hearing these deeply personal and often emotional accounts of their activism in a manner suggested by the following observation of Liamputtong and Ezzy's (2005):

> Interviews are not merely the opportunity to discover information that already exists, meaning and interpretation predate interviews and continue on after them. However, to varying degrees, these meanings are created, recreated and transformed during an in-depth interview. Part of the pleasure of doing in-depth interviews is participating in the process of people trying to make sense of their lives. (p. 55)

I have learned a great deal from this research process. Bourdieu (1999) reminds us of the anxiety of "making private words public, revealing confidential statements made in the context of a relationship based on trust that can only be established between two individuals" (p.1). In his (1999) anthology of case studies, *The Weight of the World*, where he uses the narratives of individual people to illustrate social issues of the current day in France, Bourdieu is sensitive in situating people's realities within the context of their social world. It is important to be sensitive and ethical about the use of data and to appropriately represent the participants in the study.

Data Presentation

All 17 interviews were transcribed verbatim from audio files. From these, eight were selected to be more fully developed and presented as case studies in the book. This method has been chosen to document specific stories or narratives that evolve from the research. The case writing has been used to present a retrospective view of the identity change, learning, transformation, and knowledge acquisition of individuals throughout their engagement in activism (Stake 2003).

The case studies offer a comparative focus using the typology of circumstantial/lifelong activists and reveal the differences and similarities of their learning experiences gained through activism. The initial transcripts have been analyzed by means of category construction (Merriam 1998). Constructing categories of data has focused on interpreting recurring patterns or themes, so a "grounded theoretical" approach to thematic analysis is used (Liamputtong & Ezzy 2005, p. 266). A matrix was developed to construct common themes or patterns in activists' learning practices (Liamputtong & Ezzy 2005). Recurring themes have been discussed and critically evaluated throughout the research supervision process to analyze the relevance of a particular theme, and the matrix was used to group or "chunk" themes (Miles & Huberman 1994). This provided a visual analysis of the themes and cross matched them to the participants. Most interviews went for between one to one-and-a-half hours, which generally produced a 20–30 page transcription. The potential for the research to become unwieldy was enormous. I transcribed the first five interviews myself, in an endeavor to keep close to the data and to see the initial themes emerging from the first few interviews. It was surprising that some of the first themes, such as social learning, learning on the job, and the embodied nature of activists' learning were evident early on and were reaffirmed as more data was collected. In these early days of collecting the data a short "theme list" (Liamputtong & Ezzy 2005, p. 62) was developed to lead initial discussion with my supervisors. I used a fieldwork journal throughout this process where I recorded (usually after the interview was complete or a short time later) thoughts, feelings, and reflections about the interview and the data that was collected (Merriam 1998). I wrote journal entries about the differences and similarities in activists' stories. I also recorded observations about the emotions or discomfort that surfaced in the interviews. These journal entries have been a useful reflective and metalearning tool for my own practices as an activist and as a researcher. They situate my own learning as part of the research and are a record of the process and journey thus far (Stage & Manning 2003).

There was a conscious process of looking for hidden meaning within the data by "interrogating" both the data and my own interpretation of and assumptions about the data (Liamputtong & Ezzy 2005, p. 263). For example, I considered whether the persona of the activist was contrived or constructed to portray a particular view, and whether the embodied persona was influenced by other phenomena, like the construction of a media persona. Foucault (1977) draws on Nietzschean genealogy to describe an approach to research that explores the history of the hidden, aiming to deconstruct what appears to be the truth. Often, issues and individuals are affected by multiple truths, narratives or political, social, and identity discourses that influence the actor, or, in this instance, the activists. Many supervisory meetings were held regarding the interpretation of the data and the possibility of hidden meaning within them. Attention was given to uncovering hidden meanings and exploring hidden themes during the data analysis. In essence, a "critical lens" has been used to interpret the data and the results of this are presented in the case studies in this book (Merriam 1998).

Ethics

Ethics in this research and ethical practices of the researcher have been applied throughout the research. Ethical practices have been observed from the initial conception of this study and have been applied throughout engagement in the research processes. Ethical practice is not merely a process of managing potential litigation (although it is this too), but rather a process of ongoing ethical reflection and practice. Ethical issues were considered from the early framing of the research questions to the construction of the typology of lifelong activists and circumstantial activist. Ethical questioning allowed the research process to have integrity and be disciplined. The ethical engagement with the activists who participated in this research has been paramount. I was sensitive to the ethics involved in this process. I was also conscious that activists were giving me time in their, often very busy, lives.

The issue of confidentiality arose very early on for the research study. Some activists, as noted earlier, would not participate in the research unless they had ownership of their story, requiring permission to be sought from the HREC to a change from blanket confidentiality to optional confidentiality. Activists who chose the option of confidentiality did so for various reasons. Others, particularly those whose lives had already been to exposed media scrutiny, were not necessarily concerned with being named in the research. I tried to give participants a full range of potential scenarios regarding informed consent; clarifying when their stories and subsequent data might be used in the final thesis or when their story may be used in a case study. I was careful to discuss the potential consequences and potential risks of unmasking themselves in the research. As Stage and Manning (2003) argue: "at minimum, each interview needs to be prefaced with a conversation with the respondent about informed consent" (p. 44). If an activist chose confidentiality they were either allocated a pseudonym or invited to choose their own, and, throughout the book, their pseudonyms appear in italics. All activists have been given their transcripts to edit and the opportunity to negotiate changes where stories were misrepresented or where, in hindsight, the activists may have wanted to change places and situations that were sensitive. When particular cases were used in the research process or in journal articles, the article or conference presentation was sent to the activists beforehand, as a matter of courtesy. I was rarely asked to change anything in the transcriptions—occasionally a name, or an event, or place, but rarely any of the content of activists' stories.

An ethical framework based on respect was applied in all of the dealings with the data, from simple issues such as storage of the data to larger issues of publishing a refereed article. I was conscious, at all times, of the importance of maintaining confidentiality and ensuring that the data was represented in a way that did not compromise the identities of the participants in the research. Data access was given only to my supervisors; files were kept in a locked storage cabinet; my computer and data storage devices were password protected. I was well aware that the subject matter may have the potential to be sensitive since the interviews occasionally evoked emotional responses from the participants. Access to counseling and professional support from the university was at hand and publicized in the consent form but to date has not been requested by the participants. For the most part, activists reacted in a positive way to the interview process. They appreciated the opportunity to be reflective, many stating that they rarely had the time to think about their practices and the journey of their activism, their achievements, and their disappointments. Most of the lifelong activists were reflexive about their own practices as activists. For many, their formal studies, or involvement in student politics, had encouraged reflection and, therefore, reflective praxis.

As a community development worker, a senior educator, and lecturer I am keenly aware of ethical considerations and have practiced these diligently in my professional life. Ethical practice was emphasized early in my education as a community development worker and continues to resonate in my current practices as a academic and researcher.

Conclusion

This chapter has outlined the methodological considerations that arose through the life of this research. The selection of a qualitative methodology that is interpretative yet interfaced with a constructivist interpretation of the data has been effective. The data that was gathered from the semistructured interview process was rich and provided a detailed account of activists' learning practices. Care and diligence was taken to produce a research proposal that was relevant to adult activists' educational practices and allowed for a deeply personal and rich biographical account of their history of learning. The development of indicative questions from the candidature proposal ensured that the data represented the thematic concerns and central questions asked, namely: "What are the stages and processes of learning and identity formation for activists' engagement in social action?" Revision and adaptation over time through the evaluation of the effectiveness of the initial pilot interview ensured the research stayed focused on its aims and objectives. Ongoing critical analysis throughout the research supervisory process has enabled the emergent themes to be constructed in a way that highlights the deeply personal stories and accounts of activists' learning as they engaged in struggle or resistance.

The following chapter traverses a broad range of scholarship in the sociology and philosophy of adult education, which has relevance to activists' learning practices. In doing this I am reminded of Horkheimer's (1974) critique of social theory, "all systems are false, that of Marx no less than Aristotle's—however much truth both may have seen" (p.198).

3
The Politics of Adult Education

Introduction

This chapter reviews a broad range of literature relevant to this study and explores three knowledge domains of education. The chapter commences by outlining scholarly approaches to popular education, radical adult education and transformative learning, and explores the foundations of these epistemologies and their contribution to the literature on education, activism, and social change. The chapter goes on to examine the knowledge domain of social learning, which includes literature on "informal learning," "workplace learning," and "communities of practice." The next domain of knowledge is embodiment and learning, which explores mind, body, and emotions in the development of knowledge and considers the role that identity plays in "learning to become an activist." The review concludes with a summary of the major propositions outlined in the literature.

Popular Education and Radical Adult Education

Learning through social action belongs to discourses of "emancipatory learning," "radical," "working class," "social purpose," and "radical adult" education. As a body of knowledge it is also broadly referred to as "popular education." The literature on education for social change is extensive. The international literature includes the work of Freire (1972a, 1972b, 1974), Mayo and Thompson (1995), Gramsci (1971), Crowther (2005), Lovett (1975), Darder, Baltadano, and Torres (2003), and, in Australia, the work of Foley (1999, 2001), Branagan (2003), Newman, (1994, 2006), and more recently the writing of Whelan, who explores the pedagogy of activism in the environment movement (Whelan 2005a, 2005b). The term "radical adult education" describes how people, both individually and collectively, learn through their engagement with community development activities or their participation in social movements (Newman 1994, p. 3). Jesson and Newman (2004) state that "learning in the sense we use here means learning by people acting collectively to bring about radical and emancipatory social change" (p. 251). Popular education is a tradition in the field of adult education, which broadly encompasses community development activity, activism, and social change. Learning and education in this sense is a necessary part of the effort to achieve significant social change in some way (Foley 1999; Mayo, P. 1999; Jesson & Newman 2004; Newman 2006). According to Crowther, Martin & Galloway (2005) popular education is a process of acting toward a social order that is more just and egalitarian. It includes social action and community development activities that seek to change and alter inequality, and therefore bring about progressive social and political change. Popular education generally has some of the following characteristics:

> Its curriculum comes out of the concrete experience and material interests of people in communities of resistance and struggle;
> its pedagogy is collective, focused primarily on a group as distinct from individual learning and development;
> it attempts where possible, to forge a direct link between education and social action (Crowther, Martin, & Galloway 2005, p. 2).

A significant feature of the literature on popular education and radical adult education is its focus on the impact of historical materialism on society, which draws attention to the impact of capitalism on the creation of social disadvantage for certain groups in society (Allman & Wallis 1995; Mayo & Thompson 1995; Foley 1999; Jesson & Newman 2004). Whelan (2005b) believes there are some "shared attributes" to the popular education activities associated with activism. These commonalities are:

> A curriculum or content that is anchored in the daily lives and interest of participants;
> an overt interest in progressive social, political and structural change and in strengthening resistance; and

a pedagogy or methodology that emphasizes collective rather than individual learning and development (pp.119, 120).

Whelan (2002), who analyzed environmental activists' training needs, argues that the pedagogy of activism is founded in adult learning principles and occurs through learning in social movements. This learning is often informal, as formal education among environmental activists is uncommon (p. 33). Learning includes the practices of individuals as they join together in a social movement or to work on issues in their local neighborhood or community, on issues of human rights, or as campaign organizers (Alinsky 1971). As Maddison and Scalmer (2006) remind us, "progressive activists and social movements have much to teach the rest of society" (p. 4). Popular educators such as Freire (1972b) point out the importance of understanding systems and structures in their creation of oppression. Freire believed in education that was liberating in the sense that it embraced with intentionality and purpose revolutionary change to structures in society that created oppression. Literacy education would change individuals, enabling them to take up action to change society (Freire 1972b). Through this process of awakening, termed by Freire as "conscientization (Freire 1972b), individuals would become empowered. Through their acquisition of knowledge, they would understand the impact of dominant systems of oppression and would redevelop or reconstruct these discourses (Foley 1999). Freire's connection to popular education is well known through his activism to promote literacy education in South America, and his theory of education has influenced popular education in both the developed and developing world (Darder, Baltadano, & Torres 2003). Freire (1972b) believed in the concept of "praxis;" that is, practice must be intertwined with reflection and action in order to change society:

> It is only when the oppressed find the oppressor out and become involved in the organised struggle for their liberation that they begin to believe in themselves. This discovery cannot be purely intellectual but must involve action; nor can it be limited to mere activism, but must include serious reflection: only then will it be a praxis (pp. 40–41)

Freire (1972b) frequently referred to the importance of action and he argued it was essential to not remain silent on issues of social significance. He consistently stated that the importance of acting in a way he describes as "humanly" is to "transform the world" (pp. 61–62).

While the popular education writers such as Whelan (2002), Maddison and Scalma (2006) and Foley (1999, 2001) have emphasized the important dimensions of learning through social action, they have also been concerned to address the skill and knowledge development of activists. The next section examines what activists learn through social action.

Learning through Social Action

Foley (1999) argues there are three dimensions of learning in struggle: an analysis of the political economy, the operation of micropolitics, and ideology and knowledge of discourses at play in society:

> Satisfactory accounts of learning in struggle make connection between learning and education on the one hand, and analysis of political economy, micro-politics, ideology and discourse (or discursive practices) on the other. (Foley 1999, p. 9)

Chase (2000) believes environmental activists acquire skills and knowledge in five areas: technical knowledge, political knowledge, life skills, knowledge of organizations, and skills through personal growth (p. 17). Jesson and Newman (2004) describe three domains of activists' learning:

> *Instrumental learning*—will provide the skills and information to deal with practical matters, to use existing structures and systems such as government and legal processes, but the purpose is always to bring about change;
> *Interpretive learning*—which has a focus on communication or understanding the human condition, the focus is on people, what they are and how they relate;
> *Critical learning*—activists learn problem solving skills, through reflection new meaning is produced. "It helps us understand the psychological and cultural assumptions that constrain the way we see the world." (p. 261)

Some theorists draw attention to activists' development of practical knowledge or wisdom and suggest they are concerned about protecting this knowledge and passing it on to other activists (Maddison & Scalmer 2006). Activists also learn community development–type skills such as interpersonal communication skills, facilitation and networking skills and group work (Kenny 2006). Mayo (2005) believes activists can gain a great deal of knowledge from understanding community development skills and the use of these skills in protest .They also learn how to use systems of government and develop systemic advocacy skills, so that they can challenge government policy and instigate new legislative reform (Jesson & Newman 2004). Organizers learn how to think critically about the world to challenge and change the assumptions that maintain and create inequality, and this appears to be an important part of knowledge development for activists.

Learning to Think Critically

The literature frequently refers to the way radical adult education invokes higher order cognition through the process of critical thinking, critical reflection, and the use of reason (Freire 1972a; Allman & Wallis 1995; Foley 1999; Mayo, P. 1999; Branagan & Boughton 2003; Newman 2006). Through critical thinking, activists acquire knowledge about systems and structures that create social inequality (Newman 1994; Foley 1999, 2001; Branagan & Boughton 2003; Jesson & Newman 2004). Brookfield (1987) focuses on critical thinking as a cognitive way of making meaning. Through acquiring new knowledge about political, economic and cultural systems, an enquiring mind is developed (Brookfield 1987). This is supported by Allan and Shields (1998), who state:

> Central to emancipatory or libratory education processes is developing the ability to think critically and thereby to develop a critical perspective on society and our actions for social change. (Allan & Shields 1998, p. 36)

Similarly, Foley (1999) argues that critical reflection requires the power of theory; we need to understand the way our consciousness is shaped "by social relations and ideologies." Branagan & Boughton (2003) believe "learning through the politics of protest occurs at a variety of levels, and often involved the so-called higher order cognitive processes which characterize academic study" (p. 348). This is affirmed by Freire (1972b), who argues that critical thinking and action are interconnected:

> True dialogue cannot exist unless it involves critical thinking—thinking which discerns an invisible solidarity between the world and men [sic] admitting of no dichotomy between them—thinking

which perceives reality as a process and transformation, rather than a static entity—thinking which does not separate itself from action, but constantly immerses itself on temporality without fear of the risks involved. (pp. 64–65)

However, learners can also reflect on their practice and their learning without necessarily being critical. As Brookfield (2000) points out, there needs to be a distinction between reflection and critical reflection. Critical reflection is informed by the theorizing of the Frankfurt school and the theoretical tradition of critical theory (Brookfield, 2000) represented, in particular, by the writings of Marcuse (1964), Horkheimer (1974), and Adorno (1973), and the work of Habermas (1984). In adult education the critical theoretical tradition is called critical pedagogy. To be critically reflective requires knowledge of the ideologies that influence and permeate the "self," ideologies that are often pervasive and therefore powerful (Brookfield, 2000; Brookfield, 2005).

Understanding and recognizing hegemony is a key area of knowledge development for activists (Gramsci, 1971). To understand why people accept, without resistance, discourses of power and of inequality when these may not be in their own interest requires the individual to unlace many years of socialized ideas, socialized practices, and processes; in essence, the individual's normative ways of being in the world (Foley 1999; Brookfield, Stephen 2005; Newman 2006). Gramsci (2001) links education to hegemony and claims all relationships of power are educational relationships:

> This relationship exists throughout all society considered as a whole as well as for each individual relative to other individuals, between intellectual and non-intellectual sections of the population, between governors and the governed, between elites and their followers, between leaders and led, between vanguards and the body of the army. Every relationship of "hegemony" is necessarily an educational relationship and occurs not only within a nation, between the various forces that comprise it, but in the entire international and world field, between complexes of national and continental civilizations. (p. 284)

In order to resist social forces that oppress, we need to understand the power of hegemony for, as Gramsci (1988) eloquently states, "Each individual is the synthesis not only of existing relations but the history of these relations." It appears from the literature that learning about power and power relations in society, and how these relations are practiced and reinforced through hegemony, are key areas of knowledge development for organizers. This knowledge about hegemony can be transforming as it changes activists' long-held views about the world around them (Mezirow 1991). The next section outlines Mezirow's (1991, 2000) theory of transformative learning.

Transformative Learning

Transformative learning is a domain of knowledge in adult education that explores how adult learners make meaning as they become increasingly and consciously aware of their own learning. Mezirow's (1991) theory of "transformative learning" focuses on the individual's emancipation; learners can be liberated through their own conscious awakening. By reflecting on practice and where a situation of "ideal discourse" was created between teacher and learner, a change in "meaning perspective" would happen to the learner; that is, a process of transformative learning would occur (Mezirow 1991, 2000; Cranton 1996). This is explored further by Mezirow (2000) who states:

> Transformative learning refers to the process by which we transform our taken-for-granted frames of reference (meaning perspectives, habits of mind, mind sets) to make more inclusive, discriminating open, emotionally capable of change, and reflective so that they may generate beliefs and opinions that will prove more true or justified to guide action. (pp. 7–8)

Mezirow argues perspective transformation is an integral process of adult development (Mezirow 1991). Mezirow, in turn, draws on the critical theorist Habermas (1984) who developed a theory of "communicative action." Puigvert & Vallis (2005) indicate that

> [Habermas's] theory of communicative action sheds light on the possibility of transformative action between all social subjects through inter-subjective, egalitarian dialogue based on the validity of different knowledge claims and the attempt to reach understanding without the distortions produced by powerful social interests. Habermas' theory sets a framework, which inextricably links dialogic processes among different social agents to social action. (p. 90)

Daloz (2000) argues this change of meaning perspective ascribed by Mezirow is a deep change in the person's frame of reference. Thus, learning focuses on change within the individual rather than on change that would benefit broader society. For Mezirow (1991) critical self-reflection is a precursor to emancipatory learning:

> Emancipatory knowledge is knowledge gained through critical self-reflection, as distinct from the knowledge gained from our "technical" interest in the objective world or our "practical" interest in social relations. (p. 87)

Critics of transformative learning such as Newman (1994, 2006) argues that without action transformation theory is purposeless. The intent to critically reflect is underpinned by the need to discover a desire and awareness to change, pointing to a fundamental flaw in transformation theory. Brookfield (2000) notes that "Mezirow has distinguished between transforming habits of mind and transforming structures" (pp. 143–44). In addition, Brookfield (2000) claims there is a lack of understanding regarding ideology and hegemony, which is a fundamental flaw in transformation theory. He argues for critical reflection associated with social action:

> Building on Freirean interpretations of praxis, this school of thought holds that reflection only truly becomes critical when it leads to transformation. Without subsequent social action, critical reflection is castigated as liberal dilettantism, a self-indulgent form of speculation that makes no real difference to anything. (p. 143)

Alternatively, Daloz (2000) argues, transformative learning can change broader systems and structures. He believes transformative learning can be used for "the common good" in society, referring to the change that occurs after the learner experiences a sense of "social responsibility" (p. 103). He analyses the transformation of prominent activists such as Nelson Mandela and describes four necessary conditions for transformation for the common good: the importance of the "presence of the other," the use of "reflective discourse," the availability of a "mentoring community," and, finally, "opportunities for committed action" (p. 103). Centers for learning such as the Transformative Learning Centre at the University of Toronto, do focus on transformative learning for participatory democracy, particularly in the writing of Ginieniewicz & Schugurensky (2006).

Loughlin (1996), in contrast, argues there is need for a greater holistic analysis of transformative learning. Too much attention, she claims, is paid to cognitive ways of knowing. Her research, involving women who had experienced emancipatory learning through their participation in women's consciousness raising groups, led her to conclude that learning came through informal processes that changed the individual's meaning perspectives. Loughlin (1996) argues there needs to be "an integration of rational and non-rational ways of knowing, which includes an analysis of values and value shifts that take place in the learner" (p. 56). Similarly, in empirical research conducted by Kovan and Dirkx (2003), environmental activists involved in small NGOs in the United States were interviewed with regard to maintaining their commitment to activism and the role of learning in "maintaining their long-term commitment and passion" (p. 103). While activists noted that the use of intellect and systemic thinking was important to their practice as activists, there was also a spiritual dimension associated with their practice:

> These processes seemed grounded in and derived from strong, emotional and spiritual connections to themselves, nature, and humanity. Consistently, the activists mentioned being motivated by head, heart, and spirit. (p. 103)

As Kovan & Dirkx (2003) argue, activists' learning in this sense is deeply rooted in both the conscious and unconscious "self." Activists view their involvement in activism as a calling: they claim "the call feels like a force beyond our conscious awareness that seems to be inviting or leading us somewhere, to some place, to do that which we were intended to do" (p. 110). In this sense, activists' emancipation is entwined with a perception of a shift in the self. There is a sense of fate, a sense of purpose; indeed, there is a sense of agency associated with their activism. These activists believe they are meant to be there, that becoming an activist is a part of their destiny in life.

Learning to Be Radical

Literature from the 1960s and 1970s on radicalization also has relevance to this study. Alinsky (1971) argued the education of the organizer comes from learning with others through conferences or meetings, having an understanding of power and power relationships, learning communication, learning about how to work with conflict, and educating and developing community and movement leaders. Keniston (1968) studied a number of young people involved in protests who worked at "Vietnam Summer," an organization opposed to the United States's involvement in the Vietnam War. The study found that it was not just a process of "confrontation, disillusion and reinterpretation" that made a radical (Keniston 1968, p. 133). There were many people who had a similar perception and disillusionment with the war but did not act on it. What Keniston discovered was that "a further process of activation and engagement is therefore essential in the making of a radical" (p. 133). Consequently, radicalization requires social agency; it requires the individual to act on social and political issues that concern them.

Activists do not learn in social isolation. Instead, they often learn from one another, by networking with other activists, and by observing the actions and strategies of other activists so that they become more skilled in what they do. This is explored further in the next domain of literature that focuses on social learning, situated learning and learning in the workplace.

Social Learning

Sites of social practice, including sites of social movements, are a key domain of knowledge that has relevance to this study. By participating with one another in social change, activists are able to acquire new skills, new ways of knowing and make new meaning of the world around them (Foley 1999; Mayo, P. 1999; Branagan & Boughton 2003; Newman 2006). The practices of activism are invariably connected to communities, community development and social movements. Sites of community and sites of social movements are the spaces and places where activists learn through socialization with one another (Newman 1994, 2006; Foley 1999, 2004; Whelan 2002; Boughton 2005).

Learning through struggle has a long and rich history in Australia, but initially found its most formal expression as a mode of instruction offered by the workers' education programs of the "Marxist schools" set up by the Communist Party of Australia (Boughton 2005). These workers' education groups brought together people from a variety of backgrounds to discuss workers' rights and social justice issues. This formal yet underground pedagogy was based on nineteenth-century Chartism influenced at the time by the International Communist Party (Boughton 2005). As Boughton (2005) argues, the tradition of worker education in the socialist and communist movements extended from the late-nineteenth century to the postwar period of the twentieth century:

> From the 1920's onwards, the major vehicles for this education movement were socialist and communist party schools. In Sydney, as in Melbourne and other centres all over Australia in the 1940's, the CPA opened an adult education centre, called the Marx school. For an annual fee, members and supporters enrolled to study historical materialism, scientific socialism, Marxism-Leninism—in a word communism. (p. 101)

Similarly, the consciousness raising groups of the women's movement in the 1960s and 1970s in Australia had a pedagogy based on socialism (Burgmann 2003). Influenced by radical and socialist feminism they contributed to the history of popular education in Australia, by bringing together women in women's consciousness raising groups. The purpose here was not only to educate and to raise women's awareness of their own oppression but to place women's personal experience in a political context and encourage women to take action on issues that concerned them (Burgmann 2003). This would lead to their emancipation. The learning in both the workers' education groups and women's consciousness groups was ground breaking in a number of ways. Learners were invited to participate in learning that raised their own political and personal consciousness. Yet, there was also agency involved in this type of learning: learning was purposeful in that it invited participants to act to change the world. It was learning that involved both personal (Mezirow 1991) and societal transformation (Freire 1972a).

While learning in both the Marxist schools and the women's consciousness groups was informed by a curriculum embedded in the ontology of Marxism and feminism, it was also social since individuals learned from one another's experiences. Likewise, the learning spaces of neighborhood houses, now an integral part of the Adult and Community Education (ACE) system in Australia, provide a social avenue for women to learn from one another in their communities. Through the sharing of information and by relating to each other's experiences, women are able to form new "meaning perspectives." As Foley (1999) states:

> …, the whole experience of a participant in a house is an important process of learning for women. Much of this learning is informal and

incidental, it is embedded in other activities, and is often not articulated as learning by neighborhood house members. (p. 54)

One of the most influential theories in adult education in recent years has been Lave and Wenger's (1991) theory of social learning. In their book "*Situated Learning, Legitimate Peripheral Participation,*" they outline the significance of learning that occurs informally as people interact with one another in a social site or workplace. Social learning occurs when individuals learn from one another through the processes of socialization (Horton & Freire 1990; Lave & Wenger 1991; Wenger 1998). Learning in activism is a naturally social process; through time, and the opportunity to observe and interact with others, activists become more expert at what they do. As Lave & Wenger (1991) note:

> A theory of social practice emphasizes the relational interdependency of agent and world, activity, meaning, cognition, learning and knowing. It emphasizes the inherently socially negotiated character of meaning and the interested concerned character of the thought and actions of persons-in-activity. This view also claims that learning, thinking and knowing are relations among people in activity in, with, and arising from the socially and culturally structured world. (pp. 50–51)

Because activists rarely take action without others, they need other activists to learn from and learn with. Taking action is a process of collective engagement (Foley 1999) that involves learning through collaboration and learning with one another for a broader social purpose or outcome (Jesson & Newman 2004). This was particularly important, for example, in the case of the "Highlander Research and Education Centre" established in 1932 in Tennessee. The centre provided education for activists that placed emphasis on learning from one another as well as "learning together" (Horton & Freire 1990, p. 41). Lave and Wenger's (1991) theory of situated learning directs attention to how and what people learn as they go about their daily work, and the following section summarizes some of the prominent literature on workplace learning in adult education.

Learning on the Job

The last fifteen years have seen learning in the workplace rise to particular prominence in adult education. We are now aware that learning is an inherently social process embedded in our daily interactions at work (Boud & Garrick 1999; Beckett & Hager 2002; Billett 2004). It is widely understood that adults learn all of their lives and that much of this learning occurs in the workplace (Hodkinson & James 2003). Theorists in education have argued that the "situated" nature of the workplace (Lave & Wenger 1991) is a major site where informal learning can occur (Wenger 1998; Boud & Garrick 1999; Beckett & Hager 2002; Hodkinson & James 2003; Billett 2004). There are five prominent theoretical paradigms within the epistemology of workplace learning, which are described below.

- The didactic model of workplace learning focuses on formal workplace training, which Beckett & Hager (2002) refer to as the "front-end" model of workplace learning (p. 97). The emphasis here is on education in the workplace that views the learner as a passive recipient of knowledge.
- The sociocultural model explores the relationship between learning and socialization and is primarily informal; learning, thus, is developed through social participation with colleagues in the workplace (Lave & Wenger 1991; Wenger 1998).
- The psychosocial model draws on the writing of Vygotski and links learning to psychology in the social site of the workplace (Billett 2004).
- A fourth approach, posited by Engeström, relates workplace learning to activity theory. Learning occurs through a series of activities as organizations face internal and external upheaval, conflicts and tensions (Engeström, Miettinen, & Punamäki-Gitai 1999; Engeström & Tuomi-Gröhn 2003; Engeström 2007)
- A fifth, broadly postmodern[1] model of holistic learning in the workplace developed by Beckett & Hager (2002), Beckett & Morris (2004) and Beckett (2008) that draws attention to the connection between the whole person in the processes of learning at work. This approach puts the whole self, mind, body, and emotions at the center of learning, and posits that all of these contribute to effective learning.

Clearly, learning of a similar nature takes place in the unpaid work of social activists. While learning occurs through our daily social interactions with one another as we work, it is often informal and tacit, and not always articulated or perceived as learning (Foley 1999). Whelan (2005b) describes activists' learning as often "incidental" and informal, as formal training among environmental activists in particular is uncommon (p. 122). Learning that occurs through socialization is often tacit or implied (Eraut 2000). This learning occurs as a consequence of action, an incidental outcome, rather than as a process that is engaged in formally.

The sociocultural model of Lave and Wenger, which draws on their theory of "communities of practice," and the poststructural model of holistic workplace learning developed by Beckett and Hager (2002) are noteworthy in terms of their relevance to this study and are worthy of further discussion. "Communities of practice" provides an explanation of learning and the importance of identity formation through socialization (Lave 1991; Lave & Wenger 1991), while Beckett and Hager (2002) analyze learning that occurs in the "hot action" of practice as workers make judgments at work and develop expertise.

Lave and Wenger: Situated Learning

According to Lave and Wenger, the situated site of the workplace is ripe for informal learning to occur and they argue "that learning is an integral and inseparable aspect of social practice" (Lave 1991, p. 17). Individuals may start out as newcomers on the periphery of practice, and eventually move on to full involvement and engagement in learning as they become more "absorbed in the culture of practice" (Lave 1991, p. 97). People teach and learn from one another all of the time from the "master practitioner" who passes on his/her knowledge, experience and skill to the novice in a "community of practice" (Lave 1991, pp. 94–95). Wenger (1998) believes that through participating in a "community of practice" a reification[2] of likeminded discourses, symbols, artifacts, and approaches to work occurs and, through socialization, workers begin to mirror one another. As Wenger points out:

> I would claim that the process of reification so construed is central to every practice. Any community of practice produces abstractions, tools, symbols, stories, terms and concepts that reify something of that practice in a congealed form. (p. 59)

However, critics of Lave and Wenger argue that not all learning in a community of practice is necessarily positive; individuals can also learn poor practice in communities. This is explored in the following section analyzing power and the social learning model.

Power and the Social Learning Model: Holistic Learning

Beckett and Hager (2000) argue for a new epistemology of workplace learning because they believe the focus on formal, social, and informal learning in workplaces is too narrow. They put forward a theory of workplace learning that analyses how people make judgments in the workplace, one that acknowledges the lived experiences of people as they go about doing their daily work. They claim judgment is central to practice and that if we are serious about understanding what we do in the workplace, we cannot discount that workers make judgments every day:.

> The hypothesis is that making better judgements represents a paradigmatic aim of workplace learning, and that therefore growth in such learning is represented by a growing capacity to make appropriate judgments in the changing, and often unique, circumstances that occur in many workplaces. (Beckett & Hager 2000, p. 302)

Much of what we learn in the workplace occurs through our daily business of doing tasks. Workers make judgments about what to do all day every day, and Beckett and Hager (2000) argue for an epistemology of learning that is holistic and developed through the experience of "hot action" in practice. They propose a model that

> focuses on the whole lived experiences of workers not merely their skills, attitudes and outcomes of these...such experiences of working life are manifest in daily practices, particularly in decisions when the worker is caught up in the "hot action" of practice. (p.304)

In the "hot action" of practice, workers make judgments about what to do next and how to go about doing it; in effect, they become more expert at what they do. Furthermore, Beckett's (2008) ontology of workplace learning draws attention to hitherto neglected embodied practices such as intuition, hunches, gut feelings, and instinct. Beckett (2008) argues against dualist constructions of knowledge and ascribes, in particular, an "Australian model" of "integrated holistic competencies" in the development of workplace expertise and adult learning (p. 21). Drawing on previous work completed by Beckett and Hager (2002), he believes "low status knowledge, typically called 'intuition' or 'commonsense', or 'know-how,' is now receiving long-overdue critical attention"(Beckett, 2008, p. 21). Such embodied ways of knowing need not be discounted and have a central place in understanding how activists learn.

Embodied Learning: Mind, Body, Emotions

The literature on embodiment has relevance to this study. Merleau-Ponty (1962) claims that the world is present before us without any preceding analysis, and through being-in-the-world we gain knowledge and skill through experience rather than through cognition (Merleau-Ponty 1962). The embodied nature of activists' knowing includes the mind, body, emotions, and self, all of which contribute to their effective mastery of learning. It is practical knowledge developed through the experience of being an activist (Maddison & Scalmer 2006). This way of knowing is in contrast to rationalist approaches to pedagogy, which are disembodied and largely focused on mind and thought. Merleau-Ponty (1962) argues we live through being in the world. Crossley (2001), a sociologist of the body, argues we need to move from Cartesianism and its tendency to privilege rationalism over experience, and develop knowledge about people's daily experience of being human in the world. As Hager (2000) indicates, "it needs to be remembered always, that practice is an embodied phenomenon" (p. 285). More recently, literature on social movements has discussed the role emotions play in the agency of activists (Jasper & Goodwin 2004; Eyerman 2005; Brown & Pickerill 2009; Jasper 2009). Recent research by Damouzi (2005) has demonstrated that the removal of a person's ability to think has a considerable impact on their emotional self, as shown by his study of brain injured patients, which indicated that the emotions are inextricably bound to rationality. In his book, *Descartes' Error*, he claims "that certain aspects of the process of emotions and feelings are indispensable for rationality" (p. xvii). If reason and the emotions are entwined, the emotions are not something that can be ignored or cordoned off. In understanding how we know what we know, they are central to rational thinking (Damasio 2005). Gonczi (2004) argues that if this is the case then there are implications for understanding how we learn and for education more widely.

Identity and Learning

An interest in the self, the subject, and subjectivity has become prominent in education as in other areas of sociology and the humanities. Constructions of the "self" as a unitary subject have received much criticism (Chappell et al. 2003). A discursive approach to the self and subjectivity acknowledges that the self is multiplicitous and always evolving:

> Power resides in all discourses including those economic, social and political theories that attempt to explain identity. Put simply, our

conception of who we are, our identity, is constituted by the power of all the discursive practices in which we speak and which, in turn, "speak" to us. (Chappell et al. 2003, p. 41)

The identity of the learner can be influenced by multiple discourses entrenched in social, cultural, and political institutions in education. The subject may engage or identify with these discourses and incorporate them into his or her own personal biography, or, alternatively, "dis-identify" with the discourses of these institutions by rejecting them (Hodges 1998). A discursive approach to identity looks at influences of power, difference, and otherness in identity formation:

> The self is not seen as neutral representations, of the subject/person but rather as discursive representations that do important political and cultural work in constructing, maintaining and transforming, both individuals and their social world. (Chappell et al. 2003, p. 28)

Foucault (1980) links discourse to power, language, and subjectivity; language helps to shape subjectivity and identity. Through the power effects of discourse, knowledge is either legitimated or delegitimated and what is commonly held as "truth" is constructed (Darder, Baltadano, & Torres 2003; Gore 2003). Discourses both discipline and construct the self and become embodied in who we are. Power is diffused on a systemic level of ideology, systems, and structures, and, on a micro level, to the body (Foucault 1983, 1988). As we learn to become a teacher, master practitioner, a student, a scholar, or even an activist, we make meaning and our sense of self or "identity" is altered (Chappell et al. 2003; Colley et al. 2003; Soloman 2003).

Postcolonial Theories of Education

Postcolonial theories of education have relevance to this study. Many social movements and activists, work on issues around the impact of colonization on Indigenous people and communities. Said's (1979) postcolonial theory outlines the impact of colonization on societies in terms of displacement and creation of the "other." Activists' pedagogy is often situated in sites of struggle around issues of culture, race, ethnicity, racism, and Indigenous communities. Particularly in Australia, one of the most important social issues of our time has been the struggle for self-determination by Australia's Aboriginal people (Lippman, 1981; Maddison, 2009). Similarly, displacement of millions of refugees around the globe has impacted on nation states' policies on refugees and their treatment of asylum seekers. Postcolonial theories of education explore issues of race, ethnicity, culture, racism and the subsequent impost on identity in the postcolonial landscape (Darder & Tores, 2003). Access to knowledge and knowledge formation does not often account for representations of knowledge constituted by oppressed minority groups such as Indigenous peoples. Ife (2002) argues we need to recognize the "wisdom of the oppressed" (pp.88–89), that current wisdom comes from "expert" knowledge. The practical wisdom of Indigenous communities and groups are often rooted in ancient practices handed down from elders, informally, through nontraditional forms of education.

Conclusion

Radical adult education is about how activists learn through the processes of engagement in social action and social movements (Newman 1994; Foley 1999, 2001; Branagan & Boughton 2003; Jesson & Newman 2004). Radical adult education, emancipatory learning, working class education and popular education are situated in the broad tradition of critical pedagogy (Allman 1999; Foley 2001; Darder, Baltadano, & Torres 2003; McLaren & Kincheloe 2007) that draws on the critical theory tradition of the Frankfurt School (Gramsci 1971; Freire 1972a, 1972b, 1974; Habermas 1984; Gramsci 1988; Allman, Paula 1999; Foley 2001; Darder, Baltadano, & Torres 2003; McLaren & Kincheloe 2007). These discourses of adult education view education as a project for social change in society. Activists learn skills associated with high order cognition. Activists use reason, critical thinking, and critical reflection to renew and remake their practice (Brookfield 1987; Foley 1999; Branagan & Boughton 2003). Learning frequently entails developing knowledge about social, political, and economic systems that create oppression. Learning includes developing knowledge about the impact of ideology, power relations, and discourse on society (Newman 1994, 2006; Allan & Shields 1998; Foley 1999, 2001; Allman 1999; Branagan & Boughton 2003; Boughton, Taksa, & Welton 2004; Boughton 2005; Branagan 2007; Maddison & Scalmer 2006). There is a particular focus in the literature on the role of historical materialism in the creation of social disadvantage in activists developing knowledge (Newman 1994, 2006; Allman & Wallis 1995; Allman 1999; Foley 1999; Boughton, Taksa, & Welton 2004; Jesson & Newman 2004; Boughton 2005).

Learning in activism is both social and informal, occurring through socialization with other activists and by being involved in social movements and communities (Horton & Freire 1990; Newman 1994; Foley 1999; Mayo, P. 1999; Branagan & Boughton 2003). The literature on learning in the workplace, in particular that pertaining to "communities of practice," can be applied to the process of learning as an unpaid activist because it focuses on the role of socialization as individuals learn from one another in a workplace or community (Lave & Wenger 1991; Wenger 1998; Boud & Garrick 1999; Beckett & Hager 2002; Billett 2004; Kenny 2006).

The literature that connects learning, knowledge, and identity provides insight into identity formation and activism. It locates the role of the self in identity formation as people learn to be and become activists (Focault 1980, 1983; Chappell et al. 2003; Colley et al. 2003; Soloman 2003). Literature on identity formation in adult education views all learning as a project of identity work (Lave & Wenger 1991; Chappell et al. 2003; Hodkinson et al. 2004).

The literature on learning and embodiment has relevance to this study. The historical focus on rationalism in understanding learning as a cognitive process connected to the mind cannot account for activists' learning alone. (Loughlin 1996; Damasio 1999, 2005; Beckett & Hager 2000, 2002; Crossley 2001; Beckett & Morris 2003; Kovan & Dirkx 2003; Gonczi 2004; Beckett 2008).

The following chapter outlines the data and themes from the lifelong activists in the study. It then provides detailed case studies of four of the lifelong activists—Jorge Jorquera, Felicity Marlowe, *Kerry*, and Cam Walker.

4

The Lifelong Activists

Introduction

This chapter gives an overview and analysis of the learning practices of nine of the lifelong activists interviewed for this study. It provides a context for the detailed case studies that will be examined later in chapter 5. The thematic analysis offers insight into the complexity of the pedagogy of activists, and addresses the central research question: "What are the stages and processes of learning and identity formation for activists engaged in social action?" This question and associated subquestions are used as a guide to understand the various areas of activists' learning, including: the stages and phases in the learning process; activist identity formation or learning to "become" an activist; and the role of formal and informal learning in the learning of activists. First, a biographical account for each of the lifelong activists is given. Following this is an analysis of the data for the lifelong activists, using their narratives from their interviews. The data reveals the holistic nature of activists' pedagogy as they engage in social change within and against the state. It shows that their early politicization occurs through involvement in student politics or exposure to political opinion in their families and has led to their continued involvement in social movements over the longer term.

The Lifelong Activists—Biographical Profiles

Jonathan has been involved in activism for more than 20 years. He is a committed environmentalist a long-term member of Friends of the Earth (FOE)in Melbourne. He has an undergraduate and a postgraduate qualification in psychology, and was involved in environmental campaign groups at university. He has been involved in many long-term campaigns, as a campaign organizer and participant. He is connected to social movements such as the anticorporate globalization movement, the environment movement, peace and men's movements. *Jonathan* was a key organizer of the protest in Melbourne against the World Economic Trade Forum (WETF) in 2003. He was involved in human blockades in the Middle East, assisting Palestinians to move between the borders of Gaza and Israel. He is presently employed as a counselor for men who have a history of violence towards women. He continues to be involved in a range of activist groups and movements.

Dr. Jean McLean was one of the founding members of the Save Our Sons (SOS) movement that campaigned against conscription and Australia's participation in the Vietnam War in the 1960s. She was arrested eighteen times and jailed once for her direct action against conscription in 1962. She has no formal qualifications. Her parents were active members of the Communist Party of Australia (CPA). She has been involved in many campaigns and social movements. A member of the ALP from 1965, Jean McLean made her first attempt to gain election to the Victorian parliament in 1973, when she stood as a candidate in the Legislative Council province of Monash. She served in the Victorian parliament as the ALP member for Boronia province in the Legislative Council from 1985–1992, and then as the member for Melbourne West province from 1992 until her retirement in 1999. Since retiring from politics she remains an advocate for many social justice issues, in particular, the rebuilding of East Timor. In 2003 she was awarded an honorary doctorate from Victoria University in Melbourne for her services to politics and community.

Cam Walker is the Campaign Coordinator for FOE, Australia. He has worked with FOE since 1989. He has been involved in all aspects of the organization and campaigned on dozens of issues, from forests to toxic waste, Indigenous affairs, sustainability, and climate change. His main campaign focus at present includes the social and human rights dimensions of climate change and water policy issues. He represents FOE at a national level, working with government, industry, unions, and Indigenous and community organizations. He spent six years on the Executive Committee of FOE International, attending many meetings dealing with international conventions and treaties, and has travelled and worked extensively with NGOs and local communities in Latin America, Europe and, most recently, Africa.

He presently lectures part-time in the School of Social Sciences at RMIT University. He continues to be involved in a range of social movements.

Felicity Marlowe was involved in student politics in the 1990s at Melbourne University. She was elected National Union of Students State Education Officer in 1997. Between 2000 and 2003, Felicity was a member of the Democratic Socialist Party (DSP). She has a bachelor degree in education, and has worked as a student rights officer at the RMIT Student Union in Melbourne, as a community development teacher at Victoria University, and as a research officer and youth worker for same-sex-attracted young people. She has been involved in social movements relating to free education, East Timor, gay and lesbian rights, refugee rights, and the anticorporate globalization movement. Her more recent activism focused on social and legal recognition for rainbow families. She was the coordinator of the successful Rainbow Families Council's "Love Makes a Family" campaign, which achieved legal recognition for same-sex parents and fertility access rights for lesbian women and gay men in Victoria, with the passing of the Assisted Reproductive Treatment Act (2008). Felicity was a founding member of the Rainbow Families Council established in 2006 and remained an active committee member until 2011. From 2005 until 2008 she was employed by the Australian Research Centre in Sex, Health and Society as the Rainbow Network Coordinator, providing professional development and resources for workers working with same-sex-attracted and gender-questioning young people in Victoria. In 2008, she was nominated as one of the 25 most influential gay and lesbian Australians. Currently, Felicity is a full-time parent of her and her partner's three young children and, with her young family, is about to move into the first purpose-built cohousing community in Victoria.

Garry Rothman was an anticonscription campaigner during the Vietnam War. In 1970, he attended Monash University and became involved with the Labour Club that was a radical left-wing political group at that time. Through an alliance with other left-wing groups, he became involved in the socialist/communist community in general and supported the liberation of Vietnam in particular. He moved to the UK in 1973 after traveling through Asia, and set up a business in London importing and selling Chinese medicinal herbs and Chinese arts, crafts, and books, then returned to Australia in 1985, where he started a family. In 2001 Garry enrolled in a Diploma of Community Services (Financial Counseling) course and since graduating has been employed in a number of agencies, most notably Broadmeadows Uniting Care, and Moreland Hall Drug and Alcohol Treatment Centre. He has been a member of the Financial and Consumer Rights Council. (FCRC) and held the positions of convener of the Victorian Network of Financial Counselors and convener of the Infringements Working Group, through which he sits as a community representative on the Infringement Standing Advisory Council facilitated by the Department of Justice. As a consequence of this work, he has often been able to advocate for disadvantaged and marginalized people through the media and has made appearances on *Insight*, *The 7:30 Report*, *Lateline*, *Today Tonight*, *A Current Affair* and many ABC radio programs. He continues to advocate with passion for his clients on an individual basis and, through his casework, advocates for systemic change.

Jorge Jorquera first became involved in political activity in his early teens. After fleeing the Pinochet dictatorship, he arrived in Australia with his parents and two brothers, and has worked with the Chilean exile community through the Chile Solidarity Committee in Brisbane. At 14 he joined the ALP and remained a member until the beginning of the Hawke Government years.[1] During this time, he was also active in community work especially through the St Vincent de Paul Society, serving as a state representative for the Vinnies Youth arm of the organization.[2] After commencing study at the University of Queensland, Jorge and some collaborators founded a small socialist discussion group. He later joined the Socialist Workers Party and was elected secretary of the University of Queensland Student Union in 1987. During these years Jorge was a founding member of various student organizations and national campaign coalitions against tertiary fees. Throughout the 1990s, he was a political organizer for the Democratic Socialist Party (DSP) that he left with others to form the Revolutionary Socialist Party. He is one of the cofounders of the Popular Education Network of Australia (PENA) and a founding member of the Melbourne Bolivarian Circles and the Centre for Latin American Studies and Solidarity. Jorge teaches political economy, sociology, and advocacy. He continues to be involved in a range of activist groups and movements.

Kerry is an Indigenous woman from the Yorta Yorta tribe. She has been involved in Indigenous politics since her early 20s. She has worked in a range of public service roles, mainly with a focus on education. More recently, she has been employed in a university setting as the acting director of an Indigenous education unit. *Kerry* provides lectures and talks to students, staff and community groups about the importance of cultural heritage to the identity of Aboriginal people and was appointed a member of the new Victorian Aboriginal Heritage Council, one of a group of Victorian Indigenous people who will advise the Victorian State Government on cultural heritage. She is also presently a board member of the Victorian Equal Opportunity Commission. She continues to be involved in a range of political and community groups involved in Indigenous politics.

Rose was involved in the student union at La Trobe University, where she became active in student politics. She was elected Women's Research Officer and became engaged in a number of campaigns on campus. She has a bachelor of arts in Leisure Studies and a master's degree in social policy. *Rose* has had a lifelong commitment to social justice and community development. Her research has focused on the area of neighborhood renewal, mostly in the west of Melbourne. She was a founding member of the Rainbow Family Council, a campaign group working toward fertility access rights for lesbian women, and along with Felicity Martin, *Rose* was instrumental in changing government legislation regarding fertility rights for homosexuals in Victoria. She is presently the coconvener of the Rainbow Families Council and is still actively concerned with issues of same-sex discrimination and fertility rights. She is presently employed as a research fellow at La Trobe University and continues to be involved in a range of activist groups and movements.

Max was involved in student politics from an early age at TAFE. He was chair of the student union and became involved in a range of campaign issues on campus. *Max* has a bachelors degree in social work and a graduate diploma in education, and has studied sociology and politics. He has been employed as a community development worker and is involved in an array of community engagement and community building projects. He presently teaches community development studies at TAFE. A former member of the Builders Laborers Federation (BLF) and a committed unionist himself, *Max* was elected as the vice president of a major education union for a period of three years. He continues to be involved in a range of activist groups and movements.

Typologies and Their Limitations

As outlined in chapter 1, the central focus of this book is the examination of two groups of activists: lifelong activists and circumstantial activists. Lifelong activists are activists who have been involved in activism for many years, often since adolescence. Circumstantial activists, on the other hand, have become involved in activism due to a specific life event. Naturally, there are limitations in any typology, and there are some circumstantial activists such as *Catherine* who have gone on to practice activism for a long period of time. The distinguishing feature of the typology is that lifelong activists have had a long experience of political engagement and social movements through their involvement in student union politics, their family's culture or through relationships with significant mentors. Circumstantial activists' involvement is often initiated by a life transition, a traumatic event, or a confluence of circumstances that have driven the person to act or take action.

Stages and Phases of Learning

Lifelong Activists—Early Politicization, Early Learning

The interviews commenced with a request for the activists to outline their history of learning to provide a picture of the breadth and depth of their activism. Many of the lifelong activists began with a reference to their intrinsic sense of social justice or understanding of inequality that motivated them to act against or speak up about injustice in the world. As *Max* notes, he knew as a school boy that something was unjust when he saw a nun at school behave violently towards a young girl:

> I remember at one stage there was a young girl who was taken out to the classroom [and] was strapped by the nuns! I remember I had an awareness that there was something not quite right with that. The next day I went back and I went to the presbytery where they had the altar boy list up and I went and rubbed my name off the list. That precipitated a visit home by the priest that night to ask if I knew anything about it. Yes, I rubbed my name off. I did not want to be a member of the Catholic Church anymore. Yes, I vividly remember that as a first [political] act.

For some of these activists, family, religion, or politics provided a starting point for an activist identity. Garry belonged to a Zionist Jewish family that immigrated to Australia. Garry's family supported socialism and they voted for the Communist Party in the Soviet Union. Jeannie also had parents who were Jewish immigrants and members of the CPA. She remembers being "politicized" by her mother who used to "go collecting money for sheepskins" to send to Russia. Jeannie remembered, "we always discussed politics and especially my father who was, you know, a humanist." Jeannie was a small business owner with young children and was involved with artists in craft groups when she first became involved in activism after the Australian government announced compulsory conscription in 1964. She decided, "there is no point standing around in the street. Let's try and do something about it," and with a group of young mothers she organized a public meeting. Like Jeannie, Jorge learned about socialist politics from an early age around the family's kitchen table. His parents had fled Pinochet's Chile after 1973 and settled in Australia.

Jorge believes his family was influential in building an early political awareness in him. Felicity's parents were practicing Catholics and she became concerned about social justice in her early adolescence while attending a Catholic school. Her maternal grandfather was a foundation member of the Catholic Worker in the 1930s alongside Bob Santamaria. They later had a falling out with Santamaria going on to became a leading member of the Democratic Labor Party (DLP), formed by a group of dissidents from the broader Labor Party.[3] In contrast, *Kerry* is an Indigenous woman. Her father, who was a well-known footballer and Indigenous man, never spoke about Aboriginal politics. This made her feel, from an early age, that she wanted to "have a voice" on issues. She believed that her father had faced discrimination that had led to his reluctance to claim his Aboriginal heritage. *Kerry* became involved in Indigenous politics in her adolescence. The parents of *Jonathan* were not politically minded either. He started to become interested in activism in his early twenties when he joined a Community Aid Abroad group in his first year of a master's degree at university. Cam's parents, too, are described as being "completely apolitical." Cam has a long history of involvement in a range of social movements, particularly the environment movement. In his adolescence, he discovered an affinity with nature and the environment through bushwalking. Cam made a very deliberate political decision at 17 to become an environmental activist. He became a vegetarian and then went in search of groups he could learn from and work with:

> I used to travel into [Melbourne] and just shopped around to find out all the groups I could find. [I] went to rallies [and] took everyone's leaflets, then followed up with, and went through, a vast number of groups;

everything from left-wing socialist organizations, environmental organizations, vegetarian groups [and] human rights organizations.

Rose first became politicized when she started studying women's studies at TAFE. Her parents "were conservatives" who, she felt, needed to change. She was awakened by the literature she was reading on feminism, which raised her awareness of women's oppression and made her question the gender roles of her mother and father. At that point, she thought,

> Oh my God, this makes sense to me. This makes sense to my life experience and it makes sense of what I see around me...You know, I went home questioning my mother "Why have you lived like this"? angry at my father, you know.

But she regards her motivation for activism to be fundamentally more deep-seated, always "wanting to see change" in society, whether in relation to women's issues or discrimination against the gay and lesbian community or fertility access rights for same-sex couples.

Student Politics

Almost all of the lifelong activists were involved in student politics at some time and, for some, the involvement took primacy over study and other activities. Felicity believes she learned everything that she needed to know about politics from her experience of student politics at university: "Student politics teaches you everything you ever needed to know about how state and federal politics work, I reckon, and it's all about factions!" Felicity became involved in the socialist arm of the student union early in her second year of teacher education. She was "education officer" in the student union in 1996, and then ran for National Union of Students [and] was elected as State Education Officer in 1997, then joined the DSP after university in 2000. It took Felicity seven years to complete her degree because she became involved in so many issues at university. Similarly, Jorge started an arts degree at 17 in Brisbane, and through his family's politics, was already "very politicized." He became involved in the union movement and was elected general secretary of the student union. He became involved in so many activist issues on campus, he never finished his degree. *Rose*, like Felicity, became involved in feminist politics in the student union and was quickly elected to the position of Women's Officer, "So I was Women's Officer for the next two years and that was my very first experience of taking a strong lead role as an activist." Similarly, *Max* ran the Student Association of the Bendigo College of Advanced Education and states "I got involved in a whole heap of political stuff there!" Garry, too, became swept up in activism at university in the 1970s. On arrival at university, and despite being "fairly conservative" at the outset, he became very active in the antiwar movement:

> I got swept away with the wave of student dissent at Monash and the Labor Club that was very active at the time with Albert Langer, Mike Hyde, Jim Bacon and Jim Faulk and the draft resisters, who were very prominent at that time and I quickly became supportive of the anti-war movement, the anti-conscription movement and then became involved in socialist organizations.

Garry then joined the Worker Student Alliance aligned with the Young Communists League (YCL) and the CPA, and became more intensely involved in the anti-conscription movement. Cam became involved in student politics when he joined an education action group on campus at Rusden.

Developing an Activist Epistemology

Critical Thinking

The activists in this study frequently spoke about developing a theoretical framework for practice, thinking critically about society and inequality, and learning to ask critical questions. Jorge believes he learned to think critically through his activism; he believes his knowledge about structures and systems in society resulted from his direct action. Jorge says he learned never to be satisfied with the first answer he was given. He also started to critically question issues in society or, as he says, "to keep asking questions." His philosophical mindset has required him to think critically and develop a "systemic framework." He believes that he has acquired and developed knowledge informally over many years, although Jorge argues his real ability to think critically came from his political involvement with the DSP. While he did study some sociology and philosophy at university, he believes it was through his long association with a group of socialists—the

"Stalinized left"—that he learned about Marxism. He joined the DSP and became a long-term active member:

> I joined the DSP [and] I was there with two of my brothers for over ten to fifteen years and active on and off in that time. I'd say I still had sympathy for the "Trotskyites" movement within Marxism. As people, they are generally the most critical amongst the Marxist left.

Felicity believes many of her skills came from "being critical." What she is referring to is looking beyond the immediate situation or issue, learning to understand political systems and structures that create inequality and this is reflected in the statement below:

> I mean the argument really is that if there's any social justice in the world, I mean, if there's any conflict around the human rights movement, everyone is affected. Which is the same argument about why people should not support war and they should free the refugees and they should all campaign against climate change or whatever, because it doesn't matter whether it affects you in your day to day life; any kind of infringement on human rights or social justice affects everybody.

Max believes his early days of "hammer and tongs" activism was important. He was what he defines as an "angry young man" and describes himself as being a "rock thrower" for a long time. He enjoyed the processes of direct action because it gave him a space to channel his anger. Then he started to develop knowledge about the uses of representative democracy and it was after this that he began to build his political knowledge and understanding of political systems:

> I'll simplify it by saying that everything is a representative system and if you want to change something, you just have to find out, how many votes are taken and put something together to see how you can incrementally get 52% on whatever government, party board or students' council whatever, that they all had the same fundamental weakness built into them: that they use a democratic process.

Cam found in his early days of environmental activism that he started to build an awareness of "how change happens" that involved understanding democratic systems and structures and becoming "less dogmatic" in order to "find ways to work with other people." He says he started to understand "theories of change" and then developed an idea about "a big picture" on social change issues. Cam believes his commitment to nonviolence laid the foundation of his political understanding as he began to "consciously learn models for understanding power and understanding new societies." Garry, likewise, observed:

> that once I became aware of injustice and social justice and international injustice, the exploitation of people, I just really felt in my heart, I really felt committed, that I really wanted to do something, that I wanted to be involved and that I could do something.

Some of the lifelong activists developed highly specialized skills like *Rose* who, after many years of activism, has gained expert understandings about "laws which discriminate against lesbians" and developed broad knowledge about the ways in which legislation affects and discriminates against lesbians:

> My main interest has been in lesbians having children, the laws that discriminate against lesbians in that situation, laws and actions that discriminate against lesbians once they do have children as lesbian parents.... So I've been involved in a variety of capacities over the last ten years, and in the early days the focus of my work was around lesbians accessing fertility and other services, and exploring issues around legal and social discrimination.

Jeannie's participation in the anti-Vietnam movement saw her travel to Vietnam, the USA and Europe to connect up with other solidarity groups who were trying to engineer an end to the Vietnam War. Her knowledge about the processes of war and government, and the nature of corruption and oppression developed quickly. She says that events in Vietnam equipped her to "read the signs of oppression" in Pinochet's Chile later on:

> It's very educative insofar as if you are to look into any social situation, if you look into the various Latin American countries, like what happened in Chile. Australia, as well as the United States, supported Pinochet in murdering, and getting rid of the government there.

Jonathan's environmental activism took him to Palestine and Gaza where he joined blockades to allow residents' access to Israel. He says his commitment is to "world ethics" and action against a "lack of dignity or oppression." His own involvement in activism over many years has been structured around a deep concern for trying to live and build a more sustainable and equitable society, and he argues his approach now is "much more spiritual and political," whereas previously he had a simplistic "desire to help other people and other cultures."

Formal Learning

Most of the lifelong activists have had postsecondary education of some kind, secured over protracted periods of interrupted study. Cam and Felicity are both trained secondary school teachers; *Jonathan* studied psychology at university and has a master's degree. *Rose* initially trained as a childcare worker then went on to gain a degree in social work and a master's degree in public policy, studying sociology, women's studies and politics. Similarly, *Max* has a degree in social work and a postgraduate qualification in education and has studied sociology and politics. Jorge, who never completed his undergraduate arts degree, is now studying for a master's degree in education and has a certificate in education and training. However, he did study sociology, philosophy and politics for his uncompleted undergraduate degree. Jeannie never gained a formal qualification but has been awarded an honorary doctorate for her work in politics. *Kerry*, who is employed as an Indigenous educator at a university, has participated in some units of training, including many short courses and professional development programs, but has no formal degree.

The majority of activists have not, however, had formal training in activism. For most of these lifelong activists, their learning has come from socializing with other activists, by observing other activists in their practices, or through being involved in direct action campaigning, by participating in strategy or campaign meetings and by being involved with a range of networks, community groups, NGOs and social movements. The exceptions to this were *Jonathan* who had done some training with Joanna Macy (1991) "on deep ecology and spirituality" when he attended a six-day residential training program, and Cam who had attended and facilitated workshops on principles of nonviolent activism. Activists such as Jorge, *Rose*, Garry and *Max*, who studied politics, sociology and philosophy at university, found it a useful foundation of theory for understanding systems of government and society. Nevertheless, this research indicates that formal training in activism is rare and learning is chiefly achieved through extended immersion in activist activities and the processes of socialization.

Social Learning

Most of the lifelong activists believe they have learned a great deal of their skill development and knowledge through being involved with other activists or learning through practice. *Kerry*'s initial social contact with other Indigenous Australians allowed her to learn about her clan group, the Yorta Yorta people, and to make contact with other people who were involved in Aboriginal politics. A good friend gave her access to a significant network of people involved in Indigenous politics:

> He just opened a whole set of doors for me that filled the space. There was always this empty space about who I was and where I fitted, and there was always a need to know more and not really realizing what it is that I needed to know. And so it was through those early days of working with him that I got to know about all the Aboriginal organizations around the Melbourne metro area, plus also got to know a whole lot of aunties and uncles, Yorta Yorta people.

Jorge has developed most of his knowledge and skill informally through being involved in many activist groups, but his early learning was through protest:

> In the early days [what] we learned about were really practical things, and all of the tenacity that goes with that [such as] pickets, protests. Apart from being involved in the student union we were more than that; we were a part of a really effervescent movement against Joh Bjelke-Petersen.[4]

Jorge believes that he is "a collective learner" and he believes that in the activist environment he learned a "lot of people skills." The social nature of his learning is reflected by the following quote:

> I think [from] all of the left groups I have been involved in I have learned something. Right now I could join any of the groups in Melbourne and learn something. I am very much a collective learner.

Max says he learned about politics and political systems not in a "blinding flash" but "incrementally." He and a group of community workers became involved in running a candidate against John Brumby[5]—with some success because they only lost by a few votes. *Max* recalls "it caused a big ruckus in the Labor Party" at the time.

Felicity believes that she has learned all sorts of things from observing activists in action, including:

> How to talk to police, how not to talk to police, how to do police liaison,[and] how to think about organizing large numbers of people to do something [and] how to manage volunteers in situations where they have to collect money for Timor; how to organize conferences[and] events.

In response to a question about what she had learned informally in the processes of activism she states, "I have learned all my skills through observation and practice." Felicity argues the social environment of activist meetings have been fertile ground for skill development:

> I think over the years other skills I've learnt have been around successful meetings that are action-orientated, and again that came through observing good and bad practice at various meetings. Those things I've just learnt more and more through practise.

Rose puts forward the view that her skills in community development and her work with communities have been pivotal for her work as an activist, stressing the importance of not "acting in isolation." She claims, "the community development-type group processes and engagements of people along the way are as critical as the actions you take in terms of meeting with government." The importance of acting with others is crucial. *Rose* emphasizes that building relationships with people she is working with is a vital skill in activists' work. She affirms the view that "people have been critical to my learning, [having] key people around me to learn from." For *Rose*, this is particularly important as she describes her learning as strongly experiential and action focused:

> The work that I did as the Women's Officer in the Student Union was really formative as well, that was really learning, even the Neighborhood House work, it was all flying by the seat of my pants, that's how I used to describe what I did.

In these environments, social and support networks are crucial. During these early days of activism *Rose* became "hooked into a network" of women's studies students who were interested in feminism. She then found herself "...hooked into a network of academics who were interested in women's issues, and that was a whole other level of expertise and experience that I was exposed to." Jeannie found herself working with a diverse group of women on the SOS campaign. She subsequently met other prominent activists, draft resisters, and joined the ALP, connecting herself with many different groups in the union movement. The anticonscription movement was growing and gaining momentum, so she was socializing and learning from a variety of different individuals, activist groups and political organizations.

Learning Skills "on the Job" of Activism

Most of the lifelong activists believed the majority of their skill development came from practising their activism "on the job," whether through direct action protests or through the numerous meetings and campaign groups with which they had been involved. Their skill development was rarely acquired through formal knowledge transfer at university or school. A majority of the skills were foundational skills for community development work such as communication skills and understanding group processes. They learned about group dynamics and group work, about getting groups to function well, and they learned about getting people involved on an issue or learning to work as a part of a larger campaign organization or social movement. *Jonathan* learned many skills through participating in social action, including event management skills. He learned how to organize an event, how to engage and mobilize large numbers of activists, how to manage the protesters, how to work with police, how to manage traffic and work with local government. He says that most of the actions with which he has been involved included "hundreds and thousands of people." He supports the view that learning though direct action has been significant for him and adds, "there is a whole heap of direct action stuff, a whole heap of tactics that you learn on the job and you apply before the next action." There is reflexivity in this statement: what had not worked previously would be reconsidered before the next action. *Jonathan* notes, however, that his direct action activities have not always produced an immediate outcome:

> A lot of my activism hasn't been immersed in a campaign, [which] I've [been] working on for 3 or 4 years to achieve an outcome. It has been [through] direct action or major blockading or non-violent direct action in the occupied territories. I'm quite interested in culture jamming stuff, [6]so doing things that are going to challenge the basic means of capitalism.

Jeannie, who has no formal qualifications, but who went on to have a significant career in Victorian state politics, "always read books and magazines." Yet it was the social environment of the practice of activism that really deepened and developed her knowledge:

> Whatever I learnt it was through working with people of a like mind; [and] the importance of constantly replenishing your knowledge about the issues and also about all of the [other related] peripheral issues.

Both Felicity and *Rose* also spent a great deal of time accommodating the dynamics of the various groups in which they were involved. Felicity says she often had to run meetings at the DSP so that they would reflect the broader gender representation of the group because the men tended to dominate the discussion. So she would allow time for both genders to speak. *Rose* has spent a great deal of time playing the role of "pragmatist" in her current campaign group, building relationships and trying to get the best and most useful skills out of the people with whom she is working. This role includes mentoring newcomers and matching less experienced activists to more skilled campaigners in the group. In essence, the newer members of the group become apprenticed to the more experienced activists. The following statements by *Rose* and Felicity represent their highly developed communication and facilitation skills. Felicity says, for example:

> I'm very good at making sure everyone's respected and acknowledged for participating,... to make sure that every meeting's a participatory action kind of meeting, so everyone gets a chance to speak. We might break up into small groups so people get to know each other and they come back to a meeting with their actions, we divvy up [these] actions and make sure that there's [a] shared delegation of tasks.

Rose says:

> I think one of the roles that I play in groups is a peacemaker. I'm often the one that will be doing the summing up of an argument, bringing things back as they fly off, identifying differences, identifying similarities so that we know what the common ground is. I tend to take on that role.

Cam, like *Jonathan* and Felicity, has developed event management skills that he describes as "good process and facilitation skills," but most of the skills he has "learned on the job" through "facilitating big meetings and meetings of diverse people," adding "I've learnt a lot about speaking in public and writing in a moderately coherent way." Garry gained a great deal of skill through using the media, skills that have developed to a sophisticated level in recent years. He says his knowledge has changed from his direct action days:

> I think my knowledge level and the issues that I speak out on now are much higher. I've understood that I need to be really clear and articulate about the issues that I am talking about and that I just can't wing it—I can't bullshit my way through because it does me more harm than good! Probably in those early days it was just a cause, whereas today its more specific issues I'm talking about. I've learned a lot about how to perform in the media, [and how] to get the message across in the media.

Kerry's initial learning was about developing her knowledge of Indigenous history, learning her culture and building up credibility with the Indigenous community. She says she learned "advocacy skills" and began to understand the "language of government." She learned how to build and establish relationships with key people. In particular, she found that "I was really good at writing that policy stuff in the language that the policy makers wanted to see."

Significant Mentors

Many of the lifelong activists involved in the study referred to the role that significant mentors had played in assisting them to hone their skills. *Rose* had a couple of significant mentors who were initially her lecturers at university, but with whom she later became involved in activist and community groups. One mentor was a bureaucrat who managed a government department. *Rose* believes this person was significant to her learning and development, particularly in terms of her acquisition of knowledge about systems of government and social change. She argues:

> I think that mentoring is different to observing, because I think mentoring is someone actively making a commitment to you that they will offer you something, whether that is meeting with you and talking about what is going on or what could happen or offering advice, and I

had a range of people like that in my life and they were really important ways for me to learn, very important ways for me to learn.

Rose's mentor helped her to reflect on her practices and develop alternative strategies so she could "influence the right people and [get] a decision made in the right place." Garry also had a mentor to help him develop skills, someone who had "an enormous amount of experience in community development work and advocacy work" and he would spend time practicing and role-playing media interviews with her. *Kerry*'s early politicization occurred when she became a public servant and met a significant Indigenous mentor, whom she later realized she was related to through the Yorta Yorta people. Through this relationship and by having social contact with other Indigenous people, she started to learn about her Indigenous heritage and discovered the potential of activism. She started to think "Wow! So there is stuff I can do that involves Indigenous people." She then began to immerse herself in Indigenous politics. Initially, Cam had a couple of former teachers who became informal mentors and helped him learn and connect with other environmental activists and protest groups:

> I was lucky I had those teachers in the early stages and I had some older activists, there was a guy for instance who kind of looked after me a little bit and took me to events and forums in that first year of activism.

But it was the women in the FOE collective who really challenged him to change, be reflexive and improve his practices.

> In the early days of FOE I was very basic and minimal in my communications and I was really called on that and [told] "That isn't good enough. You have to tell us what you think, you have to explain yourself," and I mean [I was] really challenged by some of the older people in the organization. You know a kind of the sharp stick prodding me out from where I was. That was fantastic in hindsight. [It was] not only my failures or shortcomings but the places where I wasn't so strong and [they were] willing to push me out of them, that was really useful.

Like Cam, *Max* had a woman as a mentor and worked with this person for a long time in various community development projects:

> She was always interested in broader social change stuff and we worked together on that and achieved some really phenomenal projects. She

now works for Red Cross and works on the Asia Pacific region. She taught me heaps and heaps about patience and she also taught me some really incredible lessons about how I used to be so rigid about enemies and allies.

Jorge had many activists in his family who were influential and there were also family friends from Latin America who were socialists. He became involved in the union movement and the ALP through members of his family. An uncle, who now resides in Paris, had been an active socialist for most of his life and this relationship had a significant impact on Jorge.

Identity: Learning to Become an Activist

The issue of identity is an important focus of this research and in all of the interviews the activists explored how they would define their activist roles. Most of the lifelong activists tended to identify as activists and this identification is connected to a large extent with their sense of "self." *Jonathan*, for example, reveals, "…activism is a huge part of who I am and I could not imagine myself without being an activist and doing activism, so it's a huge driver for me." He felt that he would always be involved in activism of some kind:

> My major meaning and purpose of life comes through doing activism and there has certainly been a period of six months in my life here and there where I strode away from it a fair bit but it was still central for me. It's massively important to my self identity and my way of life and my way of relating to others.

Rose also retains her activist identity but at times this has presented difficulties for her present career as an academic. She believes there have been times when requests for research grant funding were compromised because of her activism. Nevertheless, she says that "I would describe myself as an activist and I would say that because I am actively involved with others in campaigns for change." Likewise, Felicity says that she knew when she first became involved in student politics that she was an activist. She would rather use that term than "lobbyist" or "advocate," and in the interview she lamented the change in her role from activist involved in direct action to someone who is now involved in lobbying within the existing system of government. Regardless of her skills ("she can do advocacy") she rejects that identity:

> I'm not [an advocate], I'm an activist, because that just means you can step out of the boundaries of more formal discussions. It gives you the flexibility to do "prams on parliament"[7] or whatever you want to do!

Cam believes it is important for activists to claim the identity of activist. For him it is not just something done "between uni and your real job." He thinks that for profound social change to occur a new systemic approach is needed, saying "it is how you approach the world." Identifying as an activist is a part of that. While Cam is keen to emphasize that it is not a part of his whole identity, he nevertheless regards activism as an important part of his identity, explaining:

> I think of activism as a life path [and] it is imperative that people identify as that and say I'm really proud to be this. I'm lots of other things like a Dad or a teacher or whatever but I am definitely an activist.

For Cam this identity promotes authentic social and civic engagement. He contends that it easy to complain about problems in society and much harder to be an "engaged participant in life." He says having an "activist lens" is important so that you are not just "being cynical and complaining [and] only observing; you are actually engaging and actively trying to change society." Jorge's activism is deeply embedded in his sense of "self." He frequently referred to his activism in terms of "the trade," "the game," or "the job." His activist identity is present in everything he does; work, life, family, and friendships are very much connected to his activism. For this reason his discussion of doubts about where "the politics of the 'left' is going" takes on the urgency of an existential crisis. Jeannie, who is now officially retired through still very active in politics, identifies as an activist, but now limits and has redefined the nature of her involvement. She doesn't go to as many "demos" as she "gets tired if she walks too far." She says at this time in her life she is more "specific in the things I'll turn up to... I'm still an activist though at slightly different levels than I was."

However, some of the activists were very ambivalent about identifying with the "activist" label, although they conceded its applicability. *Kerry* is unsure about identifying as an activist, seeing herself more as a mentor for other Indigenous people. The following statement reflects her view of her social change work:

> There are probably non-Indigenous people who see me as an activist, but I do not look at myself in the mirror and think that. When I look in the mirror I see someone who's a role model and a mentor for people who can aspire to change who they are, because they can see me making changes, and they can see that if you have a voice you can do a whole set of things. You may not do them straight away, but you can do them.

Garry was reluctant to identify as an activist, because he sees some differences between his early student politics and anticonscription activism, and the social change work that he is participating in now. He advances the view that, "I would not have called myself an activist, but I am very active in my sector in working towards systemic change and I suppose this is an activist." Garry's ambivalence about identifying as an activist reflects a concern about putting labels on himself and the work that he does. He maintains that, "I just consider the work that I do as more than just being an activist, so being an activist is a part of my work absolutely. So when you say 'Are you an activist?' I always shy away from saying, putting a label on...it might be part of what I do, but it is not who I am!" *Max* says he probably doesn't identify as an activist because "I do not see anything that I am doing as being really significant," however, he links this statement with the desire to know "that he has made a difference." Like *Max* and Garry, *Kerry* also engages in social change work and has participated in direct action by attending rallies and protests despite harboring ambivalence about her identity as an activist. *Kerry*, however, attributes this to the fact that some aspects of the activist identity can be viewed negatively: "it's a harsh message when some activists get on their soap boxes." A desire to not be associated with self-aggrandizing positions is influential in her reluctance to claim an activist identity.

Emotions and Learning

An important finding of this research is the role that emotions play in activists' learning. Activists frequently referred to the role of the emotions in motivating them to act, and in maintaining their commitment over the longer term. For Jorge, his family's persecution in Chile and the decision to flee their country are at the core of his reasons for becoming an activist. He is passionate about change and he believes that he will always be committed to social action because of his family's history. The long quote that follows shows Jorge using both mind and emotions to reflect on the reasons for his activism, demonstrating his depth of emotional, intellectual and spiritual insight:

> You know, you can intellectually know something like every other person that has been involved in politics. At an intellectual level I know there is a chance of fundamental social change. We have no idea of what is going to happen, it may take another three generations to get there and total fucking destruction of the environment! I was aware of this when I was twelve that I may die without seeing any fundamental change in the country. I sort of hope that I wouldn't go without seeing it in Latin America. I still hope that and I have seen some [change] in Venezuela. This is where Catholicism and Christianity comes into it because I still have a lot of those sentiments though [no longer] religious. I still have that notion of ministering and [all of] the passion of that.

Jorge claims leaders like Che Guevara connected the place of "passion and emotion" in struggle. Both Cam and *Kerry* argue that passion and responsibility to others are the drivers of their activism:

> (Cam) I just think everyone should have the right to basic stuff, you know, food and shelter and water and we should do that without burning us off the planet. They're just inalienable truths as far as I can see, and yet both of those things are not happening so the question is "Will I do something about it or do I ignore it or do I complain about it"?
>
> (Kerry) I think it's just being passionate, and if you're passionate enough to share what you know then you share it in a way that people feel it coming from your heart and coming from your soul. They get to understand those things.

Jeannie and Garry's involvement in the anticonscription movement provided them with a real emotional connection to the human rights abuses associated with war. Both of them travelled to Vietnam and Indochina and were deeply affected by what they experienced and saw. Their emotional agency reflects the horror of seeing the impact of war on local communities.

> (Garry) A real turning point for me was when I went to Indochina and I saw people with kids [who had] their legs blown off, people who were

not a part of any political movement, they were just people in a war zone. It changed me. I think it made me more human. It humanized me in lots of ways, [and] I'm feeling quite emotional about it now. I think seeing that kind of suffering changed me forever!

(Jeannie) I mean it was just the most unbelievably difficult primitive stuff and to know that our side was creating it. It was very hard to remove yourself from the human realities of things like that, [and] I've always functioned at that level.

Jonathan found that it was important to not disconnect from his feelings and to provide spaces for those feelings as a part of his work in activism. This connection of heart and head was influenced by Joanna Macy's writing on "heart politics" (Macy 1991). He believes in an "ethical striving or ethical responsibility" for others. He argues this is a "driven" thing; there is a "passion to work with others" for social change. Felicity said that she has had "emotional responses" to individual stories when she could not help being moved by that experience. She was involved with a large protest with the Maritime Union of Australia in 1998 during which they stayed up all night in a blockade with hundreds of people. She claims the experience "was passion and adrenalin and really exciting." She believes that anger is an important emotion to feel as an activist and states, "you have to have some degree of getting pissed off with things." Similarly *Rose* firmly holds the view that in activism "there is always a common commitment and passion that is the driver." It is the significance of "wanting to see change" or a connection to an issue that drives the emotion.

Recognition and management of that passion can be part of the learning of activism. *Max* acknowledges that when he was young activist he was not very sophisticated because he was angry at everything:

I was the classic angry young person that was lashing out at the world and I think that some causes gave me the opportunity to just be angry. So I think there was a whole lot of stuff for me at a personal level that I was working though in my adolescence [and] some of my explosions were able to be expressed out there. I think that I was targeting issues "out there," rather than holding the mirror up and looking at myself.

As he became more experienced as an organizer he used his emotions as a part of the theatre of activism. Emotions are used as a way to persuade or as a strategy to achieve a particular outcome. He says that change will not happen through an "angry outburst" and that you need something "more sophisticated and strategic than that." He says "he now realizes it is more important that he put his 'emotions in the background' if he is negotiating for change" and adds, "sure from time to time you do some theatre, you stand up and slap the table and walk out, [and the] emotions are on display, but they are there in a very controlled way."

Spirituality

Throughout the interview data is the strong theme of the influence of Christianity and spirituality on activists' sense of social justice. Felicity felt the teachings of the Catholic Church were instrumental for her development of a sense of social justice at an early age and she believes the teachings rather than the institution of religion were most important:

> I think that there's the institution of the Church with a capital C and there is the good works on the ground, the kind of work that people do. It was more through the good works on the ground that people do in local communities or as missionaries or aid kind of work.

Jonathan frequently referred to the influence of Joanna Macy's writing on his awareness of a connection between mind, spirit and the environment. *Kerry* has a deep connection to "country" a word used by Australia's Indigenous people to refer to the spiritual dimension and ancestral associations of landscape and place, as well as all living things within the landscape. She expressed an affinity with Indigenous culture, place, and time, and valued her connection to an ancient people and culture.

> Well, because you can actually go and say "I'm a Yorta Yorta woman and I have these connections and I am strong in my spirit and my strength of culture, and so this is what I know." I mean you may not be able to articulate to people what that knowledge is, but that's what gives you the authority because you know who you are and you know your culture.

Max believes his sense of social justice comes from his early Catholic schooling, reflecting that "One of the things that I think is at the nub of everything I do is the concept of social justice, and that I would have got from the Marist brothers." *Max* says the symbolism of the Catholic Church and the stories told in Sunday school and at his

Catholic school about helping people who were "needy or poor" were influential in developing his social justice framework. In school settings he believes he was made to think beyond the immediate:

> There was always the classic stuff, the cardboard tins, collection boxes for the poor, the destitute children, always going on. We were forced to think of other worlds beyond the ones that we were in. Certainly that concept of social justice was instilled at a really, really early age!

Cam was involved in Catholic groups in his adolescence, and believes this was influential. His father was a practicing Catholic, and his mother in those early days he believed was agnostic. He asserts that, "I became very active in the Catholic, kind of charismatic youth kind of thing in our local parish." Cam had a mentor at this time, a prominent activist in the Catholic Church. He then said he got a "good dose of anarchist politics and kind of rebelled against being connected with mainstream religion." However, Cam, like *Jonathan*, has a spiritual dimension to his relationship with the environment. Jorge won a scholarship to a Catholic school where he became keenly interested in "liberation theology." He was inspired by the Nicaraguan revolution at the time and considered becoming a missionary because the Catholic Church and liberation theology made such an impact in his early adolescence. He describes this spiritual awakening by saying:

> I started to be interested in liberation theology and I remember doing a bit of theology in school after secondary school for about 6 months. That sort of influenced me ethically I think. I remember when I was young I certainly entertained the idea of being a missionary, and, of course, by then the Nicaraguan revolution happened and I was very excited and inspired by that and a big chunk of that was liberation theology inspired by priests who had a role in the revolution. So that was influential.

Garry, originally from a Zionist Jewish family, notes that after his experience of seeing death and pain in Indochina he moved from his earlier Maoist politics to become a humanist. He is now a practicing Buddhist.

Conclusion

Lifelong activists tend to develop their skill over a much longer period of time and usually begin to develop an activist identity in adolescence. This identity evolves incrementally, "not in a blinding flash" as *Max* observed. Almost all of the lifelong activists were a part of the student union movement that appears to be a significant social and organizational space where early learning occurs. Lifelong activists like Jorge, *Max* and Jeannie had parents who were political people, members of the communist, socialist and Labor parties. The family environment led them to an array of social and family connections with others involved in politics and resistance movements, thus forming a strong identity of resistance. Lifelong activists from a very early age had greater connection to social and political movements in general. They also remained engaged in a broad range of social issues after many years of practice. Some, like Jeannie, went onto have a career in politics. Others, like Cam and *Max*, have gone on to be paid organizers. Others, like Garry, *Jonathan*, and *Felicity*, are working in community development projects, community building and advocacy, social research and human rights roles. The majority of lifelong activists have a strong sense of commitment to activism and it is an important part of their overall identity and how they view themselves in the world and in relation to others.

Lifelong activists develop knowledge about government systems and structures about inequality over a long period of time. They are critical thinkers, reflective about their own practices, passionately engaged in the politics of change in both their paid and unpaid work, and eager to develop greater expertise through ongoing practice. Most of the lifelong activists have postsecondary qualifications in community development, education, social work, psychology, or social welfare work. They have previously studied subjects such as sociology, politics, and psychology, which contributed to their grounding in political and sociological theory and the development of their ontology and epistemology of activism. In addition, their practice of activism has been facilitated by mentor relationships and informal "apprenticeships" that have given them the opportunity to observe and socialize with more experienced "master activists" to become more skillful at their craft.

The next section of this chapter gives a deeply personal account of the lifelong activists' journeys of learning in the case studies of Jorge Jorquera, Felicity Marlowe, Cam Walker and *Kerry*.

Case Study: Jorge's Story

> *"You know as children we spent our childhood sitting around the kitchen table listening to our parents talk politics."*

Jorge has been involved in activism for most of his life through his commitment to socialism and Latin American politics. When asked about his history of activism he says "A lot of it is tied into my family background and even to this day the history is really tied to my family fleeing Chile as a result...of the Pinochet dictatorship." His family fled in 1975 in order to escape the Pinochet regime after the military overthrow of the democratically elected Allende government and subsequent establishment of a repressive authoritarian regime. The family arrived in Australia as refugees and settled in Brisbane. From a very young age he and his brothers learned about socialism from his parents and relatives, who recounted experiences of fear, persecution, and oppression in Chile. In the early 1970s he and his brothers, and many other Chilean refugees in the Brisbane community, were involved in the résistance movement against the Pinochet regime:

> I played quite a role not only in solidarity politics, but in supporting democracy in Chile in an underground resistance movement against the dictatorship. [I] also actually became very politically active in Australian politics, in fact the bulk of the Chilean community in the '70s joined the Labor Party and in fact I joined the Labor Party for a few years as well.

Jorge says that his family members, like many Chileans of the time, were

> extremely political people and like many of the people who came out of Chile they were destroyed by what happened in Chile. There were those who were left leaning but not really activists, there were some who were economic refugees if you like, yet still really left leaning.

His father's brother was a leader in the resistance movement and was arrested and endured persecution, jail, and torture. When he eventually escaped, he resettled in France, while other family members settled in Australia. Jorge joined the Labor Party at the age of 13 and became involved in the party and, more broadly, the union movement.

When I asked Jorge about key people, mentors, or family members who had influenced his practices as an activist, it was obvious that his familial and cultural connections to Latin America were very important and continued to remain so. Jorge's bond to his family's history of oppression, death, torture, and persecution under the Pinochet regime featured prominently in the interview. His anger and frustration at his family's treatment have contributed to his sense of "self" and are important in his identity as an activist. In the following narrative, Jorge indicates how his family's concerns effectively served as the backdrop for his political socialization:

> ...You know as children we spent our childhood sitting around the kitchen table listening to our parents talk politics. I think this is interesting because what they've told us wasn't pedagogical; it was really about their stories that were heartfelt and sad and bitter.... It's not like we were taking in Marx or anything like that directly, it was mainly emotions and how we were affected by those stories. I mean psychologically-speaking it is quite amazing a lot of us were obviously the average kid who wanted to do something for their parents. Well, for us it became a political thing like that, finishing a journey they could not complete.

His parents' life stories, told to Jorge in childhood, that were "heartfelt, sad and bitter," have contributed to Jorge's motivation to act and participate in activism. His early experiences of leaving Chile and escaping the dictatorship have deeply affected his cultural identity and sense of place. These representations of his cultural history and their correlation to human rights abuses have contributed to his learning practices as an activist. For example, the threat of death, torture, or simply a relative going missing in the night and never to be seen again, have been profound. I asked Jorge to reflect on his family's experiences of fleeing Chile and how it had influenced his desire to take action:

> My family's lives, like a million Chileans at least, were whole lives that were destroyed by that experience, let alone the ones who stayed who would have died. But the ones who left almost died as well spiritually, because they basically never, ever, wanted to leave the country—they never wanted to live here! My parents even till this day wanted to live there they never wanted to leave. So, yes, probably there is a hell of a lot of anger there for my people.

The narrative outlined above shows the trauma that was experienced by a family leaving a country and a society that they loved and seeking asylum in Australia as refugees. In the interview, Jorge often spoke of his anger in response to the treatment of his family and friends. Yet, his anger is reflective and measured. It is not anger that is eruptive. It is anger expressed after careful reflection on his own history and practices as an activist. It is a well-considered reflection on the oppression his family experienced under the dictatorship and the subsequent impact it has made on his own political values and beliefs. This anger has fuelled his passion for activism and socialist politics. It has been argued elsewhere that emotions are powerful motivators and play a role in the desire and reasons to take action (Gould 2004). Jorge's passion, commitment, and desire for change precipitate his need to take action on issues of concern. This desire is connected to a broader sense of social responsibility. He notes that Che Guevara famously said "if there is anyone feeling injustice anywhere in the world you cannot stand still"—such values are important to him and are ones that he would like to pass on to his children. Jorge's anger, passion, and desire stem from the postenlightenment traditions of humanism; they influence his understanding of inequality in society and contribute to his desire to change it.

In the early days after arriving in Australia, Jorge and his brothers were given scholarships by St Vincent de Paul, a charitable organization in Australia, to attend Catholic colleges in Brisbane. He believes "the Church definitely had an influence" on his activism, although his father and mother "were not Christians in any meaningful sense." However he developed, through his socialization and religious instruction at a Catholic school, an interest in Liberation theology.

In the early 1980s, Jorge commenced a bachelor of arts degree at the Queensland University of Technology, and became closely involved in student politics on campus. He was elected secretary of the National Student Tertiary Union and never completed his degree. What followed was a lifetime commitment and involvement in socialist politics. He studied sociology and philosophy in his first and second years, but found philosophy more useful than sociology for developing a "basic methodology" or framework for his ontology of activism.

> I felt like in philosophy at least there was some interest in the ancient philosophers [and] at least academically, there was a genuine pursuit of knowledge. You know with sociology some of it was crap really, you know these people are writing sometimes 200-page books and saying very little and do not improve on much of the sociology of the early nineteenth century! You may as well read Durkheim, or Marx, of course, or any of them really.

Jorge discusses in the quote below a remarkable period of "political growth" after he joined the Labor movement at the age of thirteen.

In his adolescence, he joined several groups aligned with socialist principles in the Marxist Leninist tradition. Then he and his brothers became members of the DSP[8]:

> Probably the time of my most major political growth period was when I was in my early twenties in the DSP. One of the really good things about the DSP...part of the culture was that you had to think for yourself, you were not going to be a part of a faction. You really had to bring your own ideas and be a part of this new DSP. What you had learned you had to apply. I mean basically you would come back to those comrades if you followed through with it was really a form of constructive individualism...we learned from each other and probably were over confident.

As Jorge reveals, he felt he was socialized into "being part of a culture where you had to think for yourself" rather than being pushed by a faction into a particular ideological positioning, although the DSP is well known for its critique of historical materialism, being a socialist party and therefore heavily inflected by the writing of Karl Marx, or what Jorge defines as the "Marxist left." Jorge is remarkably well read, as a consequence of his own self-learning. He has read Greek philosophers such as Aristotle and Plato and also many of the classical philosophers such as Kant, Marx, and Hegel, and he argues "that once you have a basic epistemology" you can absorb theory and writing more readily. Jorge still has an association with the Hegelian Society and, unusually for someone who did not complete an undergraduate education, gives papers at the University of Melbourne at the Hegel Summer School.

Learning to think critically is a skill that Jorge developed through situating himself in the practices of the DSP. This critical reasoning or learning to question or critique in order to understand circumstances that create oppression is what Jorge refers to as "being anti-systemic." He refers to his activism as "the trade"—like a well developed craft, he has honed his activist skills.

> Yeah well, with my association with a lot of the left, I think that is one of the plusses of the Marxist left is that most of them do tend to do a lot of reflecting. Compared to the rest of the population, compared to most academics, most of us are reflective. Even the most political minded activist probably does more reflecting than the average person and the average academic. Partly because I think it is necessary part of being anti-systemic, by being anti-systemic or those inclinations and not be partially questioning, even if you have a particularly dogmatic

interpretation of Marxism, you have to be a bit reflective to survive. I think its part of the trade at least.

Jorge's discourse of activism is at times analogous to a battlefield. He argues that some of his peers formed "the first group since the 1970s [that] were actually trained and steeled in some actual political activity, actual combat." He states that many of the activists of his generation are now major leaders in industry or politics; that their engagement in student politics made them confident people, whether they were a part of the "left" or the "right," their combat played out in student activism was no different to the combat that is played out in the present political system. Jorge has learned through his activism about politics and international systems of government. I asked Jorge whether he had learned about political, social, and international systems in university or whether it had been acquired through his engagement in activism. I also asked whether his participation in political parties had helped him to understand social systems or systems of inequality. He replied:

> I very much think ideas what I would believe to be about structures and world systems, through my direct action, it's not like I was going to seminars or anything, sometimes maybe. But it did embed for life the spirit of questioning for me if nothing else you would never be happy with the first answer, and you know I am amazed just with my own teaching and stuff how many people are happy with the first answer or, if they are not happy, do nothing.

Jorge's critical questioning is a level of metalearning in that he purposefully observes his own learning and is reflective of his own practices and adapts and changes because of this reflection. His own reflexivity and skills are not necessarily taught in a classroom, but are certainly valued in activists' practices, so that thinking critically and being reflective are, as Jorge states, a "part of the trade" of activism. Jorge also explicitly acknowledged the importance of questioning and critiquing ideas: he is discussing how important it is for activists to question and critique ideas.

> Definitely the asking questions thing is probably the main thing; tenacity, courage but they tend to come with circumstance—yet I'm a believer that even the greatest coward will be courageous in certain circumstances; passion is probably the main thing, and you need to be self conscious of what you are doing.

Jorge thinks the ability to think critically about systems and structures and how they connect to inequality in the world is essential. He links this view with what he refers to as being "anti-systemic," but what he is actually referring to is critical thinking.

I interviewed Jorge at a time in his midlife when he was very reflective about his role in activism. He was no longer a formal member of the DSP and was involved in some fragmented groups associated with the left, but his involvement was not as it had been in previous years. His activism is presently focused on the Bolivarian Circle, a solidarity movement with Venezuelan socialism and Latin American politics. Jorge argues, being reflective is an important skill that activists need to be effective:

> You have probably caught me at a time when I am particularly reflective about this in fact; I'm waking up at night sometimes thinking about this. But yes reflective, but I remember when first reading Descartes at least this guy's got one thing right at least if you keep asking questions you will get there.

Throughout the interview, Jorge continued to reflect on what he described as his "disillusionment with the left" of Australian politics. He spent a great deal of time in the interview reflecting on the decline of the left in Australian society in comparison to the rest of the world. Jorge lamented his present lack of involvement in socialist groups and indicated this was something he was missing greatly. He acknowledged that his own social learning has been paramount in the development of his knowledge and skills. When I asked him about the social aspect of his learning he responded by saying:

> I think I have learned a lot of people skills working in team scenarios. I really enjoyed and now have missed the collective polemical activity.... In the educational sense of learning precisely because I am a real communicative learner, in that environment I probably learned a lot of those people skills.... It gave me more tenacity through the heat of political moments. I think even courage really came through all of that. It stopped me from just sitting at home watching TV.

Attending meetings, contributing to discussions and being actively involved in groups, networks or solidarity were important aspects of his learning that he now saw as in decline. Jorge stated that his involvement in groups and collectives had been important and believed there is a great deal to learn from other people in the group process:

> I am very much a collective learner. I like to learn from other people and impart knowledge... You know, I do not like to learn alone. I have always learned from people in collectives. I am a real collective learner in that sense.

Jorge described his present lack of social involvement with other activists as "killing me literally." This reflection shows the importance of the communal aspect to activists' learning practices; to act alone and be outside of a group is the antithesis of activism. There is a sense of community and a solidarity that develops when individuals participate in a community of practice. Significant learning has occurred for Jorge through socializing on the job of activism, and his expression of frustration is a harbinger of his desire for activism to provide another new learning experience.

Conclusion

Jorge is knowledgeable, skillful and reflective. The interview was constantly filled with his self-deprecating humor and his liveliness is representative of someone who is articulate and intelligent. He displayed insight into the learning of groups, reflecting the social nature of his own learning through activism. His passion for socialism and social justice are evident in how he articulates his desire for love of change. The embodied nature of his learning cannot be underestimated, motivated by anger, hurt and resentment, and a sense of betrayal at the politics of place, race, and identity in Pinochet's Chile and his plight as a refugee child fleeing a brutal regime. This family history has contributed to his purpose and agency as a learner. Passion, desire, and love of humanity influence his learning as an activist, and they contribute to his ongoing desire to understand the world around him. The narratives within this case study show Jorge's high level cognition and his ability to think critically. They confirm that Jorge's learning is holistic and that by working with groups and by socializing with other activists he has developed greater expertise.

Case Study: Felicity's story

"I've learned all of my skills through observation and practice"

Felicity's story is a journey of lifelong activism. Like many of the lifelong activists in this research, Felicity became an activist in the student union. Felicity comes from a middle class family and she attended a private Catholic girls' school. Her parents and extended family were Catholics, whom she describes as conservative in that they just did not do anything; not necessarily that they had conservative politics, although she does remember "attending a rally when I was in a pram." She jokes that her family were a part of the "Catholic mafia of Melbourne." Her grandfather was involved in the ALP, and supported the subsequent split that resulted in the formation of the Democratic Labor Party. So there certainly does appear to be a history of politicization in her extended family life. Felicity appears to have been a child who was a high-achiever. She was involved in lots of extra-curricular activities at school, including social justice activities, debating, drama, and performance, and was very engaged with ideas and her school work. Felicity was also heavily involved in the Catholic Church from a very young age and, as a consequence of the stories told within the Catholic Church, at one stage considered becoming a nun:

> I was all ready to become an African Missionary Nun when I was 15 because that was the sort of thing you were taught about. I was very active in my local Church. I was a special minister and I was the special minister of my school as well. I did all that kind of pastoral care [and] social justice stuff!

Although her secondary schooling was important, she claims,

> I felt that when I'd left school that I'd been kept in the dark about a lot of things, and I think it's because I had a real thirst for understanding the politics of the world, and that just wasn't discussed.

While her Catholic school was influential, and she still believes in the good works of the Church, she is critical of the institution, holding strong views about the homophobia in the Church and the oppressive nature of Catholicism:

> It was only really later on when I became an activist that I realized just how fucked, basically, the institution of the Catholic Church is...! and you'll go to hell and all of that kind of influence.

The change in her religious beliefs was influenced by Felicity coming to terms with her own sexual orientation and awareness of the church's homophobia. Against the backdrop of her recent activism around legal recognition for same-sex couples and their children, as well as access to assisted reproductive treatment for lesbians and single women, she claims the Catholic Church is "one of our biggest nemeses."

Felicity went on to the University of Melbourne to study education, and became heavily involved in the student union and student politics. It took her seven years to complete her degree because she became involved in so many issues on and off campus. Being involved in student politics was the commencement of a lifelong commitment to campaigning and activism covering a number of areas such as refugee rights, student politics, and support for East Timor and, more recently, a long period of activism and lobbying on behalf of Rainbow Families. Talking about her early days of activism and her involvement in student politics, Felicity recalled:

> Yes, I was 18. So that's where it all kind of started, and I did not do a great deal in the first year, but then I decided to get involved in the Student Union through theatre and in activism around the issues of free education and East Timor.

She was elected Education Officer for the student union in 1996 then became State Education Officer for the National Union of Students (NUS), before joining the DSP in 2000 and becoming an active member of the party. Like Jorge, she was inspired by the effervescence of those around her. They were groups of people who were involved and engaged with many different political issues on campus and she found this inspiring:

> It was a collection of really vibrant people in the student union from say 1994 onwards....[W]hen we were elected on the left focus ticket in 1996, we won every position, and it was just a really vibrant group of people, and the people before that had been ALP and some Liberal and right-wing...it wasn't as active a union and they had a different way of organizing,...but there were some women's officers too, who did some really great activism in 1995.

Felicity brought an existing level of experience to her activism. These were skills developed as a part of her drama studies and student theatre experience, so she was often involved in building props, stage craft, and stage management. She learned to network and became skilled in "establishing and creating or maintaining relationships with different organizations and people." Yet she believes the most significant skills she developed while with the student union were learning to facilitate good meeting processes, and the community development skills of active listening, facilitation, chairing meetings, and conflict resolution:

> I think over the years other skills... came through observing good and bad practice at various meetings. I've also learnt skills in doing things like police negotiation and legal support, which I've done for many protests and sit-ins where I've taken on that kind of negotiating role. Those things I've just learnt more and more through practice.

During the nineties, Felicity and her partner became involved in coordinating a support group for prospective lesbian parents, with Felicity also taking on the role of coordinator of the Fertility Access Rights (FAR) lobby, then part of the Gay and Lesbian Rights lobby. In 2006, the FAR lobby became a formal organization called the Rainbow Families Council. "Rainbow," or same-sex-parented families and same-sex marriage are what Felicity refers to as the "last bastion of gay and lesbian rights." Felicity has learned to be strategic in her lobbying and over time moved from a direct action phase of action to lobbying within the system for legislative reforms for same-sex-attracted people. She claims that when she first began her activism it was all direct action processes with not much of strategy. She now knows, in intricate detail, the machinations of the Australian political system and its representatives:

> I probably know quite a few of them, know what their electorate's like and have a much more sophisticated understanding of advisers and chief of staff and who you talk to and how it all works, because I've had to engage on that high level of advocacy.

The motivation for Felicity's present activism is deeply personal and has urgency because she is in a same-sex relationship and has two young children, which as a result of the laws existing at the time, she had no legal rights or responsibilities for. Consequently, a lot of her advocacy and lobbying work has a direct relationship to her sense of self:

> I guess from the very beginning of our relationship that was always a personal part of what we were doing...there was more personal

agency to it because we were going through exactly what we were arguing to change, so having to access IVF, travelling interstate, finding a donor, dealing with bureaucracies when [her partner] was pregnant.

Although she acknowledges that these issues are close and personal to both her and her partner, she nevertheless believes that they connect up with other issues of social justice in the world:

> I mean, the argument really is if there's any social justice in the world, if there is any conflict around the human rights movement, everyone is affected—which is the same argument about why people should not support war and they should free the refugees.... Because it doesn't matter whether it affects you in your day to day life; any kind of infringement on human rights or social justice affects everybody.

Central to her learning has been the development of a critical framework or "being critical" that has developed over many years through student politics, being involved in the DSP and other activist groups. She has also done a lot of reading and self-learning over the years. Her activism took her overseas to Prague to be involved in a large antiglobalization rally. Her involvement with the DSP and its international focus gave her access to a lot of knowledge about international systems of government:

> Particularly in the Asia Pacific region and that was fascinating too, you know. I got to meet Dita Sari and a whole range of amazing activists from Indonesia and Asia Pacific countries who just know a lot more about Malaysia and Thailand and the movements there.

Felicity left the DSP in 2002 because she felt she was constrained by the patriarchal processes of the party. Women were not always listened to and she believed the group processes were not inclusive. As with most social movements, she argued, there are always some people who join who are looking for care and nurturing, and she believed that the DSP failed in that area with some of its members. She did not agree with the debating processes for issues because they were didactic and gendered, and when she had tried to instigate change in this area by suggesting that if a man spoke then a woman should speak too, she found change was very difficult to achieve. So even though her ability to learn may have been thwarted through the DSP, in spite of this she developed facilitation skills for being more inclusive. She outlines a progressive speaking process that she had developed by observing other activists:

> The people who have not spoken will be asked if they've got an opinion. If you've already spoken you're put at the bottom of the list and we'll go male, female, male, female through the list so that's how we'll run it. So if there were ten men and two women in the meeting, well the likelihood is the women would get to say more things than each individual man.

Felicity is reflective about her practice. She says this maybe a part of her "being a perfectionist," but she will always evaluate or take notes on her teaching and learning. She still uses these skills in her day-to-day work as an educator for same-sex-attracted young people and in her unpaid work with the Rainbow Family Council where she runs groups and meetings. She firmly holds to the view that she has learned all of her skills from observing good and bad practice.

Conclusion

Felicity's pedagogy is typical of many of the lifelong activists in this research. Her early exposure to the teachings of the Church was extremely influential in her learning about social justice issues. The discourses at school and at home in her family environment were important in establishing an identity associated with benevolence. Felicity began to be heavily involved in a range of social justice issues once she started at university where she also became active in the student union. A member of the DSP for many years, Felicity became heavily involved in politics in the student union, a fertile grounding for the development of her outstanding facilitation and group process skills. It appears that the organizational context of the student union provided a setting to learn group communication skills. Felicity developed event management skills typical of those learned by lifelong activists who develop expertise over the longer term of practice. She has learned how to plan rallies, how to talk to police and how to maintain a sense of cohesion in the midst of a large protest.

Her more recent activism has concerned an issue close to her personal life, campaigning with her partner for legal recognition same-sex couples and their children and access to assisted reproductive treatment for lesbians and single women. She believes she has now taken on the characteristics of a lobbyist rather than an activist because she is no longer arguing for revolutionary change to structures in society, but rather arguing for legislative reform for gays and lesbians. This was a clear conflict for her: the change from direct action to being an advocate or lobbying within the system. However, it has been argued previously in chapter one that lobbying can coexist with direct action as a part of a broad project of activism. Nevertheless, she has been a key player in building and developing an organization and social movement agitating for change and legislative reform for same-sex marriage, legal reforms, and access to reproductive treatment for same-sex couples.

Case Study: Cam Walker's Story

Cam became actively involved in activism towards the end of high school. He says he had always been interested in the environment and had done a great deal of bushwalking and ski touring and, through this, saw a lot of "gorgeous places being trashed through logging operations." It was at this stage of his life that he "consciously" made a decision to become an activist:

> I had a bit of a revelation that everything was special. It wasn't just about the wilderness areas that mattered, and when I put those things together, I decided to become an activist and probably the first thing I did was to consciously become a vegetarian, which I remember I did at the end of Year 12.

Cam describes his parents as being "completely a-political;" they were not involved in any political party, were not members of the union, there was no discussion about politics in the family that he can remember. He grew up in an area of Melbourne that he described as "working class." He believes his parents were conservative thinkers and probably "quietly voted Liberal." Cam became actively involved in the Catholic church for a few years. His father was a practising Catholic, so he had been influenced by Catholicism from an early age. His mother at that stage of his life was "agnostic." He was a part of the charismatic youth group in his local parish. He developed a very strong friendship with a teacher, who he believed later became a priest, who was a very prominent activist in the church. This was influential," but as he states "that probably only lasted for two years" and he was then exposed to "a strong dose of anarchist politics and kind of rebelled against being connected with a mainstream religion."

Apart from the influence of Catholicism, Cam has not become a member of any political group, and in his present role as a paid campaign organizer at Friends of the Earth, he has remained non-aligned with any of the political parties or political groups. He was, however, influenced by two older male teachers in his local community that he went bushwalking with, both of whom were "very deep spiritual thinkers" and by his mother. She encouraged him to not just talk about something if you believe in it but to actively pursue it. As Cam states, she was "so very, incredibly generous as a person." She stayed with him through some of the Franklin Blockade in 1983, and camped out with the other activists and eventually "for the first time in her life" handed out leaflets, "so [she was] engaged in politics and gave out leaflets for the ALP."[9]

In his earlier activist days, Cam said it was quite amazing to start coming into the city of Melbourne. He was networking with people from the DSP and was surprised to find that some of the political literature that he was reading at the time affirmed his own developing ideology and values. The DSP was focussed on the revolutions in Latin America and, in particular, in El Salvador:

> That had a huge impact on me. That was the first kind of overtly political stuff I read so I was like a kid eating candy. It was amazing I'd assumed there were people out there that had that kind of approach [and] having the sense of this is not just in my head or something I saw on TV was quite significant.

Cam then started to seek out individuals and groups of people that he could relate to and network with. He made a conscious attempt to find people he could work with at university, but it was a small campus at Rusden at the time: "activists could be counted on one hand really!" He became involved in political issues on campus by starting an anarchist student network. He started to campaign about education issues on campus and became involved with green groups at university. He eventually became interested in ecofeminist work and consensus politics. He describes these emerging and developing ideas and the people around him at the time:

> I started to fall in with people who were very interested in non-violent politics who were working on the Franklin Blockade or the pre-work to the blockade, [and they] were training people around non-violence but were exceptionally interested in consensus politics and eco-feminism

and the kind of peace activist analysis of the environmental campaign. They were not kind of traditional greenies in that sense.

Cam's skill development over many years of activism is wide and varied. He learned practical skills through the Franklin blockade campaign and he passed on skills by training people in nonviolent action. He learned knowledge about the political environment and system of government; he learned to perform direct action protests and blockades at the Franklin. The following dialogue outlines his early learning and knowledge development. It appears an early scaffolding of skill has been developed almost layer-like over many years. It shows the reflexivity of Cam and his own metalearning after many years of practice. He has the agency to learn, the ability to reflect and identify his weaknesses, and learns in order to increase these perceived gaps in his knowledge:

> (Cam)I think that early non-violence action phase that was a really strong laying down of values that came through the training I was doing, the non-violence training. After that probably the next big influence was the bioregional phase in terms of consciously learning models for understanding power and understanding new societies. I think [what I learned] was just that individuals can make a difference.
>
> (Interviewer) What did you learn as you became more experienced, looking back now, if we did some sort of reflection on the learning that has come from some 25 years of activism?
>
> (Cam)I've become more of an all-rounder. I'm really much more aware of my limitations with skills, and I've realized I have my areas where I'm comfortable and I can learn all day in those realms but there are things I'm useless at. So I think as I've gotten older I'm better at identifying my weaknesses and my blind spots and then [have] sought to try and learn in those realms.

In Cam's early days of activism he used his physical body skillfully in activism. He was a good climber and skier and he was able to apply those physical skills to his activism in the environment and, in particular, by using them in blockading actions. But, as Cam indicates, his major skill development was in the area of group processes and facilitation:

> I think skill wise, I [have become] very good at maintaining a sense of group process in [the] chaos around protests. So around the World Economic Forum, [for example], how can we have a space where it's

not just the person with the loudest bull horn or the most charismatic speaker that sways the group?[10] How do you actually create safe spaces where people can have informed conversation and decision making in spite of the physical and time pressures of doing blockading?

Cam says he has become "reasonably good" at "facilitating big meetings" and "meetings of diverse people" that can at times, depending on the issues at hand, become "incredibly fraught." His facilitation skills have been further developed by being involved in large mobilizations of people through his involvement in social movements. He has learned how to manage crowds of people and be involved in the planning and development of large public events. He has learned how to organize speakers, how to negotiate traffic, and how to negotiate with police "on the job." He has also learned how to write "in a moderately coherent way" and honed his communication skills, especially his public speaking skills. Being a naturally "introverted person" he has really had to push himself to develop these skills and he has often been out of his comfort zone as a learner:

> I think [I have] good process skills, facilitation skills which have served me really well through the years. I was very interested in practical skills for a long while because I was getting involved in anti-forestry activity, doing tree planting. So I focused for a long while on the practical. I would think process, facilitation, consensus type skills are probably the strongest I've got and the rest I've just learnt on the job.

He became more effective in honing these skills through consistent evaluation, critical reflection and "really being quite hard on myself." For example if he was delivering any training there would always be an evaluation process that included feedback, so he would often get "peer support" and "feedback from friends." This has allowed him, through frequent practice, to review, revise, and remake his practice. He is mastering his craft as an activist, through the processes of metalearning.

Like most of the activists, Cam has read widely on the environment, bioregionalism[11] and non-violent activism. He became interested in Mahatma Gandhi's philosophy of nonviolence, the women's movement and Quakerism. He claims that at this time there was "a really strong laying down of values that came from the training I was doing, the non-violence training." He did read some Marxist texts but found he had "a reaction against it" because "a lot of my friends who are

Marxist could explain motivations away: they all came down to historical struggle!" In his early days of activism for the Franklin River he was a "bitser" in terms of his developing ideology: "So I was interested in eco-feminist work, in consensus politics, in non-hierarchical politics and I had a number of interests around the environment." He was cautious about organizations because of his experience of hierarchy within the Catholic church, so he gravitated towards people who were interested in "anarchist politics." He was socializing with a lot of people who were a part of the squatters movement, they were very "anti-God and very anti-Marxism and isolationist." He developed an understanding of feminism and issues around patriarchy and masculinity from many of the older radical feminist women at FOE, where they "fed him" books on feminism:

> I was quite influenced by a considerable number of older, very switched on women activists and then that led to reading a lot of eco-feminist literature in [the] early days and that was probably my biggest single political influence in my early twenties was reading all of that '80s era women's press books.

These radical women were extremely challenging and important to him in his developing activist epistemology. They frequently challenged him to be careful and observant about his communication, encouraging him to participate, to express his ideas and acknowledge his privilege in society as a man and reflect on his masculinity. They challenged him to move from his introverted ways: "It was fantastic for people to see, not just my failures or shortcomings, but the places where I wasn't so strong and being willing to push me out of them that was really useful."

Cam's reading of feminist literature and the influence of these women formed the foundation for his profeminist politics. He became involved in the Men Against Sexual Assault (MASA) collective, a collective of men who were profeminist and concerned about male violence towards women. Cam left Australia and worked with different social movements in the United States and South America. He found activism in those countries quite liberating, away from the constraints of western activism where there were limits placed on practices and processes because of activists being "co-opted" into political discourses. He found the environment of Latin America "inspiring in terms of commitment to the long haul" and the emphasis on "doing what you think is right regardless of what's going on around you."

> I spent bits and pieces of time in Mexico and Columbia and Ecuador and Chile, [with] social movements [that] are very collectivist and very kind of rowdy and radical, [or] unreconstructed compared to here where it's all toned down. By that you cannot speak to people or use arcane terminology, [the activism] is so co-opted and nervous about upsetting the horses!

Cam found the activism of the social movements in South America "less intellectual" and more passionately engaged in social change, and he gained knowledge about the differences between social movements in Australia and South America. He became deeply involved in FOE and found this environment seemed to fit his politics because it was "radical but engaged" and it was radical enough to sustain his practices as an activist and less pragmatic than many of the other activist groups. The opportunity to work alongside other activists who had a similar vision was very important to him. There are people at FOE who have remained with the organization over many years, and he cannot imagine doing activism without them:

> I'm not a vanguard, I'm a collectivist in terms of change so it's important that I can look along the line and see other people who are walking with me who have been there for a long period of time. There's been a lot of people [who have] worked here over the last 10 years that I've admired.

Cam repeatedly stated in the interview that a great deal of his knowledge and skill has been developed "on the job" of activism. He commenced work at FOE first in an unpaid role and then as a paid campaign worker in the late 1980s and has worked there on and off ever since. This is the longest period that he has been involved with an activist organization. In this time, he has been an international organizer for International FOE and his present role is as campaign coordinator for FOE in Melbourne. His role is to identify, coordinate, and promote campaigns that focus on the environment, human rights, and social justice. His on-the-job skill development has included learning to write press releases, learning to use the media and engaging with the media to promote FOE as an organization, as well as learning to make representations to other activist groups, community organizations, and NGOs. However, he argues his greatest learning has still been in developing community development skills such as facilitation and group process skills. These community development skills have been crucial when working from a nonviolent perspective within a collective environment where the purpose is to promote consensus decision making.

Conclusion

Cam's learning in social action has continued over many years of practice. There appears to be an early scaffolding of values, ideology and knowledge, that he has continually updated, developed and renewed over time. He has high level expertise in community development skills such as communication, facilitation and networking. Cam went actively in search of other activists and groups that shared his vision of sustainability and human rights. He needed people he could socialize with and learn from, and he deliberately sought out other activists to assist him. He has taught and passed this knowledge on to other activists through his commitment to nonviolent activism, revealing the interrelationship between learning and teaching in activism. Cam's learning is constructivist; he has sought out opportunities to learn that would build on his early developing anarchist politics. He actively constructs knowledge through his practice in the world of activism. While learning at times was disconcerting, challenging, and confronting and he found himself out of his "comfort zone" as a learner, his agency as an activist pushed him to further his knowledge and skills. Through FOE he is encouraged to reflect on his practice and to extend his knowledge and skills and has the opportunity to evaluate and reflect, and reconstruct and renew his practice. Cam repeatedly stated in the interview that a great deal of his knowledge and skill has been developed "on the job." In Cam's activism there are no transmission models of knowing. He learns through his active construction of meaning through the world of activism and by socialization with other more experienced activists. There is a continual scaffolding of knowledge about systems, structures and processes in his political and social world. He knowingly seeks ways to work with and change systems of government. This is education with a social purpose—over a long period of activism, Cam has developed high levels of expertise).

Case Study: *Kerry's Story*

Kerry has been involved in Indigenous politics since her early twenties. An Aboriginal woman who is proud of her Indigenous heritage, her family is a part of the Yorta Yorta clan in Victoria. She is currently employed by a university as director of an Indigenous education centre. Her father was Aboriginal and her mother was of Anglo Celtic heritage. *Kerry* was born in rural Victoria in a country town called Thornton. Her father was a local AFL football hero. Indigenous politics were rarely discussed at home and *Kerry* did not have the opportunity to socialize with Indigenous children or develop early connections to other Indigenous communities. While her father acknowledged his Aboriginal heritage he refused to be drawn into Aboriginal politics and rarely spoke about his Aboriginal culture with his family and children. *Kerry* explains her father's reluctance to embrace his Indigenous background in the following way:

> [Dad says] I'm an Aboriginal man and I belong to an Aboriginal nation, but I don't get involved, because his mother moved off the riverbank into town, into Echuca, so there's all sorts of issues around my Dad growing up and then about him not telling us any stories about Aboriginal life and what that meant for him.

Kerry believed her father was concerned about the lack of opportunities for Indigenous young people and wanted to avoid being identified with the perceived disadvantage and stereotypes associated with being Aboriginal. Her paternal grandfather had been moved onto a mission during the era when government policies resulted in Aboriginal people being removed from their traditional land and placed in missions or reserves.[12] She claims that her father's denial of his Indigenous heritage was linked to his father's generation and what he had learned about the dangers and discrimination faced by those who identified as Aboriginal:

> He [Kerry's father] was very silent about the things that may have happened to him and the way that he was treated. I make a lot of assumptions about the way he may have been treated, particularly at that top level of sport. I know that Pastor Doug Nichols who's a great uncle [said] when he first started playing football the trainers wouldn't touch him because he was black. My Dad never told us anything like those sorts of things that happened. He just wouldn't talk about it.

Kerry believes the processes of placing Indigenous people on missions caused an erosion and loss of culture that resulted in traditional practices and language no longer being passed down to her family. The experiences of *Kerry*'s grandfather irreparably damaged the transmission of her family's cultural heritage. It was *Kerry*'s mother who spoke to her children more than her father about Indigenous issues. She felt a heavy burden of being judged by others for having married an Aboriginal man because her father actually said to her "if you marry that man I'm never going to speak to you again!" Consequently *Kerry* believed her mother was fastidious about keeping the house and children clean and ensuring they attended school because she was always concerned about a potential visit from the "the welfare:"

> I have had chats with my Mum where she said "I always had to make sure the house was clean because you just didn't know who was coming around." She never actually got to the point of saying that welfare might have come round and taken the kids away, but you can hear that sort of fear in her voice: "What does the rest of the community think of the fact that I'm married to a black man? And so I have to make sure that everything's just right."

In Thornton, her family was the only Indigenous family, so the only exposure that she ever had to Aboriginal culture was during an Indigenous youth leadership camp:

> I got to go a youth leadership camp, but they were really reconciliation camps, because they'd get a whole set of young Koori youth and non-Indigenous youth, and they'd get together in this camp and they'd do all sorts of activities. I met a whole mob of young Koori women that I caught up with years down the track. But the worst part about it was they all got to go on the bus to go home and I had to wait for someone to come pick me up. And so those sorts of connections that I made with those young people felt like they were torn apart.

These camps clearly sparked an interest in her Koori culture and she felt the need to learn about this history in order to understand her own sense of self and identity as a young Aboriginal woman. Yet it wasn't until much later in her early twenties that she fully understood the significance of what her culture entailed to both her and her broader Koori community.

Kerry attended a local high school but had difficulty completing her schooling. She failed at her first attempt to gain her Higher School

Certificate (HSC)[13] but, after a period working at a factory, she returned and completed her HSC successfully. After that, she applied for a job in the public service as a clerical assistant and was soon promoted to work in Aboriginal Affairs. It was here that she developed significant relationships with an uncle who acted as an Indigenous mentor, and a Yorta Yorta man. Through these relationships *Kerry* was introduced to many tribal relatives and learned that "she was a Yorta Yorta girl," something that she had never known before. It was a shock to her in the first few years of her working life to realize she had a clan connection with the Yorta Yorta people in Victoria:

> I was at one of the pubs in Frankston and I think it was "Jimmie" who was there with a couple of his mates. He's a long-time Koori activist too, and somebody that they were talking to said "There's an Aboriginal girl here that I know," so they dragged me over and introduced me to them. "Jimmie" said to me "Well where do you belong?" And I said "Echuca", and he said "Well, that's Yorta Yorta." And of course I didn't realize…well I had a bit of an inkling but I had no notion, and he just went "You ought to get yourself into Fitzroy and find out what's going on in the world, rather than hiding out," because we lived down in Frankston then…And so that sort of sunk in and I thought "Wow! So there is stuff I can do."

Kerry began to establish a connection with other Kooris who became friends and linked her with family and relations. Through her role in the Victorian public service, she began to work with other prominent Aboriginal activists in the Department of Human Services, writing policy for child protection and developing polices for the care and protection of Indigenous children. This policy work was pivotal in establishing the Victorian Aboriginal Child Care Agency (VACCA). She explains the political environment of Indigenous child protection at the time:

> Koori kids then were being put into white foster placements and being adopted out, rather than looking at extended family and how to find relationships within the family where those Koori kids should go, and part of that work was also helping to establish VACCA.

It was through the relationships that were developed with these two key senior Koori public servants that *Kerry* was then introduced to a network of Indigenous activists, policy workers and public servants that were involved in Indigenous politics. This gave her a community of Indigenous people or, as *Kerry* calls them, "other blackfellas" that she could work with towards social change. In her early days of participating in Indigenous politics, and through getting to know a large group of people with whom she could socialize, network, and connect, she learned about her cultural heritage and its relationship to present Indigenous political issues. This social network also provided her with the space to construct new know-how. Through socializing with other Kooris, she was able to discover new knowledge, to learn about historical issues regarding her culture, and to gain the opportunity to pass on her skills, knowledge, and experiences to other Aborigines.

Her mentors introduced her to a significant network of people involved in Indigenous politics. They were key people in the public service in Victoria: lobbyists, activists, social policy workers, many of whom had the attention of government.

It was a time for great social reforms in Indigenous affairs and *Kerry* took advantage of this political environment. *Kerry*'s learning focused on policy and legislative systems of government. She was developing knowledge about failed government policies and their impact on Koori people; she was learning to lobby significant people in both government and the bureaucracy in order to get changes to policies affecting Koori children in Victoria. She was learning social policy skills, learning to write in the language of government, and learning to recognize the key players in Indigenous affairs who could assist her as well as those who could be resistant to change. *Kerry* was employed in a number of different government departments at this time. She worked in Indigenous health issues, aboriginal employment and training and on the Royal Commission in to Aboriginal Deaths in Custody (RCADC). *Kerry*'s role in the RCADC was to plan and prepare for the hearings and also to listen to the Aboriginal community, "to listen to their stories" and develop strong networks so she knew who would work effectively with the community in order to promote social change. Her Indigenous networks were vital to this and were at the time linked to her own developing sense of self and Indigenous identity. The following exchange outlines her developing ontological framework and leadership skills. When she was asked where her knowledge of Indigenous community came from, she was hesitant about whether she actually had important knowledge:

> (Kerry) I think it's just inherent in who you are. If you're strong in your own identity and you know your own community, then you understand how best to work with your own community, and that basic

notion of how to work with your own community helps you take that notion to other communities. So as a community person, and knowing my own identity and being strong in my knowledge of who I am, I think that gives me the basis.

(Interviewer) So you're learning on the job, you're watching other people, you see them stuff up and you think "I'm not doing it like that ever?"

(Kerry) Yeah (laughs). And then when you say to those people "You stuffed that up, you know. Next time you go out to do that, don't be so rough at it, give people the space to have their own views."

(Interviewer) So really, from working with these people every day and having some good key relationships with people and just hanging around with them every day you learnt on the job what to do? But your instinct for your culture really enforced that?

(Kerry) you may not be able to articulate to people what that knowledge is, but that's what gives you the authority because you know who you are and you know your culture.

It seems her identity and her cultural knowledge allows *Kerry* to have the authority to be able to make judgments, and to pass on her practical wisdom and experience to other activists and Indigenous people. This strength of knowledge about her "self" and who she is as "a Yorta Yorta woman" and now an elder in her community, provides *Kerry* with the opportunity to speak with and on behalf of other Indigenous people. The knowledge, skill, and the networks that she has established have been skillfully developed over many years of practice. This is not knowledge acquired through studying theories of social change, racism, society, or culture. This practical knowledge is derivative of her experience of being a Koori woman and learning exactly what this identity means and the responsibility she believes and feels goes with this identity of being Yorta Yorta.

Kerry believes passion for Indigenous issues is a driving force in understanding her activism. She is passionate about change for Koori people; she says small changes often motivate her to be involved in social change, like seeing an Aboriginal young person get a degree. She frequently works with other Indigenous people on projects and recently assisted the development of the Western Suburbs Indigenous Gathering Place, a space and place for Aboriginal people to be with one another. *Kerry* has learned a great deal from socializing with other Kooris and by observing both good and poor practice:

> I think it's through socializing, sitting around and having the conversation with a mob of people, a mob of black fellas, and going "Yeah, well

we did that down there and we did this here" and "Oh those bastards over there, they never listen..." Yeah. See and I don't...I think it's just being passionate. And if you're passionate enough to share what you know then you share it in a way that people feel it coming from your heart and coming from your soul, and they get to understand those things.

Kerry believes it is this spiritual connection to land, place and community that inspires her and is her motivation for being involved in social change. *Kerry* is presently completing a master's degree in education. She returned, in her late teens, to complete her HSC, and then went on to study some subjects in community development, although this qualification was not finished. She has attended a great deal of work-based learning and professional development in her time employed in the public service and the university. *Kerry* is highly skilled in leadership, policy development, and, in particular, Indigenous education. Her knowledge, acquired through practice and socialization with other Indigenous people, is broad and highly developed. *Kerry* uses critical reflection as a tool to improve her practice. When she was asked if she was reflective, she responded by saying:

> Sometimes it takes me a while to be reflective. Normally I come out and think "Bloody bastards, they're still not listening to me!"...And you go round to the other mob and think "We went there and we tried this and they said this"...then probably a day or two later without realizing I've thought about it, I just do [this] subconsciously now – I think "Oh, need to put it in that format, need to talk about it in this way, need to link it to that..." and so I'll redo the paper.

In this sense there appears to be an emotional response to her disappointment of not being successful in negotiating the paper or project she is working on. The emotional response connects her to being reflective in order to be successful in her lobbying. Annoyed with not being "listened to," *Kerry* pushes herself forward to find a solution to the issues she is working on. In essence, she revises, renews, and remakes her practice through reflection. In order to move the project forward, she uses critical reflexivity and develops a strategy. In effect, she is carefully developing a mastery over her craft. Her present role as executive director of an Indigenous education centre is often a frustrating one, requiring her to let universities and government know when their views, policies and procedures are not in the best interests of Indigenous people. She frequently has to point out that racism exists on many levels of systems of government. As she claims "you're always knocking on the door, you're always trying to get your foot in."

Conclusion

Kerry's knowledge development was initially tied to her search for her identity as an Indigenous woman. This led her to meet other Kooris who were politically engaged, opening up significant networks of people involved in Indigenous politics. *Kerry's* way of knowing is inextricably bound up with her identity and her search for knowledge about her country and ancient culture has found her involved as a significant policy player in Aboriginal affairs.

Conclusion to the Quintain of Case Studies

The case studies of Jorge, Cam, Felicity and *Kerry* are diverse because they cross a variety of social movements and social issues. All have been involved in activism or politics for a significant period of their life, ranging from 15 years to more than 30 years of practice. All except *Kerry* identify as an activist; *Kerry* is reluctant to identify herself as such as she views herself more as a lobbyist or a role model for other Indigenous people. Jorge, Cam and Felicity became involve in activism at an early age as teenagers. All were involved in student politics and Jorge and Felicity, in particular, took on roles in students unions. Cam has been involved in a variety of social movements over the years, but still remains particularly focused on the environment movement and social change.

The knowledge of these lifelong activists is wide and varied. As these case studies demonstrate, activists are critically reflective about their practices, they are passionate and skillful, but are also critical thinkers; they use their intelligent bodies to motivate themselves and others to learn and develop knowledge through social change. They are able to readily discuss the current political, social, and policy environment of their social issue and have developed and learned from significant social networks along the way. These lifelong activists are embodied and engaged learners.

5
The Circumstantial Activists

Introduction

This chapter provides a thematic analysis of interviews with the eight circumstantial activists in this study. The research shows that while there are some similarities between the learning of these activists and the learning of lifelong activists, there are also significant differences in their learning practices.

Circumstantial Activists: Biographical Profiles

Andrew is the director of a not-for-profit nongovernment organization that works toward developing leadership skills for people with disabilities. Before taking up this role, *Andrew* was the director of Social Action and Research at the Brotherhood of St. Laurence, an Anglican welfare agency in Melbourne. He has also been the senior advocate at the office of the Public Advocate; the executive officer of VICSERV, the peak body in the nongovernment psychiatric disability sector; and the executive officer of the Attendant Care Coalition. *Andrew* has also founded and managed his own businesses overseas. He is the chairperson of the Victoria Legal Aid Community Consultative Committee and a board member of Arts Access Victoria, and the RMIT Disability Advisory Committee. He is a fellow of the Leadership Victoria community leadership program. He has recently left the community sector to work in private industry.

Bahar decided to return to study at TAFE[1] as a mature age student. She initially went there to study landscape gardening and someone gave her a brochure for a community development course instead.

She decided the course was for her. Through her fieldwork placement, she found a significant mentor who was an experienced advocate for women and against family violence. She began her activist work among Turkish Muslim women in the North Western region of Victoria. *Bahar* spends a great deal of time giving women and children support in dealing with domestic violence. Most of her activist work is still conducted underground and in an anonymous way, because attitude change is slow in the Turkish community. Many of the values and practices that discriminate against women are firmly entrenched in the Turkish migrant culture. *Bahar* advises women about support, income, and available services including women's refuges. Her feminist activist work is largely unpaid. Several years ago *Bahar* organized a women's group reminiscent of the consciousness raising groups of the women's liberation movement. She is still employed as a financial counselor and continues her activist work with Turkish Muslim women.

Tim Forcey has been involved in social activism since 2006. A corporate engineer who until recently worked for a major resource company in Australia. Tim's research for a solution to peak oil led him to understand the importance and impact of climate change on the world. Prior to this, Tim had never been involved in social or political activism; he had never been a member of a political party nor a member of a union. He has become involved in a range of activities with other campaign groups and social movements. Tim is one of the cofounders of a bayside Environmental Action Group, a local activist group that has been instrumental in organizing several large-scale public protests on climate change. He has trained with Al Gore[2] and is a frequent speaker on climate change in Victoria, while continuing his work as an engineer.

Terry Hicks is the father of David Hicks who was arrested by the Northern Alliance in 2001 and handed over to the US military, then detained on suspected terrorism charges at Guantanamo Bay, a US military prison in Cuba. Terry campaigned for more than five years for David's release, launching a national and international campaign. He travelled to Afghanistan to retrace his son's steps prior to his arrest, which became the subject of a documentary. He concluded his travels with a major public action in the middle of New York City, where he stood in a cage of exactly the same dimensions as the cages in which prisoners were kept in the open at Guantanamo Bay. Terry retired recently after working as a printer. He lives in suburban Adelaide with his wife of 20 years, Bev, and they now enjoy travelling together. He continues to be interested in human rights. David has recently married and lives and works in Sydney. He is slowly settling down to a normal way of life.

Tricia Malowney became involved in activism following her retirement from Victoria Police where she was asked to be the First Disability Liaison Officer. Tricia has worked with various government and nongovernment agencies regarding access to mainstream services for people with disabilities. She is currently president of the Victorian Disability Services Board and deputy chair of the Victorian Disability Advisory Council, as well as a number of other disability and mainstream boards. Tricia has been an influential activist and advocate for systemic reform for inclusion of disability issues in the mainstream agenda in Australia. Although retired, she continues to work in an unpaid capacity for the rights of people with disabilities.

Eva is a former school teacher and artist lives in the bayside suburb of St. Kilda. She has been involved in a local campaign against urban development called "Unchain St Kilda" in opposition to a proposed development called the St. Kilda Circle, a high density shopping development. After several years of campaigning, the City of Port Phillip has recently announced that the development will not proceed. *Eva* still lives in St. Kilda and is active in her local community.

Catherine is someone who came to activism in mid life after finding herself divorced with two young children to support. She returned to study welfare work and community development and, during her fieldwork practicum, was placed in a union. She became heavily involved in the "Fair Wear campaign," a campaign for fair pay conditions for outworkers in Australia. She has been a significant campaigner on human rights for refugees and was a participant in the "No One Is Illegal" campaign to challenge government policy on the mandatory detention of refugees. She is now employed as a campaign organizer for a large NGO and still pursues issues of human rights for asylum seekers in Australia.

Grace, a former veterinary surgeon, initiated a campaign in rural Victoria for access to children's services. She campaigned for four years to get a childcare center and kindergarten funded by the federal government, and then oversaw the project management of the building. She became involved in a campaign for saving public space in the middle of her rural community. She is now employed as a rural community development worker by the Department of Planning and Community Development.

Stages and Phases of Learning

Circumstantial Activists, Early Politicization, Early Learning

Unlike lifelong activists, none of the circumstantial activists were involved in political action as young people. Tim, who is an engineer, came from a family of conservative farmers in the United States. He says "they were country people, who kept to themselves." He describes himself as a "conservative," involved in the corporate world and working for a multinational resource company. Until 2006, he was never involved in activism in any capacity. *Bahar*'s family were conservative Turkish Muslims and she was raised to observe gender roles for men and women. She says women were not expected to become involved in the community or with activism:

> In my community [the focus] is family. You go to work, come home, you have your family. Work is work, there is no activism, family is family, men are men, women are women, and kids are kids, no ifs or buts about it. That was the upbringing I had with my parents, my house was very male dominated, and he [the man] is the ruler of the house.

Grace grew up in Melbourne, trained as veterinarian and moved to Gippsland in country Victoria. Her family, too, were "conservative" and quite isolated. She states her family "had very little community involvement," her mother and father were not very outgoing or political and there "was very little exposure to anything that was political or community minded." Similarly, Terry came from a working class family without any interest in politics. Terry had been coaching a local football team for many years, but claimed he never became involved in administrative or organizational roles: "on committees I tend to stay away from that because they are usually political." None of his family has ever been interested or involved in politics. Terry recalls that they would watch the day's events on the television but, "like 90% of Australians, did not take much notice."

Catherine was very influenced by the early teachings of the Church in Sunday school. Both her parents were practising Catholics. She remembers her father and mother as being "very kind to people" and always helping others in some way. She says her family's politics were "quite conservative" and she is "sure my father never voted Labor." *Catherine* remembers herself as being outspoken and getting into quite a lot of trouble for this. When she found herself a single parent in midlife after the break-up of her marriage, she decided to enroll in welfare studies, and it was through her work-based placement that she became involved in activism.

Like *Catherine,* Tricia came from a family influenced by Catholicism. Within her large Irish Catholic family there was "a strong sense of social justice; my parents were always doing things for other people." Her father "was a shunter on the railroad" and her mother was a "homemaker" who, even though she had ten children of her own, did unpaid work for other women "who weren't coping; ironing and things like that." Tricia contracted polio at four months of age, which gave her a significant physical disability—"I had calipers, I had paralysis on my left leg. I still have calipers." She maintains however, that her disability had not held her back until late adolescence when she applied for a job with a bank and did not get it. "I was mainstreamed in my schooling long before everybody did this. I never thought of myself as having a disability." She believes her sense of social justice came from her family: "very few of my family have remained in formal religion and yet each one of them is doing social justice in their work."

Eva came to activism long after she had raised her family. She was a trained teacher and artist who had, like *Catherine*, found herself a single parent in midlife. She states her family were "very well read" and she "came from an engaged Irish Catholic family." From an early age she was aware of the politics of being an Irish Catholic and believes that a culture of resistance was a very strong part of her Irish heritage:

> I was very aware of the DLP and the Bob Santamaria issues. I did not understand it but I was very aware as a descendent of Irish settlers that I came from a culture of dissent and a very anti-establishment culture. It was in my nature to not want to support the establishment and its givens.

But it wasn't until she was in a second marriage and semiretired that she actually became involved in a campaign group against the urban development that was proposed in her bayside suburb in Melbourne. *Andrew*, like Terry, came from a working class family, albeit one with strong aspirations for social mobility. His parents did not want him to work as hard as they had to. A congenital eye disease found him almost blind at the age of eleven. But it wasn't until midlife, after returning from Germany where he had run a landscape business as a social enterprise, that he actually became involved in disability activism.

Circumstances and Activism

Circumstances have propelled these individuals to become politicized and engaged in social change, and their lives have been changed as a result of initial experiences and then because of their activism. Unlike the lifelong activists who incrementally became involved in political and social movements, these people experienced identity change through their practice as activists. This is not to claim that lifelong activists are not changed through their learning as all learning is a process of identity change. However, for circumstantial activists the change is abrupt and sometimes monumental, and characterized by a heightened pitch of emotional intensity. Terry Hicks, for example, suddenly found himself being woken in the middle of the night by the Federal Police and the Australian Secret Intelligence Organisation (ASIO), who had come to search his house for evidence that his son David was a terrorist:

> We had nothing to tell them anyway so that really started to give you a bit of insight into how these organizations work with their threats, mainly verbal threats I suppose. The other thing that was told to us is that you do not speak to the media until we give you the all clear.

Unlike the lifelong activists whose learning is incremental, Terry was thrown into the unknown and his life is changed. Terry's street was blocked off, the police and the media were camped outside. The story of David's alleged terrorist activities and arrest was big news after September 11, 2001. Terry realized that he had to act in some way to assist his son. This was the impetus for Terry to take action and his first experience of learning through activism. He recognized that he had to get into the public arena to protect himself and his son:

> I realized what had happened [and] after a while I started to think, particularly with the demonizing of David, you know, there was no trial or anything like that, the only way we could keep David's issues up front was to keep the whole thing up front.

So Terry decided to speak to the national and international media about his son's arrest and his campaign for David's release commenced.

Like Terry, *Bahar*'s activism was circumstantial as well. Unhappy with her marriage and her own experience of gender oppression, she decided to pursue a course in community development after reading a brochure:

> When I got…the brochure, there was something about community development that this was what I was meant to do. I did not really know what community development was at that stage [but] I thought "this is what I need to do—this is me."

She said the "years and years of frustration" had drawn her to community development study and to work as an activist in the Turkish community. Even though she knew her activism would bring "a lot of conflict in the community" she says her activism was born out of "frustration, just a bundle of frustration." Her activist perspective provided her with the insight that women in her community were oppressed; they were dominated by patriarchal values, had limited freedom and faced violence when they resisted. Her work led her to recognize that male resistance to women's education was rife in the Turkish Muslim community:

> [Because] they do not want their women to be educated this will cause conflicts at home. Women shouldn't be educated because they will [then] have a mind of their own and that's not what they want.

At 37 years of age, *Bahar* became an activist in her own cultural community, working towards social change for Muslim women.

Tim is an environmental activist, although, unusually, he is employed as an engineer in a major resource company and, before 2006, had never been involved in any form of activism whatsoever. He lives in a bayside suburb of Melbourne and has been involved in the establishment of a local environment action group. The group's main concern is climate change and its impact on the local environment. His public protest started with a simple campaign using a pole that would measure advancing sea levels if climate change continued at its current pace. In the narrative below, Tim outlines his first experience of activism after he became frustrated as he felt that people were unconcerned about climate change:

> Living down near the beach in Sandringham, you know, it's a nice spot that I'd like to see preserved and a lot of Australians live near the coast,

so I thought "Aha, this is something that might get their attention." I mean at that point, drought hadn't really even gotten their attention, and the threat of disease or what this was going to do around the world; nothing seemed to be really getting the attention. And so I thought this plastic pole, maybe that can demonstrate to people what happens with the sea level.

Eventually, Tim assisted in organizing a large campaign to mobilize thousands of people onto the beaches at Sandringham to make a human sign that read "Halt Climate Change". Tim is a self-learner whose interest in the concept of "peak oil" fostered his realization that the world's dependency on oil was having a devastating impact on the environment and was unsustainable. Tim, who identifies as a "conservative" and comes from what he acknowledges as the "corporate world," began to immerse himself into the campaign about the impact of climate change.

In contrast, *Grace* was recovering from postnatal depression when she commenced a campaign to get a childcare centre in Mirboo North, a town of just 1,400 people, in country Victoria. She had never been involved in a community campaign before, and had no involvement in politics or community-based organizations. However, after realizing there was no childcare available in town, she decided to embark on a campaign to lobby local, state, and federal politicians prior to an election to improve children's services by getting a childcare centre. *Catherine's* activism began in midlife after she returned to Australia and began Welfare Studies at TAFE as a mature-age student. She saw a documentary on the exploitation of women outworkers in Australia and decided that something needed to be done about their poor working conditions. She gives an account of her first stirrings of activism below:

> I remember in 1995 seeing a *Four Corners* program. It concerned outworkers who were paid at just $2 an hour. I just thought, hang on, we've got structures in this country, in this place, to make sure that people do not have these sorts of working conditions. I went and spoke to the union and to churches. I talked to various groups and there was a project [the union] was starting up around outwork and had an idea that unions and community could work on together and try to expose, create awareness and also ultimately change things.

Catherine was able to obtain a fieldwork placement with the union and she was involved in a significant and influential campaign to change the working conditions of predominantly migrant women outworkers. She then became involved in one of the largest political campaigns in Australian history, working for greater rights for asylum seekers.

Andrew became involved in disability activism in midlife after returning from Germany, where he had lived and worked as a landscape gardener and small businessman for 13 years. He met some people at a barbeque who were involved in the disability rights sector and was asked to write a book on attendant care. *Andrew* reflects on the significance of this accidental meeting in the quote below:

> I'd been on the end of a shovel and been working as a businessman in Europe. So here I come back to Australia and I meet some people at a barbecue and they say, look, "Are you blind?" and I said, "Yeah" and they said, "Well, can you write?" I said, "I do not know." They said, "Well, we need somebody who can do a booklet for us."

After *Andrew* had written this book, the same group of people asked him if he would be willing to "organize a political lobbying campaign around attendant care." He had never been employed as a political lobbyist before and had no experience whatsoever in this area, but he said that he "would give it a shot." He then became employed as a political lobbyist "to work with Victorian politicians in Canberra, to try to get attendant care up as legislative framework for people with disabilities." This series of circumstances and learning on the job have now led *Andrew* to be director of one of the largest disability organizations in Victoria, "Leadership Plus." *Andrew* identifies "two sets of reasons that led him into disability activism." He argues that "being disabled means that I have an understanding of vulnerability." Supporting an understanding of "what being discriminated against means," he argues the circumstances of his blindness are not confined to a theory that he has no relationship to, it is something "that he has experienced." He argues this experience is a great catalyst towards "personal development." He has then been able to transfer that personal development "into a passion that's about causing broader social change."

In her sixties *Eva* became involved in a campaign against urban development in her local suburb. She says that although she had always had an interest in politics and social justice she had mostly been an observer because her time was taken up with "raising babies" and, as a single parent, she was "too busy." She had participated in a consultation for a proposed development on the beach front of St. Kilda, but when the developers and the local council finally announced the plans for the development, she realized that the proposal did not reflect what the community wanted. It would end up an enormous development "with something like 380 shops." She said her anger about this false form of consultation motivated her to act:

> It just seemed that something had gone hugely wrong and that got me so angry that I sent off a few emails around and the emails clicked with the people who were sending them and we had a meeting to see what we could do about this. Now that was completely spontaneous. It just really made me very angry when I saw what had come out. It was spontaneous anger by a few people who did not even know each other and we had a group in three weeks working on it!

Tricia, now a disability activist, became politicized when she realized women could not be promoted in the public service if they had not completed their secondary schooling, while men could be promoted regardless of their level of schooling. This awakening led her to become a feminist and to challenge this policy of the public service:

> You know my activism wasn't something I planned on doing. It wasn't a conscious decision...I got a job in the public service on the railways and I really started being an active feminist then when I realized that women could not get promoted. So you could not become a clerk if you were a woman, I could not get a promotion. This was the early 80s...while equal opportunity had been passed, it had not reached the public service and I agitated to get a promotion.

Tricia applied for a position at the Victorian police force and was offered a job as disability liaison officer. Even though Tricia had a physical disability at the time, she claims "I knew nothing about disability issues." Thus, Tricia became a disability advocate in the police force and had to learn rapidly: "I had to develop my knowledge very quickly." Tricia has gone on to be involved at a senior level in disability rights activism and has been involved in the Victorian Equal Opportunity Commission and is presently the Chairperson of the Victorian Women with Disability Network.

Formal Learning

Most of the circumstantial activists had postsecondary education of some kind, though not necessarily related to politics or social sciences.

Eva is a trained teacher in the creative arts and has taught in secondary school; she also has a master's degree in Australian studies. Tricia left school after Year 11, and then commenced an undergraduate degree later in life. Terry has no formal qualifications at all. Tim has a science degree and is a qualified engineer. *Grace* has a degree in veterinary science. *Andrew* never completed his undergraduate degree, but later on in life completed a master's degree in business. *Grace* and *Andrew* have completed short courses in leadership. *Catherine* and *Bahar*'s qualifications in community development and welfare studies have a closer link to activism with their emphasis on social change practices, advocacy, social policy, and social action.

Developing an Activist Epistemology

Rapid Learning "on the Job" of Activism

The learning of circumstantial activists has a particular sense of urgency. They are suddenly thrown into unknown situations and frequently describe their experience as a "huge learning curve" or a "steep learning curve." Terry suddenly had to address the media at the front of his house because of his son's arrest. He had to learn to speak publicly for the first time and to practice this skill time and time again through his social action. From a strategic point of view, he knew that he needed to keep the issue in the media if David was to be assisted. He also had to develop rapid knowledge about terrorism, civil liberties, and the politics of the war on terror. This involved understanding both the Australian and American systems of government. Terry reflects about his changing worldview and states, "the blinkers were off and I started to see the world differently." He demonstrates this shift in his political knowledge, remarking:

> Well I started to see other things; you start to see the broader picture. You see what is happening in the background. You can see how governments try to influence things to their situation. Yes it's been a pretty big learning curve, you've got to work your way through.

Entering into the unknown was difficult for Terry; he said what made his learning particularly "tough" was that "no one really knew how to deal with this, it had never happened before." But Terry began a journey to acquire new knowledge, to rapidly learn about international systems of government to connect disparate aspects of national and international policy and to identify the hypocrisy of governments. He also found that governments were more likely to intervene depending on where the electoral cycle was at the time. This learning underpinned new critical thinking:

> Here is our government who wouldn't even have anything to do with [David's case], until last year, when things started to heat up; the election [was] coming on so David just became a "political football." The government said [David] would never become a political issue, it did, and it started them moving to get this thing "speeded" up as they call it.

However, in realizing that he could not become a complete expert and could only tinker "around the edges," Terry recognized the importance of accessing the deeper knowledge of "the experts," stating that if you "start heading into it you get yourself into trouble." Thus, while he does not regard himself as an expert in terrorism or international law, he has been able to learn from and draw on the skills of those who are specialists in these fields. Terry has also developed knowledge about how to engage and use the media. He has become skilled in public speaking and running a campaign. He has learned how to "speak to influential people" and has developed an understanding of the art of lobbying, going to Canberra, talking to politicians, backbenchers, independents, and cabinet ministers. He also quickly learned about the frustration of dealing with governments and bureaucracy:

> So what I was doing I was hoping was to put pressure back where it belonged with the government because they weren't doing enough. Really that's where it all developed, it's been a hard road, the amount of times I fronted up in Canberra and no one wants to speak to you!

Tim spent a year prior to his initial activism researching climate change "mainly on the internet" during which he realized there would be no ready solution to the problem of peak oil. Through this knowledge acquisition he knew that he had to act to influence the politics of climate change.

> Peak oil led to climate change and then working in the oil business, our ability to supply oil has peaked, so that's why the prices keep going up all the time. So we need to switch and we could switch over to coal, but given that just generates more carbon it would just totally wreck things even faster than are happening now. We have to switch to something

else. So given that we have to switch we might as well get started, so I'm a pretty practical person and so the time has come to change. Actually it's probably about 20 years ago but better late than never.

He and his wife cofounded an environmental action group in bayside Melbourne. Other residents of the area slowly began to get involved. This then led to his action on climate change on the foreshore with the climate change pole. People were curious about the pole so he was able to engage with them in discussion about climate change. For Tim the shift from corporate engineer to climate change activist was life changing. He outlines this abrupt change in attitude below.

The first time I walked down the street related to climate change was probably June 2006, and so I'd done research into climate change and the peak oil on my own and I suppose somewhere in the back of my head I knew eventually I was going to have to do something.

Tim was anxious about taking action and was completely out of his comfort zone. He said he was so nervous on the day of his first action with the pole, he felt the same way he did when he was a young child on the morning of the school spelling bee. Tim decided he had to develop knowledge about the key players in the environment movement who, he believed, were initially suspicious of his involvement in climate change because of his background in the corporate sector and because he was working for a multinational resource company. Tim is a person who is meticulous about researching everything, so he says his initial research "slowed him down a bit." He found he needed to, "try to work out what all these different NGOs stood for with respect to climate change; who was going to be useful to me, who I could be useful to." He made contact with people from Greenpeace and Environment Victoria and he began to network with a whole range of people in the environment movement, community groups and NGOs. He started to learn how to communicate and work in groups, something he had never done before in the corporate sector: "speaking out in public, working with community groups. I'd had no experience at that, and I'm still not that comfortable in the group." His connection with NGOs and his local climate change group led him to become involved with one of the largest protests about climate change in Victoria: the "Walk against Climate Change." In little more than three years, Tim has developed extensive knowledge and skill on the job as an activist.

Grace's initial campaigning for a childcare centre led her to develop skills in campaign and project management. She claims the project dominated her life for four years:

> I lived that project from the start to finish. I led the steering group and then I led a community project team and I ended up project managing some of the building in the end, and some of the budgets and all sorts of things that I never would have considered being involved with.

Grace says in some ways her naivety about activism helped her. When people claimed that achieving a childcare centre could not be done she refused to believe this. "You know, when people said that can't be done, I just said 'baloney' and kept going." She points out she wasn't "politically savvy." *Grace* frequently spoke about her science background and being a logical thinker, and that she was someone who liked to see the facts before believing something. Her greatest learning has been in understanding the machinations of government and bureaucracy:

> I've learnt so much, I think I'm still stunned by the complexity that exists in bureaucracy.... Things like how do you speak to politicians, how do you get to speak to politicians, why would you want to speak to a politician? At what time in the electoral cycle do you speak to politicians, on what level do you talk, with what amount of information?

Catherine's rapid learning was reinforced by her community development studies, but she argues that the actual practice of activism is more important than any formal learning she had done and deploys the argument: "you do need some theoretical underpinnings, but the practice is more important, the last few years have been a steep learning curve for me." Through her practices, *Catherine* argues she has learned to be "more strategic" about her campaigning and lobbying. She has learned that you need to have "a multilayered approach to community activism," that you needed to bring along in the journey community groups, churches and NGOs who "will stand up on social justice issues." In the quote below, *Catherine* reflects on the stages and processes of activism, from taking direct action to influencing change in government policy and legislation:

> The extroverted activist things that we did were necessary at the time to waken up the conscience of Australia and to let the Government

know that they could not keep a curtain pulled on what was happening. But then you know with any campaigning you have there are stages. There is no point standing around detention centres continuing to do that forever.

Bahar's initial rapid learning was in the form of personal development, learning to become stronger. "What seemed like huge steps back then seem like little steps now" she remarks. *Bahar* needed to find the strength to work through her own oppressive relationship and describes herself now by saying, "I'm a stronger person. I've learned that I can speak up!" *Andrew*'s experience involved learning how to bring his existing skills and business acumen to the community sector. He was able to hone his communication skills, but his rapid learning was really in relationship building and networking.

> I guess what I've learnt is really around knowing the importance of building networks and relationships with people, being able to call on those relationships to deliver certain outcomes that you might be wanting to achieve in your work. I think my biggest, my strongest competency, is my ability to find a message...that's holding people together in a movement and then to build a network around that.

Andrew argues that what he has learned is to change the existing discourse around "rights activism" to a discourse of leadership, which is about building relationships with people to achieve mutual goals. The focus on "entitlement and need" in the disability sector has not achieved a great deal. He says what is needed is a discourse of leadership, because leaders always talk about "what they can contribute and what is possible as opposed to what my entitlements are and what I need." He argues that change will not occur while the movement still focuses on need:

> But, for me, the reality is that the change – the force for change won't happen as long as we are talking about need. If I can talk to you about what I can add, how I can make a contribution, then we've got a relationship.

Andrew's approach of moving from a rights discourse of entitlement, to a discourse of leadership and mutual opportunity has enabled his organization within the space of three years to raise two million dollars in grants from government and become a very influential organization in disability policy and politics.

Critical Thinking

As with the lifelong activists, circumstantial activists learn to think critically about the world around them. *Catherine's* present involvement in refugee rights and the movement for change to the Australian government's treatment of asylum seekers has led her to think critically about policy, the legal system and human rights law. She has seen, under the Howard government, a systematic silencing of dissent, which has contributed to the ongoing oppression of refugees. The following statement gives insight into her critical thinking about asylum seekers:

> [After] Silencing dissent ... the next step is criminalizing dissent, then once you criminalize dissent, you are locking up people who oppose the government. ... That's what I'm worried about and that's what I see happening in this country.

Eva says she has learned so much more about the processes and machinations of government, "I've learned more about how the council actually works in terms of the role of the paid officers and the CEO as compared to the elected representatives." Terry claims that once he started advocating for David's rights he began to understand other political issues and how these were linked to David's incarceration. Rather than being intimidated by politicians and influential people he started to speak up:

> Just because they are in higher positions than us doesn't mean that we can't have a say, we can still stand up for our rights. That's what I have been trying to do is to stick up for David's rights. And as you go along you start to pick up on other issues, other people's rights, like the other people at Guantanamo Bay, like Mamoud Habib when he was incarcerated.[3]

Tricia believes that her ability to network with people is her greatest asset, but she is also very skillful at seeing the broader issues of discrimination and being able to influence people with this knowledge:

> I am president of the Victorian Disability Board. I have access to the Minister and Minister's advisers. My real activism has been advocating for changes to the justice systems. I brought with me some excellent networks from the police and had gotten changes there on issues relating to family violence, real change, actual reform to the systems.

> I often think that my biggest skill is my ability to get an issue on the agenda, to get people to take things seriously by understanding and learning about systems advocacy. Individual advocacy doesn't change systems. You can theorize about advocacy, but how can we practically get things done?

Andrew began to think critically about the disability sector after many years of working within it. He couldn't understand why the disability movement wasn't as powerful as other social movements such as the Indigenous rights movements and the women's movement:

> I'd been a part of helping this group thinking about what it was that was holding the disability sector back from becoming as sustained a social movement, as the women's movement or the Indigenous movement or multiculturalism; [What the] group came up with is the lack of leadership by people with disabilities. So the notion of self-determination; [and] people with disabilities started to develop these slogans: "Nothing About Us Without Us," "Why Aren't We Involved?"

Andrew found he had more success using a discourse of leadership for people with disabilities than using rights based discourse. This project saw the commencement of a new organization that would focus on developing the leadership skills of people with disabilities. Working with other activists is an integral part of their pedagogy, the importance of their social learning is canvassed in the following section.

Social Learning

Like lifelong activists, circumstantial activists learn through socialization with other activists. They learn through observing other activists at work, by watching both good and poor practice. Tim decided that he had to act on climate change. He needed to build up credibility with environmental groups so that he could participate in climate change activism. He adopts the view that his success was in building relationships with other groups:

> So just learning the players and building up credibility. Once my wife was on board, we took the Greenpeace rep and the Environment Victoria rep out to lunch. Even to this day, there are people that I meet with at forums or whatever from activist groups and I'm really not sure that they trust me.

Tim says he has learned a great deal from other activists and academics about climate change after he and his wife started their own group. He has attended the training by Al Gore and has listened to most of the significant speakers on climate change such as Clive Hamilton and Peter Christoff. He notes that he is only now, after three years in the environment movement, starting to be more comfortable working in groups because of his natural impatience. He repeatedly stated that most of his learning has come from his interaction with other people interested in climate change: "I mean I'm talking to somebody every day, like you and others, on the issue. I'm learning all the time and I'd like to do more of it. I wish I had more hours."

Bahar started a Turkish women's community group. The initial intention was to provide a space for women to come and socialize and support one another, to diminish their isolation. The space of the group allowed women to explore issues of discrimination and oppression in their community. She describes the membership of the group below as well as its educational purpose:

> There are Kurdish women in the group, Muslim women, scarfed women, women who are very open, some who are not. There should be no barriers if you want to do something we need to lift all of the walls.... We are focusing on developing skill, on being more skilled. We are linking them into professional development through workshops and training.

Bahar says she is not a "great public speaker" but she loves being involved with other people in groups. She has found the networking side of activism very important for her skill development. "I love to get into the crowd and talk to people one on one. I love communicating and networking. I love meeting people from other organizations, I find when I meet one person I link up with others." *Grace* says she learned to be more inclusive in her dealings with people and has developed her communication skills:

> I think I learned a lot more about dealing with people...I started out being very gung-ho about what I wanted to achieve, and kind of "damn the consequences;" but I think as time went on I became much more in tune with what was going on around me and being more open to that. So I think I became more astute with dealing with people in particular.

She had realized through working with various community groups that she "needed to take as many of the other people in the group on the same learning journey as me." She did this by sharing her skills, teaching others to write media releases and funding submissions. *Catherine* became engaged with a number of groups connected to the refugee movement. She was a key player in one of the biggest actions for asylum seekers at the detention centre in the central Australian town of Woomera. The broadly aligned coalition of groups came together to protest about the plight of the refugees in Australia and *Catherine* keenly observed the social diversity of this coalition:

> I mean we are a very diverse movement. I mean I've been out to Woomera and when you go out there you will be with young students, with lefties, with people referred to as Ferals, you will be there with conservatives, with old people, the church and young people. The diversity of people involved in the refugee movement is amazing and what has contributed to its success.

Eva found that she really needed to develop her skills when working with groups, especially in the initial stages of the campaign when there were many people who wanted to be involved. She learned facilitation skills, how to chair meetings, she learned how to use the skills of other people in the group, she learned how to delegate tasks in the group. *Eva* says that she has gained a great deal of knowledge from other people in the campaign group who are confident, educated and highly skilled. Working with groups, chairing meetings, facilitating discussion is key area of learning for Tim, who had little involvement with community and campaign groups prior to his activism:

> I've still got some skills to develop there in the group situation, or how to handle, how to run a group and handle somebody coming from a strange position which may or may not be helping. I probably do not have the patience for a lot of that and do not have the political savvy to work through how to deal with it.

Terry says many of the people he has met as a part of the broader support group for David have now become his friends. He has learned to trust their judgment and let them run with the campaign because, as he states, "they usually do the right thing." He has found that in any forum he attends he always learns a new slant on something from somebody that he speaks to. Tricia has exemplary networking skills and finds that because she is highly social and "will talk to anyone," these skills assist her to influence people who could be useful to her campaign for disability rights. "So much of this work is about systemic advocacy, individual advocacy is not effective alone to bring about change."

Mentoring

A prominent theme of this research has been the significant role that mentors have played in the developing ontology and pedagogy of activists. Being able to observe other activists in practice has been beneficial in their own developing pedagogy. *Grace*, *Catherine*, *Bahar*, Terry and Tricia all had significant mentors. *Grace*'s mentor was a woman who held an important leadership and management position in a government department. *Grace* admired her skill and the tone she used to get things done. She was able to block impediments to the progress of an issue through her use of strategic communication. *Catherine's* mentor was a highly skilled unionist and a passionate advocate for people working in poor conditions.

> They were launching the "Fairwear Campaign" so I got involved in that and working with Jane who was a seasoned community development activist [and] was very instructive. She really has a very clear mind and a clear strategic way of thinking and I found that really useful.

Terry had a significant mentor in Stephen Kenny, David's first lawyer. He said he learned a great deal from him. If he needed advice about David's situation or advice about the campaign he would talk to Stephen. Terry says Stephen was "the go-to fellow." Tricia has had many high profile mentors who have assisted her in her disability activism, many of them senior bureaucrats in government and ministers' departments who have been "very generous and encouraging of [her] advocacy work."

Identity Formation—Learning to Become an Activist

The identity formation of circumstantial activists occurs abruptly and can be challenging for the person, their family and activist colleagues. There is little opportunity beforehand for the person to socialize with other activists in order to develop this sense of self at an earlier stage. Terry, for example, was in his sixties when he embarked on the international campaign to help his son. He regarded himself as a "concerned father" responding to his son's needs and also described himself as an "ordinary bloke" whose life prior to his activism was "fairly boring." He says he really likes to think he is the "same person." Terry had a close connection, over many years, to his local community football club, and undoubtedly would have developed many skills in networking, communication, and social interaction with local parents and children in this voluntary role. While Terry represents himself as unchanged or having changed very little, from the moment he walked out the door to address the media about his son, his life changed in some way. His social action has ensured he became identified with a high profile campaign. Terry now believes "he will always be interested in human rights" and if he can help other people in situations similar to David's he will if he can. His direct action has instilled in him a firm commitment to human rights, a significant change for someone who had no previous interest in social issues or politics. He is changed forever by his learning; as he states, the "blinkers are off" and he now views global injustice and human rights in a different way.

In chapter 7, the concept of learning as a process of becoming is further explored. However, it is clear that these activists varied in their willingness to identify as activists. *Grace* believed there was a radical connotation to it. *Andrew* said he would have identified as an activist five years ago, but now identified as a leader. Terry insisted he was just a concerned parent doing what any concerned parent would do in similar circumstances.

Tim's sense of identity has completely changed from his self-described working identity as a "corporate engineer" who once thought it easy to sit back and let the "money roll in." He now identifies as an activist and has no problems with this identity. This is a large shift in self from corporate engineer to environmental activist in a period of three years. *Bahar* has only recently come to identify herself as an activist. When I asked *Catherine* whether she identified as an activist she confirmed that she did. So, too, did Tricia:

> (Catherine) Look, this is the problem with Australia. We have a democracy and people think that the practice of democracy is waddling up and sticking a paper in a box once a year.... Being an activist is being an active citizen and active democrat, an active participant. If you do not like something stand up and say it!

(Tricia) Yes I do, actually I have no problems with it, I'm quite proud of it actually. Do not mind the term lobbyist either. I did not always understand it before, but yes an activist—I do not have a problem with that term.

Eva frequently referred to her Irish Catholic heritage of "dissent" and spoke about the work of activists being important, but never fully claimed this identity.

For some of the circumstantial activists such as Terry, *Bahar*, *Grace*, and Tim there is a fundamental change to their initial ideological beliefs prior to their activism. This change in the self is substantial; they are changed forever because of their learning. *Grace* was a veterinary surgeon who had no prior involvement in activism. Tim, of course, was an engineer in a multinational resource company, he identified as a corporate player living a corporate lifestyle. *Bahar* came from a conservative Muslim family, resistance was not a part of her life nor her identity, and particularly not a part of her identity as a Muslim woman. Yet it is important to note that all of them had a connection to their own community. *Bahar*'s sense of connectedness about Turkish women's oppression led her to work with her community. *Grace* had worked as a veterinarian in country Victoria, so undoubtedly she would have had some connection to community and the values of place and space in a rural community. Terry had volunteered with the local football club for more than 37 years. This would have intrinsically linked him to his own community through sport in various ways. Tim was involved with the local bushwalking group, but said he always had an affinity with nature.

For all of these activists, the shift in the self was monumental, unlike the lifelong activists whose identity had being firmly established in adolescence. These activists, in their mid- to late-lives, suddenly found themselves working on a political level that they never thought possible. *Grace*, who had struggled with severe postnatal depression, found working on campaigns empowering. She is now adopting the discourses of community development and activism and has left her job as a veterinary surgeon to work as a rural women's community development worker for a government department. Tim is still working with his local bayside community group and has organized, with Environment Victoria, two very large direct action protests mobilizing people onto the beach to develop a human sign reading "halt climate change" (see Tim's case study in Chapter 7). *Bahar* is doing paid and unpaid work to further social change for migrant women.

Emotions and Learning

One of the major themes of this research is the role that emotions play in giving the circumstantial activists impetus to act and also to maintain their commitment to activism over the longer term. In all of the interviews, activists were asked to comment on why they decided to take action. Many people feel annoyed and disillusioned with social inequality and the political system from time to time but not everyone chooses to be proactive. Frequently, the activists in this study referred to passion, anger, rage, and frustration as contributing to their motivation to act.

> (Bahar) At the end of the day you've got to have that passion, it's got to come from the heart; if you do not have that passion [do] not think of this work as a career. All these people in the environment movement they are not working because the trees are going to thank them, the oxygen is going to reward them, they are doing it in their own time because they want to.
>
> (Catherine) There are a lot of people who engage at the head level, they can look at a piece of legislation and say yes it has certain injustices and it's not right, but unless you engage maybe it's engaging with the heart that enables you to see another person's pain you then want to change it, you can't just walk away.

Eva felt a sense of "betrayal" after the consultation in which she had been involved appeared to discount the views of the community. *Grace* said she was "pretty angry" about the lack of consultation on the use of public land in her local community. On the other hand, Terry says that he tried to keep his emotions in check. He was often frustrated, anxious, and cynical about the Government's treatment of David. There were times that he found the campaign "very emotional and very draining." He said, initially he found it overwhelming when the international media and prominent politicians were talking about his son, but as time went on, he shifted from being intimidated by government and the media to becoming more assertive and believing he had "a right to speak to them" about his son. *Catherine's* emotions were intrinsically connected to her motivation to become an activist: "I realized then there are two different sorts of human beings in Australia; there are citizens who have human rights and there are non-citizens who count for nothing!" *Bahar* claims you must "have a heart" to be an activist because domestic violence work is often traumatic: "you see the tears of children, you see people who are desperate!" This connection to her heart is the most important motivation for *Bahar*'s activism.

The Learning Edge

Many of the circumstantial activists reported having times of tension and anxiety in their activism. Phrases like being on a "learning curve" or "out of my comfort zone" or "on a huge journey" were frequently used by the circumstantial activists in this study. *Grace* found she had to learn rapidly to control her feelings of being overwhelmed by her lack of knowledge.

> I get very nervous before I've got to speak in public, if I've got to speak about something I'm not one hundred per cent on I feel very nervous.... I've discovered, so you can see how often I've been out of my comfort zone. So I guess my strategy of not staying outside of my comfort zone is to find a way of getting back into it, and that's probably what's driven my learning to some extent, is a desire to be credible and to know what I'm talking about.

Terry's activism led him to be involved in a documentary tracing the footsteps of his son in Pakistan and Afghanistan. He says the biggest step he took was "getting involved in the overseas thing" as he had never been overseas before. His entry onto the global stage was brought home to him when he realized his protest in the cage in New York had occurred outside the same hotel where John Lennon was assassinated. Terry was also very fearful when he realized that David had decided to plea bargain with the military tribunal in the United States. If David was found guilty, he could potentially face the death penalty. Terry brings up his anxiety about this: "when the charges were first laid there was a [possibility of a] death penalty. That was a panic session; it's probably the most fearful thing the death penalty." *Andrew*, however, argues that in those edgy moments of tension "change occurs," that this is the time when personal "change happens."

> That's where change happens; some of the wankers call it creative tension, so that's where creativity happens. That's where new ideas are born, people build alliances, you change. One of the classic definitions of "leadership" that we work with is "leadership is a force for change."

Eva was pushed completed out of her comfort zone at a council meeting that was full of protesters; it was noisy, and the crowd was angry. The councilors threatened to walk out if the meeting continued to be disruptive and the protesters yelled at them to go. Eva in an "impulsive" moment stood on a chair and asked all of the protesters to please resume their seats so that the meeting could go ahead. As Eva states, her action was completely spontaneous:

> I had no idea that I was going to do it, because we really had no idea what that meeting would be like. You see, we had too many people, they could not all fit in and there was a lot of anger. It was quite impulsive and I'm not really an impulsive person.

Eva managed to persuade the crowd to come back inside and the meeting was able to continue.

Religion, Social Justice and Spirituality

Like the lifelong activists in this study, some of the circumstantial activists were influenced by Christianity, particularly Catholicism. *Eva*, *Catherine* and Tricia all believed they were influenced by the religious stories they were told in childhood about helping other people. *Bahar* articulated her involvement in activism as a calling, believing that she was meant to work in her community with Turkish women. She believes it is "God's will" that she is here in this time and space:

> I think I now know why I am here in this world and I think that is one of my main purposes to be here. I do not want to rush things and do something that I shouldn't, thinking I've only got so much time left. But I know there is so much that I want to do...I am here for a reason.

Unlike *Bahar*, however, *Eva*, *Catherine* and Tricia are no longer actively practising their religion. They distinguish between the Christian teachings about benevolence and charity that they were exposed to and their current outlook, which is more a form of humanism. Nevertheless, they all agreed that religious teachings had instilled in them some sense of social justice:

> (Eva) The gospel messages about looking after people less fortunate and the sermon on the mount that were really incurring and a lot of

those pictures were all about helping St Christopher, there were things about lepers and poor people and loaves and fishes all of those people were going to get very uncomfortable and hungry.

(Tricia) I come from an Irish Catholic family, it had a strong feminist focus. I had not realized this before but it was there. They certainly had a strong sense of social justice; my parents were always doing things for people.

(Catherine) I guess it's my commitment and we were talking here the other day about where that comes from, whether it's religious or humanist or atheist underpinnings. I have a Catholic background and while I am not a practising Catholic the commitment to social justice is something that comes from there.

It appears that religious socialization contributed to the readiness with which they connected social justice to their identities. The following section provides a concluding summary of research findings for both groups of activists.

Conclusion

Circumstantial activists undergo a significant and rapid process of learning and identity formation over a short period of time. They have usually had a series of life circumstances that have motivated them to take action. For Terry, his son's incarceration sent him on a journey of activism for more than six years. Tim's initial "wacky" idea of going out on the streets with a pole noting rising sea levels, saw a huge shift in his sense of self. In a short period of time, Tim went from being a corporate engineer to being a committed environmental activist, he is changed forever because of his learning in activism. This theme is familiar with most of the circumstantial activists and differs to the identity formation of the lifelong activists, whose identity is formed slowly and incrementally in young adulthood. The circumstantial activists in this study very quickly have a monumental change in their sense of self, they need to learn to become an activist very quickly and their change in ideology is very dramatic. They are changed in significant ways because of their learning practices.

Circumstantial activists are rapid learners; they develop knowledge of systems, structures, and processes of government that cause inequality, at an extraordinary pace. Knowledge and skills develop in a short period of time, usually over a couple of years, as opposed to the incremental, slow development of knowledge that occurs much earlier for lifelong activists. They are on the periphery of practice and must develop expertise very rapidly and are frequently taken onto a learning edge where they are out of their comfort zone and need to develop new knowledge and skills very quickly to be effective as activists. Not all of the circumstantial activists are engaged in social and political movements. *Bahar*, *Grace* and *Eva* are not a part of any broad based social movement. Similarly, Terry refers to groups involved in his campaign as "support groups" rather than social movements; he has not completely immersed himself into the social movement. *Catherine*, Tim, *Andrew* and Tricia became involved in social movements in midlife, rather than in their adolescence. Finally, the question of formal qualifications should be addressed. Few of the circumstantial activists participating in the research had studied for qualifications supporting their activism. Terry has no formal qualification, *Grace* has a science degree, Tim is an engineer and *Andrew* has a master's of business administration.

The next part of this chapter explored, through case studies, the deeply personal accounts of knowledge development and skill outlined in the stories of Terry Hicks, *Catherine*, Tim Forcey and *Grace's* activism.

Case Studies: Introduction

Four case studies have been chosen to illustrate the learning practices of circumstantial activists. The first case study outlines the activism of Terry Hicks who campaigned to have his son released from Guantanamo Bay where he was held without charge by the US military. The case study of *Catherine* reflects the journey of a woman who returned to study after the breakup of her marriage and became involved in seeking justice for asylum seekers in Australia. Tim, an engineer with a major resource company, commenced his activism with a small campaign on the Port Phillip bay of Melbourne with his "climate change pole" and his story forms the third case study. Finally, the case study of *Grace*, a veterinarian living in rural Victoria, considers her campaign to get children's services in her town, which led her to become active in a number of other local campaigns. Each of these stories reveal significant personal growth,

136 A Critical Pedagogy of Embodied Education

skill development, and identity change as the individuals learned to become activists.

Case Study: Terry's Story

> *"I'm just an ordinary bloke... I'm not an activist, [I'm] a concerned parent."*

Terry's activism is "accidental," triggered by a series of events that would dominate his life for more than five years starting "when a friend alerted him to the fact that his son had been captured fighting with the Northern Alliance in Afghanistan" (Debelle 2003). His son, David, was handed over to the US military in Afghanistan by the Northern Alliance in late 2011. David was subsequently imprisoned in Guantanamo Bay in Cuba, beyond the ambit of the established American legal system. In response to these events, Terry advocated for his son's release and learned skills to further the campaign along the way or on the job. Prior to David's arrest, Terry argues, he "had lived a fairly boring life." He had had no previous involvement in activism, politics, or NGOs prior to David's arrest. His only community interests had been coaching the local junior football team for some 25 years. However, in that time, he had never participated on the board or management committee of the community group because, as Terry put it, "they tend to be political." Debelle (2003, p. 1) states "Terry Hicks has been on a steep learning curve." David's arrest had occurred at a time when the world was still coming to terms with issues regarding security and terrorism after the September 11 attacks by Al Qaeda in New York and Washington. "David, a Muslim convert... was not a member of al-Qaida but trained with them, as did all Taliban fighters who underwent military training" (Debelle 2003). Terry's campaign started at the local and national level and eventually became an international campaign. The "Fair Go for David" campaign became one the most high profile campaigns in Australian recent history, highlighting the fragility of civil liberties and shocking Australians who expected the US to observe the human rights of a citizen from an allied nation. I met Terry at his suburban home in Adelaide in South Australia in July 2007. His son had been released from Guantanamo Bay only a few weeks earlier and extradited to Australia to fulfill a prison sentence of nine months for aiding terrorism.

Terry Hicks commenced the interview by describing the shock that he and his family experienced when the Australian Security

Intelligence Organisation (ASIO) and the Federal Police (FP) arrived on the doorstep to search his house:

> When we had the first visit from ASIO and the FP we had nothing to hide. They had a right of search and if we did not cooperate they would have gutted the house and I said to them "well you will have to fix it!" We had nothing to tell them anyway so that really started to give you a bit of insight into how these organizations work with their threats, mainly verbal threats I suppose. The other thing that was told to us is that "You do not speak to the media until we give you the all clear."

This first experience of dealing with ASIO, the FP, and the media was overwhelming, after which "a week and a half of them camped out the front started to get a bit annoying!" Terry had agreed with the authorities' initial requests to not go to the media, but Terry felt he needed to get the real message out about David. He states:

> I realized what had happened after a while. I started to think particularly [of] the demonizing of David. You know, there was no trial or anything like that; the only way we could [raise] David's issues was to keep the whole thing up front.

Terry recalled that the media and government labeled David a terrorist before any legal process had been commenced. Because of September 11 and the "War on Terror," David's story "was big news" and everybody wanted a piece of it. He realized that he had to take action and speak to the media, at which point the campaign commenced:

> The police shut off the end of the street to come into the house. This of course gave us insight into how they all work. After about a week and a half I went out and spoke to the media and of course then them [the FP, ASIO]. It was as easy as that.

Terry's learning was fast-paced. In the interview he frequently referred to the huge "learning curve" he had been on. Terry started out as a newcomer on the periphery of practice (Lave & Wenger 1991). He was learning about international systems of government and developing new knowledge about legislation and terrorism. He was learning about Australia's foreign policy alliance with the United States, about Muslim culture and politics in Iraq and Afghanistan, about the Australian government, the processes of making legislation, and the workings of international bodies like the United Nations. He was learning about the Australian political system, and the machinations of government, and the making of legislation. He was also learning about the hypocrisy of politics and what he refers to as "the imbalance":

> You start to see things... well, the detention centres here, and Christmas Island it just goes on and on, there's Abu Ghraib and then you start to see certain principles that arise. Like the Australian Wheat Board can start selling wheat to a regime that they were trying to throw out, nothing happened with them they are not arrested for supplying material aid to a terrorist regime, nothing happened and yet here we have David who has not even lifted a finger being treated this way and you start to see the imbalance.

He was also learning to speak publicly for the first time, and then to perfect this role through practising time and time again at forums across Australia:

> Oh yeah, public speaking, I suppose if you look at that one it's a skill, the other thing that you develop ... is when you speak to a cross section of very influential people. A lot of people would say they could not do that talk to high profile people.

By being an advocate for his son he learned "out of necessity" through the process of activism that he acknowledged by saying:

> ...To be honest it's just something you develop along the way through that process; whether you call it a skill or something that you do out of necessity. I've never really looked at it as a skill...

Terry's strategy was to "keep the message simple so that everyone could understand the issues that concern David." His learning was also social as the people he met became increasingly diverse:

> In Sydney, you were speaking to the converted sometimes... but as time went by you started to see different faces. I approached some of these people and they were just "normal" people like myself who were concerned.

I asked Terry whether there had been any stages or phases to his learning. He claimed that from his early learning his formed a strategy that he deployed prior to the federal government election in 2007:

> I've only ever developed one strategy and that is I leaked a thing last Christmas. I'd looked at all of the marginal seats, they only needed a swing of 3.5% and we could bring the government down. So I rang a friend of mine in The Advertiser, and the story went national on Christmas day. It would have made Howard's weet-bix go soggy. But the point I wanted to prove was that if you say anything about John Howard (and I thought I would test him), he usually ignored you. Well, he responded the next day, so I knew that I had him, you see because of the opinion polls, you see he had said David Hicks would never be a political issue, and it worked, it worked!

Terry had clearly developed the knowledge and strategic thinking that comes through involvement in a long term campaign. His longer term strategy involved community education and educating the public about issues relating to his son's incarceration. Through careful planning and by using strategies such as the one outlined above, Terry's action ensured David became a political issue, the Australian government was on the back foot, in a tight election campaign, and the issue of David Hicks needed to be dealt with expediently. Terry had a significant mentor in David's first lawyer, he was the "go-to man" if ever there was an issue or a problem. Terry would seek advice and guidance from him. His lawyer's skill and expertise in advocacy were significant in showing Terry the way that they could approach David's case and keep the issues going in the media. Terry believes his development of expertise in relation to terrorism and anti-terrorism legislation is only on a surface level, that he relies on the knowledge of experts, his lawyers, supporters, human rights groups. His role, he believes, is to keep promoting David's case out there in the media and to keep the message plain and simple. There is significant strategy being used here: the allocation of resources, input, and skill brought in by a range of experts, groups, networks, and social movements to further the campaign. The following dialogue explores Terry's firm position of not stepping out of his role, or taking on the role of 'expert" in relation to his son's incarceration. He speaks intelligently about the possible consequences of moving outside of his role and being viewed as an expert:

> (Terry) That's why I say you have to go to the basics because I'm not a lawyer or a politician and [if] you get in over your head you can't answer their questions, then you're in trouble.

(Interviewer) So as a strategy you really tried to keep things at a simple and basic level?
(Terry) Simple and basic so that everybody understands.
(Interviewer) To get the message out?
(Terry) That's right, these forums you know we have lawyers, political people they talk the in-depth. All I do is pass on the basics and I think that has been working pretty well.

Terry is cautious about acknowledging his skill and expertise. The following quote about developing a basic level of knowledge contradicts the premise of "surface" knowledge espoused by Terry. It shows his critical thinking abilities and his ability to analyze the flaws in the legal case about his son. He clearly understands the illegal nature of David's incarceration and subsequent conviction and the systemic nature of the inequality about David's incarceration:

> I think that [what] you do is you touch around the edges; you never get right into it. You look at the basics, because I find that if you started heading into it you get yourself into trouble. You look at the basic principles of law which is if you have done something wrong you go to courts. The evidence is brought up against you and if you are found guilty you wear it. Now that principle has never been applied to David! The principle that I have to stick to right through is if David had gone through a proper court and he is found guilty then he is found guilty, he goes to jail. Not [that] you plead guilty to a charge that has been retrospective even though they say it hasn't. The same principle then applied to David falls apart which to me is about [how] David has faced an illegal system. He pleaded guilty under an illegal system and that's not good enough to me.

Terry and David's lawyers started to develop direct action protest strategies that would be effective in gaining international media coverage about David's plight in Guantanamo Bay. Terry, for example, stood inside the cage the same size as one of the prisoner cells at Guantanamo Bay, first outside the national Liberal Party conference in Adelaide, which the prime minister, John Howard, was attending. Later, the same action was performed outside a hotel in downtown New York in 2003. In this action, Terry wears an orange-colored suit representing one of the suits that the prisoners wear at Guantanamo. He invites passersby to step into the cage to feel what it is like to live in such a small space. Terry says, for a long time David was held in a prison cage outside in the open like this. In the quote below, Terry describes his anxiety about performing this action in New York:

> I invited people to go into that cage and they would not do it. Look it's an eerie feeling; this is where David was kept in one of those for quite a while in the open. Yeah, it wasn't a good experience, but we got the message across. Look the Americans are quite strange because they knew about Guantanamo, but they did not know how these people were being kept. So it opened up a few eyes. Also put a few people on the back foot and then they needed to check what the hell was going on.

The international media coverage was successful in highlighting the plight of David and other prisoners. David's story was also presented in a documentary called *The President Versus David Hicks,* in which Terry traced the life of his son and his conversion to Islam, his fight for what he perceived an injustice towards Muslims, his travels to Kosovo, Kashmir, then Afghanistan.[4] Terry claims he learned a huge amount from his mentor Stephen Kenny, who provided strategic advice about his trip and campaign overseas and assisted Terry with the idea of using the cage to show the human rights abuses of those imprisoned in Guantanamo Bay. In the process, however, he has also learned about the vulnerability of becoming a public identity. Terry said that he was lucky that he developed skills of using the media very early on in the campaign and he refused to deal with journalist or media organizations that misrepresented him or David's story:

> ...you are vulnerable and you have to be very careful. Look, in the first instance, you suddenly realize "I shouldn't have said that." I was very lucky that I'd developed that [sense] very quickly, because I could have made a hell of mess of things because of the media. So I just took the hard line and I said if you do not print what I tell you or how I put it I won't talk to you.

Terry has learned to deal with the political discourses of David's case. His has had high powered and high profile people talking about the case including the prime minister of Australia and the US president and voicing their positions and opinions on David's guilt or innocence. Terry is very clear about both his own and David's human rights. With all of the attention that David's case was attracting, Terry described the process of people such as the president of the United States speaking about his son's case as "surreal." But as he gained more experience in dealing with the issue on a day to day level, speaking to prominent people about the case, dealing with experts and lawyers and human rights groups he became indignant about the discourses of David's case. I asked Terry what he felt when he heard the president discussing David's case in the media:

> I think you get to a stage where you get sick of it, you do not care what they think, after a while you think gee this is surreal it's the President of the United States talking about David. Well I think he's not talking he is just pushing the circumstances – I call it the "fear factor" and here we have this so you try to turn it around, you go from "God, the President's talking about my son!" to "Why are they talking such bullshit!?"

Terry does not identify as an activist. He does not like the sense of radicalism behind the word. He says he is just an ordinary bloke doing what most ordinary people would do in the same circumstances. However, he does say that he will always be committed to human rights and in this sense, for someone who had no involvement in politics and activism beforehand, he is changed politically and his ideology has shifted. Terry spent some time in the interview stressing that he hasn't really changed over the long years of activism in David's campaign. Terry has never fully reconciled with the identity of an activist, and he still remains outside of involvement with social movements. It appears that he has never fully immersed himself into an activist community and still remains on the edges of social movements.

Conclusion

Terry's case study centres on one of the most high profile campaigns in Australia for some time. Terry's learning is accidental, since he was never involved in politics, political parties, social movements or campaigns before; and, unusually, he had no formal education or training. In midlife he took on a national and international campaign in order to release his son from prison. Thwarted by both the Australian and US "War on Terror," Terry pursued a long term campaign over many years and developed knowledge and skills along the way. Terry's learning is extraordinarily rapid. He has learned about government and bureaucracy and international systems such as the United Nations, and his life has been changed forever because of this campaign. As

Terry states, "the blinkers are now off and his whole world view has changed." He believes he will now always be committed to human rights and if he can "help" other individuals or groups in some way in the future he will. Terry's learning typifies the learning that occurs for the circumstantial activist, a person who describes himself as nonpolitical, but becomes politicized, knowledgeable and highly skilled along the way through learning in the practices of activism.

Case Study: Catherine's Story

> "I realized then there are two different sorts of human beings in Australia. There are citizens, who have human rights and there are non-citizens who count for nothing!"

Catherine became an activist in midlife after she found herself separated from her husband and responsible for two children. Prior to this, *Catherine* had been a trained pediatric nurse and had also worked in midwifery. She had travelled widely and set up a restaurant business with her husband. They moved to Holland and the marriage failed. It was at this time *Catherine* returned to Australia with two young children in tow. Prior to this she had no history of activism, although she states that she has always been "outspoken." I commenced the interview by asking *Catherine* how she became an activist.

> When you are in your fifties it can be a long journey, I can't say that I was always an activist....I've done a lot of things done a lot of travelling; when I was travelling I could not always be nursing. I have run a restaurant with my husband, I have done all sorts of odds and sods, but I suppose my present path began back in the '90s. I went to Holland with my husband and children. He was Dutch and I left Holland about 18 months later with my children a single parent, at which point you are making new decisions about your life.

As her marriage ended, *Catherine* decided that nursing and the shift hours were not conducive to bringing up two young children, so she decided to study at TAFE and commenced study in a diploma of welfare studies at Victoria University in Melbourne. "I did not realize that I would take to it with so much joy," she says, "being able to study, being able to think, talk about ideas; it was so stimulating." *Catherine* began to pursue a journey of study, which led to a fieldwork placement and being placed in a prominent union for her fieldwork practicum, working on a campaign for reform for "outworkers." Her passion for changing injustice commenced when she viewed a documentary that showed poor working conditions for, mainly, migrant outworkers. *Catherine* then went and spoke to the churches and the union and got involved in "The Fairwear Campaign," which was a campaign to ensure that outworkers were paid reasonable wages by fashion companies.

Catherine comes from what she describes as "a fairly conservative family." She states "my family's politics are quite conservative actually, I'm sure my father never voted labor, although he's gone to heaven a long time ago." Her parents were Catholic and she grew up with religion being an important part of her childhood, the family regularly attended church and Sunday school. Her father was very involved in the church, a practising Catholic. Her mother, who was a real estate agent for some of her childhood, unusually brought home clients who were homeless and they would stay temporarily with the family. Her parents had a Christian ethos and "believed in helping others...they were caring people." The philosophy of service to others taught within the Catholic Church, *Catherine* believes, had an impact on who she is today; in essence, the values she absorbed at this time inform her sense of "self." They set a framework for her own values and ethics around social justice and human rights.

Her activism was well-established some years later when she joined a campaign on refugee rights called "No One is Illegal." The campaign was a coalition of church, welfare and other NGOs resisting the former Howard Government's policy on asylum seekers.[5] The interview uncovered the emotional connection that *Catherine* had to the issue of refugee rights, particularly her anger. This anger is used as a motivating force and a driver in her activism, as shown in the following quote:

> Well, it's very easy to get enraged about something, to find that you want to do something, but you've got to be strategic and I think a lot of activists let's face it we've grown a lot, the community. Let's face it, ten years of a Howard Government, ten years of some pretty tough stuff – we've learned a lot....So when it came to the refugee stuff...when they started coming in and they were locked up in those camps in Woomera it just distressed me.

Catherine points to the momentum the campaign gained as women and children were detained and people saw images of the often remote areas of Australia where detention centres were located. *Catherine* helped to organize a public vigil to educate the community about the brutality of detention. Initially, very few people attended, but eventually the numbers started to increase week by week:

> ...So that was kind of the beginning there was no awareness, [about the refugee situation] some days you'd get no one, six or seven, some days you would get thirty. I remember one Sunday all of these people turned up and we were standing under this shed, the water was this deep around us [it had been raining] they had come from some churches they had heard about the vigils, it was amazing.

Catherine has contributed to reversing the discourses of prejudice about asylums seekers and refugees in Australian society. She points to the government who had, in her view, commenced a "dehumanizing" campaign against refugees to build public support for detention with the assistance of the media. *Catherine's* role as an activist was to talk to journalists and raise public awareness about the realities of refugees lives in detention:

> I suppose we talked about people and humanizing them. That was really important because the government had been demonizing them and removing their humanity to justify what they were doing to them so they were called "illegals" and "unlawful."

With a broad coalition of church groups and activists, *Catherine* attended the Easter vigils at Baxter Detention Centre in the country town of Woomera, South Australia. Observing how diverse the movement was, she notes "a lot of people said 'Why did not the refugee movement just get together under one neat little hierarchy?', but it doesn't always work out like that!" This diverse group of people included "young students, lefties, with people referred to as ferals. You will be there with conservatives, with old people, the Church, with young people; the diversity involved with the refugee movement is quite amazing." *Catherine* began to immerse herself in this diverse group of people—all coming to work together for the purposes of changing the inequality experienced by the Australian government's stance on refugees.

The Woomera campaign attracted a great deal of media attention. It was controversial because the "cyclone fence" that imprisoned the refugees and surrounded the detention centre was torn down by some of the protesters and subsequently some of the refugees escaped. So there were moments throughout the protest that were tense, anxious, emotional, and even dangerous. *Catherine* highlighted the trauma that was experienced at the Woomera protests:

> I arrived the day after the escapes and what I saw was a very traumatized community. The activists were in shock, many of them had spent the night in tents sitting and listening to the stories of the refugees. Many of the refugees were still there, the police were clomping around in their heavy boots, batons and shields, and it was surreal really. People were just quietly going on around these things. We knew that some of the people who had escaped had gone back in, but some hadn't. We did not know where they were and of course there was a huge road block. There was one way in there and one way out. They [the police] were searching the cars; in the middle of the desert.

Due to an unusual conflagration of events, the Woomera campaign captured national and international attention. It was Easter, generally a slow news time in both Europe and Australia with people away on holidays:

> You have this sort of dead media space and into that came the Woomera crusade where you had people coming from all corners of Australia, they came from Perth, Sydney, Brisbane and Melbourne, they came into the desert—it was pretty amazing!

I asked *Catherine* whether her formal study influenced her understanding of government systems. She responded that "practising activism" was more important.

> (Catherine) I think that you do need some theoretical underpinnings, but the practise is more important, the last few years have been a steep learning curve for me.
> (Interviewer) Can you elaborate on that?
> (Catherine) In the beginning I suppose I took an activist approach, standing on the gates beating on the gates metaphorically speaking. Now I'm still standing outside the gates, well, we all are outside, but I'm finding ways to get the doors open and slip inside.

Catherine demonstrates that she has become "more strategic" as she gained more experience through practising her activism, by being involved, by meeting with people, organizing vigils, by being engaged in public protest, she has increased her skill as an activist.

Catherine has also had some significant mentors that she has worked with on campaigns, sought advice and guidance from and whom she has also observed in their activism. She appreciated these mentors' "clear and strategic way of looking at things" and expressed the important role one mentor played, in the following statement:

> Jane always had believed in a multi layered approach to community activism so I guess we looked at a campaign that worked on a grass roots level. We engaged players like the churches who have a lot of credibility because they are seen as conservative, yet they have that social justice underpinning, that they will breach that conservatism in standing up on social justice issues. We needed the political machinery to acknowledge what was happening because the ultimate solution was a change in legislation.

Catherine is now employed as a paid organizer on refugee rights and she says that she has now made a transition from her "activism to advocacy," not a role that she always feels "comfortable" with. I asked her about what she had learned in the early stages of her activism compared with what she had learned as she became more experienced as an activist. She said that the early phases of the refugee campaign were about doing "extraverted" direct action tactics in the campaign, which you can only maintain for a certain period of time, as she emphasizes "there is no point standing around detention centres forever." The next phase was consolidating the momentum gained from creating awareness in the community and in the public arena:

> You've then got to move on to the next phase. OK, you have the awareness, some people are aware, some people are disquieted, and so what are you going to do with that? How will you take it to the next stage which is to change the legislation, to get the release of people? To diminish the pain of those suffering from the policy and that is around approaching the government getting people to sign petitions creating a wave of resistance but at a different level.

Catherine's learning with, from, and by others has included many of the refugees themselves whose stories she has listened to over a long period of time. Many of the stories from refugees, who have been traumatized through their experience of escaping a country or society where they and their families' lives are in danger, have been poignant.

She states she has learned many things from the refugees' own experiences but more particularly:

> ...how easy it is for a country to lose that respect for human rights and you can go down very quickly on a spiral where people suffer, where people are murdered, where people disappear, but you know you learn a lot from the refugees, they have come from countries and have seen these things happen.

Conclusion

Catherine identifies as an activist and does this "proudly;" she believes her major motivation to be an activist is "at very basic level human rights." Her story is one of change and learning through experience.

Case Study: Tim Forcey's Story

"This climate change business is serious"

Tim is an environmental activist with a particular interest in the impact of climate change on the world. Unusually for an environmental activist, Tim was employed as a chemical engineer in a major resource company and prior to 2006 had never practiced as an activist at all. He lives in a bay-side suburb of Melbourne, and is one of the founding members of a local environment action group. The group's main concern is about issues relating to climate change and its subsequent impact on the local environment. Tim was born in the United States. His parents were dairy farmers and he was brought up with an appreciation of the land and the environment and what that meant for people who lived and worked on the land. He thinks this link with his family being "farming folk" is important, because growing up on a dairy farm gave him an early affinity with the land. It is surprising that an engineer who works for a major resource company would eventually assist in organizing a large campaign that mobilized thousands of people onto the beaches at Sandringham to make a human sign that read "stop climate change." Tim is a self-learner who began doing research in 2005 to understand the issue of peak oil. His "informal learning" (Foley 1999) led him to the realization that the world's dependency on oil was having a devastating impact on the environment and could no longer be sustained at its current levels. At this time, he read anything he could about climate change and started to develop a desire to do something about it. The issues were becoming important to him and he was no longer content just to work as corporate engineer for a major resource company and "let the money roll in." He had found that the community and governments were still skeptical and questioning whether climate change was real. His public protest started with a simple campaign, using a pole that would measure advancing sea levels if climate change continued at its current pace. His wife and family became engaged and actively involved in the journey. He says he was anxious because he thought taking action on climate change to the streets of Sandringham kind of "whacky." He remembers telling his wife he felt nervous and excited like he used to feel when he was a kid and had the weekly spelling bee. In the narrative below Tim outlines his first action:

> I went out on the street in about September 2006, I'd worked out that something needed to be done on climate change and there wasn't enough happening. I came up with an idea that I felt semi-comfortable [with], where I could take some action that might have an impact. I built this 13 meter tall plastic pole, 13 meters signifies where the sea level could get to if we lose all of the ice on Greenland and West Antarctica.

Tim identifies as politically "conservative" and comes from what he acknowledges as the "corporate world" where, prior to his activism, he was quite happy to work as a corporate engineer and "let the money roll in" until through his own self-learning he realized "this climate change business is serious." His community education of the Climate Change pole was his first stirring of taking action, his family then became involved so on weekends they would take the pole to the foreshore of bayside Melbourne to talk to the community about climate change. He says his motivation to act came from realizing that it would not be scientists who publicized the dangers of climate change:

> I know that something had to be done, and the scientists had been saying "something needs to be done," for 20 years, and it finally clicked. I've worked for scientists in my job. Scientists do not get anything done; they come up with ideas, they do the research, they write the papers, and then it's the engineers like me that actually come in and turn it into something useful.

He says it was important for him to find a strategy that he felt comfortable with, given how he viewed himself:

> I'm an engineer, very conservative, not the type of person to just stand on a street corner and hand out something or try and get somebody to talk to me. But with the pole, I knew that would be hard for them to ignore.

Tim, with his wife and other local people, founded a climate change action group. The group's purpose was to raise awareness on climate change and to influence policy and public opinion about the dangers of rising climate change. He needed to become involved with other activists and people who had an interest in the environment and climate change. He started to learn about some of the key players, speakers, activists, NGOs, and community groups in the environmental movement that he needed to get to know. He needed others with whom he could act on climate change, he needed to find out about these groups and players:

> [It took a while to know]…who was going to be useful to me, who I could be useful to… that slowed me down a bit, just getting that research together and understanding it, and then going out and meeting people, which in Melbourne's not hard, because it's not a big place.

Tim and his wife began to meet with NGOs and some of the key players in the environmental movement, and he began to learn about the discipline and strategy that is involved in working with smaller groups of individuals in community-based organizations and, on a broader level, the environment movement. His learning has included getting used to the culture of small community groups and NGOs, which was very different to the corporate culture of multinational organizations he had worked in:

> Oh well we were kind of going through this the other night with the community group, the Bayside Group, we were thinking through things that we'd do for this year. And you make this nice long list of ideas, and then at that point it becomes different from work. At work you'd work out the top priority and you'd put resources onto it. In a community group it's more you're waiting for someone to get excited about something and putting up their hand and saying "I want that to happen." And so the list can just sit on the shelf and nothing happens unless somebody puts up their hand. Because in the community groups

it's top priority for no one; everybody else has got something that is a higher priority, and so this has got to fit in around that and so you may not end up accomplishing anything.

Tim is learning "on the job" and the "job" is activism. He knows he has to learn about "the players" and, as an outsider, the importance of building up his credibility with other environmental groups:

> Well, I always feel the need to research everything and know everything that's going on before I step into an area, and that was very confusing, trying to work out what all these different NGOs stood for with respect to climate change.

Tim's self learning on climate change, his research, and his synthesis of data and literature on climate change science is reminiscent of many of the activists in this study. He is using reason and critical thinking skills, his activism is still developing and emerging. His own research has led him to realize a systemic connection between government, the world dependency on oil, and governments' lack of willingness to do something about it. Tim said he "kind of took it personally" that Australia (the country of which he is a citizen) and the United States (his country of birth) had both chosen not to sign the Kyoto Protocol on climate change. Tim's ability to think critically about the costs of climate change and how he could attract the attention of the average person on the street to engage with discussion about climate change is spelled out as follows:

> I know that something had to be done, and the scientists had been saying "Something needs to be done, something needs to be done" for 20 years, and it finally clicked with me. I've worked for scientists in my job and scientists don't get anything done; they come up with ideas, they do the research, they write the papers, and then it's the engineers like me that actually come in and turn it into something useful. And so that kind of clicked with me, and I said, "Right, well the global warming pole is something that I can do as an engineer that will actually connect the scientists to the average person."

Tim's initial action with the "climate change pole" has now grown into involvement in other area of activists' work, such as organizing major public actions where activists use their bodies as a symbolic way of promoting climate change. The first action was to develop a human sign that would show concern about climate change. This is an example of his developing event management skills. He was learning about communicating and portraying ideas, learning to meet with planners and politicians in local government, to deal with the media, to work with other activists and to promote an issue using community education processes, learning about how to promote an issue in the media, which included organizing helicopters and photographers so that the protest could be photographed in order to further promote climate change.

Tim started to immerse himself in the climate change movement after this and became involved in the "Victorian Walk Against Warming." In 2007, "we had 50,000 people here in Melbourne and both of those probably should be in the Guinness Book for the largest climate change rallies in the world at those times." He now identifies as an activist, but claims "he is not a greenie" and seems to delineate between the identity of a greenie and the identity of a climate change activist. It seems that he is not completely immersed in the climate change movement. He believes there are still some people who are suspicious of his participation because he is an engineer who works for a large resource company. When I asked him about whether his activism conflicted with his working world as an engineer, he said that his employer has largely turned a blind eye to what he is doing and he is careful about trying to remain anonymous, although, as he claims, his activist practices are widely reported on the internet. He also sees that his company is becoming more aware of climate change issues and it is useful for someone in the company to be attuned to issues of climate change. There was one occasion when he was asked to read the ethics policy, but apart from this, they have largely ignored his climate change activism.

Conclusion

Tim's learning journey is extraordinary considering that prior to late 2006 he had no involvement in activism whatsoever. He has rapidly learned about climate change and has become involved in a number of climate change groups and issues over a period of four years. His knowledge and skill development has been acquired rapidly. Tim is now frequently called upon to speak to the public about climate change, by the Australian Conservation Foundation and other environmental organizations. He studied under Al Gore, a Nobel Prize winner and creator of the movie *An Inconvenient Truth*. He has been involved in a more recent action on climate change in the lead up to the Climate Change conference in Copenhagen in 2010. Tim, along with other climate changed activists organized a human sign to read "climate emergency." This action again attracted national media coverage, successful in drawing attention to an important social issue.

Case study: Grace's Story

Grace is a newcomer to social change issues. She had worked as a country veterinarian for about fifteen years before she became involved in her local community and has been an activist for only a few years. Her life took a dramatic turn after her second child was born and she experienced severe postnatal depression. She was living in a rural area of Victoria that had limited infrastructure in general and no children's services. So with no previous experience of community development, campaigning or politics or social movements, *Grace* commenced a campaign for a childcare centre in her local community. She begins by saying, "We went on a very long journey"

> engaging local government and then state government and then federal government. It was all around the time of the federal election, so there were some political opportunities there which we took advantage of.

Grace grew up in suburban Melbourne. She claims her family were not very political people and she had "very little political exposure to politics." She says she "came from a family that had very little community involvement". She cannot remember politics ever being discussed at home, although she had a sister who, as an adult, became very heavily involved in student politics and was eventually employed as the women's officer at a student union. However, Grace claims she had no interest in politics, campaigning or social action at the time and thought her sister was "a bit weird." She describes her lack of experience in social action in the following statement:

> I guess I've come from a level of absolutely no community involvement and a family that doesn't really have opinions about anything in the community or politics, to a place where I have quite strong views on some of those things. I'm still not a very political person, but I have views about what's right and wrong and what communities deserve to have and that sort of thing. So that's sort of more my interest.

Grace believes what drove her involvement in activism was a "sense of social justice" that she claims she has always had, along with a strong sense of right and wrong. She assumes that she got these qualities from her parents but is not completely sure. She does remember as a child always feeling that she should have the right to speak and, if she wasn't given the chance to say something, she would be upset and ask herself why. These qualities remain with her to this day. Like many of the other activists in this study, *Grace* spent time at church and Sunday school because she was raised a Catholic by her parents. Her father never attended church, but her mother and the children did so regularly. However, she claims she always tended to rebel against religion and, at the first opportunity, she "bailed" from the Catholic Church and "still hasn't aligned herself with a religion," adding "I wouldn't say religion's been a strong influence."

Grace describes herself as a very "intellectual person" who thinks constantly—"when something doesn't need to be intellectualized, I still do it.' In her campaigning she asserts she has always tried to "think of every possible scenario that could happen." She says she loves to think logically and, at school, was very good at maths and science, but when it came to anything philosophical, she couldn't give a toss!

Grace's initial activism took her completely out of her comfort zone. She had to learn a great deal of detail about local, state, and federal governments very quickly. She needed to learn about political cycles and which moment in time would be best to lobby the right person who could be influential. She recalls:

> …it was a huge, huge, learning curve for me, huge! Because I'd never, ever been involved in anything that was so complex. Most people who had known something more about it would never have embarked on it because they thought it would fail. But we just had a determination that we would succeed at what we wanted to do.

Grace says she already had "good communication skills" but these were "really honed" by her campaigning. She learned to speak publicly, which she had never done before, and to become a leader in her local community and apply for grants. As she became more experienced, and after the project group had received funding from government, it became "a different sort of learning curve," which involved learning about tenders, builders and project managers. *Grace* says she began learning how to be an advocate for her local community.

Grace was also learning to work with others and pass on her developing knowledge and skill. She argues that much of her skill development was in the area of group practices and processes. She was a very individualistic person prior to her involvement in the campaign for the childcare centre, describing herself as a "deep thinker" who usually worked alone and just "gets on with it." She had never really thought about working with other people until she realized that to achieve her goals she would need the help of other people. This was her greatest level of learning. *Grace* was learning how to work with community, about group work, learning to communicate within a group environment, and, more importantly, she was learning how to pass on her skills to other people in the group. As she notes, "my role is all about empowering people and empowering communities and giving people information, helping them get into processes, to help them navigate government." As she became more experienced as an activist, she began to take other members of the campaign with her when she was meeting with politicians, recognizing the importance of passing on skills and taking people along on the journey:

> I started to say "Well, hang on I'm going down to the Valley to see this politician, come with me" and we'd do it together. Because I could see that although everyone was gaining skills, I was getting more than everybody else.

This was an exciting time of skill development for *Grace*. Aware that her community was in a marginal electorate, she decided to lobby the Federal government for funding prior to the election. "I had to get really savvy about how we were going to make a strong argument to these departments." She recalls that as the project proceeded and they received funding for the centre, she went onto a different phase of skill and knowledge development. She was learning how to oversee and actually manage a large building project, learning how to employ staff, how to deal with tradesmen, and how to oversee building work. Yet, *Grace* argues that she was most aware of becoming "more astute at dealing with people" and sensing group dynamics. She had to learn to be "more inclusive." To bring the group along with her in the project, to pass on skills to other people in the group, in essence to show leadership skills to mentor, nurture, and encourage skill development in the project group. These were skills she learned by watching highly skilled people and then practising those skills herself. By observing people who were more experienced than herself, *Grace* learned skills in how to negotiate with people and, in particular, navigate the complexity of government and community.

Grace claims she learned a great deal from a significant mentor who was a senior manager in a large government department. She used to meet frequently with this woman or telephone her for advice. She was a highly skilled communicator and leader very familiar with community projects and spent a lot of time with *Grace* going over issues in the community and advising her about committees because *Grace* had never been involved in a committee before until she campaigned for the childcare centre. *Grace* spent a lot of time discussing community building and community strengthening strategies with her mentor and was impressed by the respectful way her mentor dealt with people.

> And I think I did a lot of that with her, learning by following her example. She has a real dignity about her and a way of maintaining a professionalism that I was very impressed with. I probably learned a lot from watching her, and then debriefing [with her] as well.

She recalls a meeting where she saw her "experienced colleague stop a community member from de-railing the project."

> Now I went away from that meeting and dissected that. How did she do that in a way that did not demean him? We still got our outcome but he was left in no uncertain terms that he was not going to derail the process. I knew I did not have the skill to do that, and I'm not sure that I still would now. But I remember just sitting back watching the whole conversation unfold at this meeting and thinking "Wow, she is so good at this!" So I recognize that she had skills that I definitely did not have, and I guess by osmosis you learn the ways of dealing with complex and delicate situations.

Grace's mentor was a senior manager who worked for the local shire, and *Grace* realized that her mentor had skill and knowledge that she didn't and she sought to emulate those skills. *Grace* realized that her mentor was a master practitioner in working with community, and recognized that her own skills were "intellectual" rather than social. *Grace*'s mentor would debrief with her after difficult meeting and *Grace* notes "she never told me what to do, but when things got tough she would support me and she would encourage me to look at different ways of doing things." Slowly but surely, *Grace* developed expertise by observing her mentor. I asked *Grace* if she felt she could mirror her mentor's skills in a similar situation and she replied, in conversation:

> (Grace) Yeah, I think so, with some practice.
>
> (Interviewer) So you were learning from watching her?
>
> (Grace) Yeah, definitely.
>
> (Interviewer) Learning from being a part of that process and seeing it unfold?
>
> (Grace) I think I did a lot of that with her, learning by following her example, I suppose. She has a lot of dignity in dealing with difficult situations even if they were personally affecting her. She has a real dignity about her and a way of maintaining a professionalism that I was very impressed with. So yes, I probably learnt a lot from watching her, and the debriefing side of it as well.

Grace commenced her social change work in 2002 and the childcare centre was completed in 2006. She then became engaged in a campaign to save local parkland that was allocated as the site for a police station. *Grace* was concerned at what she saw as a lack of consultation about the development of the site. She is still shocked at the level of bureaucracy and lack of organization in government and by how policy decisions are made. Sometimes she attends meetings and thinks to herself, "Wow! How did this system ever arrive?!" As *Grace* became more skilled and experienced in her campaigning, she became astutely aware of lobbying processes and strategies for accessing government within the political cycle.

> ... it's [learning] things like how do you speak to politicians. How do you get to speak to politicians? At what time in the electoral cycle do you speak to politicians, on what level do you talk, with what amount of information? So I guess it's that level of sophistication when dealing with people who are busy and may have their own agendas and that sort of thing.

In the early days of her activism, *Grace* was frequently out of her comfort zone as a learner and she says that her way of dealing with this was to do everything she could in terms of research and self-learning. She describes herself as "a bit of a perfectionist" so she would always try to cover all of the "what if scenarios" in her campaigning, which reveals a level of reflexivity in her practice. *Grace* had to learn rapidly about submission writing, how to get grants, who to influence in order to get a grant. She was learning how to speak publicly and even though she claims she already had reasonable communication skills, she really had to hone her communication skills very quickly, in order to be effective. *Grace* claims that in her early days of learning in the campaign, she was completely out of her comfort zone, she was anxious a lot of the time and her way of dealing with this "is to find a way to get back into [her comfort zone];" as she states "this has driven her learning to quite an extent. It is a desire to be credible and to know what I'm talking about and to have an informed opinion." *Grace* also claims that the processes of campaigning were healing for her in a way, given that she was recovering from her postnatal depression. The process was empowering and she attributes a lot of her own personal recovery to her involvement in these community building projects.

Grace says what drives her commitment to an issue is "passion:" She won't become involved in everything, but she also won't sit back if she thinks there is an issue that is important and needs attention. She says she has a sense of justice that drives her "I'm never happy unless I've had a say!" However, she manages her commitment quite carefully: if there is a sense of injustice "and in my heart I know it's not right, I will say something."

> …I don't get passionate about too many things…Oh no, I probably am pretty passionate about a lot of things, but I never get involved with things just because they're a hot issue, or…It's got to be something that sparks something in me or I just don't have the energy to do it.

Like many of the activists in this study, there is an intrinsic connection between the mind and the emotions. *Grace* is a thinker who likes to look at an issue logically, but her activism is driven by her passion for an issue and, in the case of the police complex being built on public land, by her anger about government processes and lack of consultation with community. *Grace* does not identify with the term activist and claims she feels quite uncomfortable with it, feeling there is "a radical connotation to it." Yet, she is committed to working with community and is now employed as a rural community development worker, working with the rural women's community development network on drought and climate change issues.

Conclusion

Like many organizers, *Grace* initially balanced work and family commitments while campaigning and project managing the building of a childcare centre. *Grace*, a self-confessed intellectual, someone who likes facts, recovering from an illness, became involved in a campaign in her local community. Through this, she experienced a level of personal development and she felt empowered by being involved in her local community. *Grace* found that being engaged in local community issues brought meaning to her life. She was able to develop existing skills and gain new knowledge about the machinations of government. She learned about dealing with the media and how to speak in public at a rally. Like many of the novice protesters, *Grace's* learning was varied. But, most importantly, she learned about group processes and realized she needed to leave her intellectualism behind in order to be effective and bring other members of the community to the campaign. *Grace* learned by simply being involved in the daily practice of community. Her significant engagement with an experienced community development worker enabled her to further hone her skills and, through reflection on and observing her practices, she was able to build on her own expertise. *Grace's* rapid learning frequently took her out of her comfort zone as a learner and she pushed herself to acquire new knowledge and skills in order to be authentic in her campaign. This anxiety about her knowledge pushed her to further develop her skills. *Grace's* campaign helped her to realize her passion for social change and she is still heavily involved in her community.

Conclusion to the Quintain of Case Studies for Circumstantial Activists

This chapter has presented the case studies of Terry, Tim, *Catherine*, and *Grace*, who became involved in significant campaigns in midlife. Terry, *Grace*, and *Catherine* became involved in campaigning after a significant life event created the space for them to pursue activism and learn throughout the processes of the campaign. Unusually, Tim's life changed dramatically from a corporate engineer to becoming a climate change activist in a period of four years. Terry, too, had been involved in an international campaign for a period of five years, yet they have both developed a level of knowledge and skills not dissimilar to the lifelong activists in this research. What is similar about all of these circumstantial activists' learning is the rapid pace at which they develop new knowledge and skills. They were frequently on a learning edge, trying to synthesize their new knowledge into a developing schema. Like the lifelong activists, they learned through socialization with other activists and they learned most new skills informally. *Grace*, Terry and *Catherine* all had the benefit of learning through a significant mentor, someone who had significant expertise in campaigning.

Both Groups of Activists: Findings

A significant finding of this research is the holistic nature of how activists learn. The embodied learning of both groups of activists is important. Activists develop knowledge and skills in critical thinking; they are communicative and social learners. Emotions play a significant role in motivating and maintaining activism over the longer term and emotions sustain and nourish their practice and are central to activists' learning. This prominence of the emotional agency of the activists is expressed in virtually every interview. Frustration, passion, anger, being annoyed with government and bureaucracy, anger at inequality in society, and the impact of advanced capitalism on the creation of disadvantage, were frequently revealed in the interviews. These stories demonstrate the emotional agency of activists, which is a major theme of the research.

A significant finding of this research is the importance of the social space and socialization in the development of an activist epistemology. Both groups learned to develop communicative and social skills in the social space of activism. Through socializing with other activists, they developed greater expertise, new friendships were formed and newer activists mentored by those more experienced. They started to form a repertoire of practice, reified by learning with others in the group. Both groups developed their knowledge mainly through informal learning practices. Very few activists attended formal training in activism; many of the activists had never heard that you could have formal training in activism. Both groups frequently referred to their learning occurring through the experience of situating themselves in the practices and processes of activism, they learned to develop their expertise on the job with other activists.

All of the activists learned to think critically—it appears that thinking critically about society, social, political, economic, and international systems of government is an essential part of activists' developing knowledge. Both lifelong and circumstantial activists develop an array of skills through practising activism. They develop skills in public speaking, group processes, running a picket line, negotiating with politicians, crowd control, and managing the media. They meet with influential people, political parties, government, and private industry. They learn how to educate the community about their issues of concern. Learning through using the physical body in a skillful way was a theme in the research—by marching in protest, or by being present in picket line, by envisaging the visual and actual power of the body, both symbolically and physically, some environmental activists climb large trees as a part of a blockade or protest. This physical use of the body in protest extends the finding of embodied and holistic learning.

6
Embodied Learning

Introduction

This discussion chapter is the first of two and focuses on embodiment and activism. How can we understand the holistic nature of activists' learning? Activists' ontology is embodied, and this research demonstrates that activists learn with intention and purpose: they are "there" and act for a reason. The pedagogy of activism happens in the life world of practice, by being engaged in action and protest in communities and by participating in social movements. Put simply, it occurs through being present and being there in the practices of activism. Activists' learning involves the whole body, including the mind, the physical body, and the emotions. Their learning is interpretive rather than rational and this holistic pedagogy will be demonstrated in detail in this chapter. The chapter commences with an account of embodiment and activism, and examines closely the important role emotions play in driving activists to learn and develop knowledge. It is argued the emotions are central to activists' pedagogy. Activists develop empathy through their emotional agency and this contributes to sustaining their motivation and their commitment to social change. The role of emotional work (Hochschild 1979) is explored to reveal how activists use and manage the emotions to portray or persuade a particular outcome, ideal, or issue. They frequently use the physical body in protest, and they develop creative and expressive (including physical) skills that are used in the art of protest. The research establishes that activists are reflexive about their practices; they learn to develop critical thinking skills about the world around them and read widely to expand their existing knowledge. There is also a spiritual dimension to their learning—these activists believe that they are meant to be there.

Learning and the Whole Body: Being There

Philosophers of the mind-body relationship such as Merleau-Ponty have long understood the importance of not just knowing why, but also knowing how, we gain knowledge. They know that understanding occurs through experience (Merleau-Ponty 1962; Merleau-Ponty & O'Neill 1974). This inductive, rather than deductive, way of knowing challenges the dominant epistemology of behaviorism in adult education in Australia, behaviorism being predicated on the notion that learning can occur through a focus on behavior change, rather than taking the learners' social world and subjective experience as central starting point for ways of knowing.

As a review of the literature has shown, a great deal of the theorizing on radical adult education in Australia to date has given prominence to cognition or critical thinking in activists' pedagogy (Newman 1994; Foley 1999; Chase 2000; Foley 2001; Branagan & Boughton 2003; Whelan 2005b). Foley's (1999), important and much quoted text, *Learning in Social Action*, situates learning within emancipatory struggle in the adult education tradition of Marxist political economy, which explores the impact of historical materialism on society. Foley (1999) presents a case study of learning that takes place in social action at Terania Creek, a 1979 antilogging campaign in NSW, in which the activists learned knowledge about government systems, rainforest ecology, and the use of the media. Another significant aspect to their learning is associated with Freire's (1972b) conscientization and Mezirow's (1991) perspective transformation; for these activists, a significant change in their own frames of reference has occurred through their learning. Although Foley (1999) doesn't explicitly articulate this as a change in the activists' sense of identity there is significant change taking place in the views of these activists. Their knowledge and skill development are embedded in their direct action, not always understood as learning but "significant and empowering" nonetheless (p. 39). Foley (1999) believes activists' learning in this sense is "mainly informal" (p. 39). However as this research has demonstrated, learning in radical adult education is also social. Activists develop significant expertise through their engagement with one another in the practices of direct action.

Foley (1999) has drawn our attention to recent scholarship on radical adult education and its focus on the construction of ideology as presented in the writing of Foucault and Habermas (p. 134). He argues that an overly reductionist approach to adult education and social movement theory relegates political economy and agency to the margins (Foley 1999, p. 135). However, much of this theorizing emphasizes emancipatory ways of knowing that are cognitive, rational and focused on the role of critical thinking (Foley 1999, 2001; S. D. Brookfield 2000; Branagan & Boughton 2003; Boughton, Taksa, & Welton 2004; Boughton 2005), or emancipatory learning through the processes of conscientization as in the writing of Freire (1972b). This research has established that, in order to fully understand the learning of activists, we need to expand and broaden this focus on cognition and rationalism to include non rational ways of knowing (O'Loughlin 2006).

The nature and complexity of learning in social action includes the role identity formation plays in learning to become an activist. These activists' learning is embedded in emotional and corporeal agency. Like the activists in the struggle for Terania Creek, these activists develop frameworks of resistance and "really useful knowledge"(Johnson 1988). However, activists' learning is also holistic, often driven and sustained by the emotions; there is much to learn from these activists' use of their intelligent bodies.

Other theorists have, to some extent, included the emotions in their theorizing on radical adult education, such as Freire whose humanistic materialism focused on emotional agency in his use of the term love—in particular, a love of humanity and love of teaching (Freire & Freire 1997, Darder 2003). More recently, Newman's (2006) book, *Teaching Defiance: Stories and Strategies for Activist Educators*, included a focus on the emotions in understanding activists' learning. Newman explores the role of calculated and creative anger, and the role of the educator who "... can help people develop, articulate and explore their anger" (pp 54–55). This largely informal learning of activists is enhanced through their participation and socialization with other activists. In short, activists learn from one another all of the time. Foley (1999) has argued through his writing on emancipatory adult education that activists' learning is informal, often tacit, and not always articulated or recognized as knowledge or learning. This research affirms Foley's view of activists' learning in radical adult education, but will expand on this existing scholarship in Australia to include embodied ways of knowing. As this empirical research has revealed, activists use reason, the emotions and the physical body in acquiring skills and knowledge. However, in order to understand the focus on critical intelligence in activists' learning practices, we need to understand the historical focus on rationalism in adult education and in education epistemology in general.

Rationalism and Adult Education

Rationalism has always dominated western educational thought (Beckett & Morris 2003). Since the Enlightenment and Descartes' dictum, "Cogito ergo sum" (I think therefore I am) (Descartes 1983), the focus on rationalism has taken primary importance in understanding learning. The emphasis on cognition through the development of critical thinking leaves the focus on learning as an intellectual activity alone (Brookfield, 1985), denying the connectivity of mind, emotions, and the body in learning (Hunter 2004; O'Loughlin 2006). Dewey claims education has moved away from its initial intention, "It ceased to mean ways of doing and being done to, and became a way for something intellectual and cognitive" (Dewey, 1930, p. 312). A focus on disembodiment in adult education denies the reality of somatic learning (Beckett & Morris 2003). As Dewey rightly claims, being human is about experiencing the world around us and learning occurs through experience, "...every experience influences in some degree the objective conditions under which further experiences are had" (Dewey, 1938, 1999, p. 30).

It is demonstrated in this book that learning is embodied , including the physical body, not just with speech and communicative actions but the physicality of actually being present in a classroom or learning space (Beckett & Morris 2003). We physically move the body as we learn and teach—we interact with others, teachers, students, and colleagues, we move our bodies in the space of learning when we work in groups with other learners; learning, therefore, requires a physical presence. We bring our bodies into learning when we walk into the classroom or workplace. Our bodies represent our present and past experiences of learning and our constituted educational discourses (Hunter 2004). Students bring their own lived experiences of class or privilege into the classroom (Hooks 2003a). They bring their own experiences of education both constituted by their corporeal experiences of education and by the hegemonic educational discourses and practices that have been worked on them (Hunter, 2004).

The dualism of Descartes, including the focus on disembodied learning or the "split" between mind and body, nevertheless, continues to dominate Western European education discourse (Beckett & Morris 2003). Recently, sociological theories of the body have called attention to embodiment and social movements (Crossley 2002). Similarly, the focus on the sociology of the emotions gives insight into the role that emotions play in both understanding individuals and society (Eyerman 2005; Maddison & Scalmer 2006).[1] It is important here to explore the role of embodied learning for these activists. Throughout the processes of learning, a significant change in identity occurs. The activists' participation in the work of activism shifts and moves within and against the political, economic, and social discourses that are embedded in their life-world of practice. Merleau-Ponty (1962) argues that our perception of things influences the way we interpret the social world:

> My field of perception is constantly filled with a play of colors, noises and fleeting tactile sensations which I cannot relate precisely to the context of my clearly perceived world, which I nevertheless immediately "place" in the world (p. xi).

Merleau-Ponty's (1962) existential phenomenology tells us that in experiencing the world we develop knowledge. We become who we are through our incorporation of lived experiences of social structures, language, habits and or action of being-in-the-world (Crossley 2001). This book draws on the philosophy of the body to make some sense of activists' holistic way of knowing. In the same way that Marx turned Hegel's dialectical method on its head, Merleau-Ponty altered our perception of the rationality of Descartes's "Cogito," turning rationalism on its head to be "I experience therefore I am." Merleau-Ponty (1962) contends the world is always present in our development of knowledge:

> A philosophy for which the world is "already there" before reflection begins as an inalienable presence; and all of its efforts are concentrated upon re-achieving a direct and primitive contact with the world, and endowing that contact with a philosophical status. It is a search for philosophy which shall be a "rigorous science," but it also offers an account of space, time and the world as we "live" them (p. vii).

Crossley (2001) claims human beings are both "mindful and embodied social agents" (p. 123). He firmly argues there is sensuality in human perception that includes emotion and desire in the agent's corporeal schema. The emotions are vital to activists' pedagogy and are an important finding of this research. There is a crucial connection between the emotions and learning and this will be reflected on elsewhere in this chapter by exploring the connection between activism and emotions. Crossley (2001) puts forward the view that "the corporeal schema is an incorporated bodily know-how and practical sense; a perspectival grasp upon the world view from the 'point of view' of the body" (p. 123). This is reflective of Aristotle's concept of phronesis, which is practical knowledge, mastery, or skill. Phronesis is knowledge not necessarily derivative of formal study or theorizing, but gained through practical experience (Beckett 2008). Crossley (2001) further argues the dualist concept of the Cartesian system, which privileges mind and thought even in its definition of human ego, is unfounded, and he supports Merleau-Ponty's view that being and action in the world occur before any reflective thought takes place. This is not to suggest that cognition, or thinking processes, are not a part of activists' pedagogy—for indeed they are—and this will be explored in further detail in this chapter. However, the "Cogito" is not removed from the consciousness of being in the world of practice (Merleau-Ponty 1962). Merleau-Ponty (1962) encourages us to see that the body through being in the world gains knowledge, that we develop knowledge through our lived experience of being in the world and that the body cannot be removed from this way of knowing. Moreover, he puts forward the view that analytical reflection begins from actually experiencing the world and, in doing so, rejects the dualist position of Cartesianism.

> Analytical reflection starts from our experience of the world and goes back to the subject as to a condition of possibility distinct from that experience, revealing the all-embracing synthesis as that without which would be no world (Merleau-Ponty 1962p. x).

The world is present before us and therefore there, preceding any analysis (Merleau-Ponty 1962). The embodied nature of activists' knowing, including the mind, body, emotions, and self, all contribute to their effective mastery of learning. It is practical knowledge developed through the experience of being an activist. As Merleau-Ponty indicates, we are present in the world through simply being there without consciously thinking about it:

> Insofar as I have hands, feet; a body, I sustain around me intentions which are not dependent on my decisions and which affect my surroundings in a way that I do not choose (1962, p. 440).

To understand embodied subjectivities in relation to activism we need to break away from dualism, and acknowledge that how humans learn is embodied rather than rational and conceptual, opening up space to explore the corporeal and the discursive in education (Hunter, 2004). The ontology of adult activism is not explicitly outlined in any single theory or tradition of learning, although it has been argued that it is broadly represented in the theoretical tradition of critical theory and its corollary, critical pedagogy (Brookfield, 2005). Critical pedagogy encourages an exploration of learners' experiences, discrimination and oppression in their various manifestations in the classroom to hold up to view inequality and why only some people have access to education (Darder et al., 2003). The foundation of the theory of critical pedagogy is the pedagogy of social change and activism. As Steinberg, cited in McLaren et al. (2007), shows us, there are direct linkages between education and activism: "critical pedagogy takes language from the radical—radicals must do" (p. xi).

The epistemology of critical pedagogy is a radical remaking of education discourse and is a process of acting to change conservative educational paradigms of learning dominated by the liberal education tradition in the last 20 years and, more recently, the neoliberal tradition of education (Darder et al., 2003). Critical pedagogy, particularly in the writing and theorizing of Paulo Freire, draws attention to popular education and social movements and their revolutionary possibilities (Freire 1972a, 1972b; hooks 1994; Darder 2003; Darder, Baltadano, & Torres 2003; Kincheloe 2004; Kincheloe 2005).

What epistemology of education could be more important than an education for social change? Activists do need theoretical knowledge, but their skill is developed through practice, sometimes referred to as practical knowledge (Maddison & Scalmer 2006).

The Junk Category of Practical Knowledge

Activists are active in communities and social movements. They are connected to communities; they meet with politicians, advocate for reform or change, resist dominant discourses of oppression, they socialize and meet with other activists. They develop knowledge about systems of government by understanding key players and stakeholders in their area of interest, sometimes advocating for change within the existing system and, at other times, marching in protest and taking direct action. In doing this they actively construct, renew, and remake their practice. This constructivist and interpretive knowledge is in contrast to the abstract and immaterial learning founded in behaviorism and in contemporary education pedagogy and practice. It is at times referred to as lower status knowledge or practical knowledge (Beckett & Morris 2003; Maddison & Scalmer 2006). Lower status knowledge, which stems from our concrete material experiences of the world, is often viewed by educators as the "junk" category of knowledge (Schön 1987; Beckett 2008;). There is a need to understand why some people have more knowledge than others, but rather than view the whole person as a site of knowledge, "outstanding practitioners are not said to have more professional knowledge than others, but greater 'wisdom,' 'talent,' 'intuition,' or 'artistry.'" (Beckett 2008, p.13). Schön develops this point further:

> Unfortunately, such terms as these serve not to open up inquiry but to close it off. They are used as junk categories, attaching names to phenomena that elude conventional strategies of explanation. So the dilemma of rigor or relevance here reasserts itself. On the basis of an underlying and largely unexamined epistemology of practice, we distance ourselves from the kinds of performance we need most to understand (p. 13).

Beckett (2008) raises the importance of taking seriously embodied knowledge and believes "low status knowledge, typically called 'intuition'; or 'commonsense', or 'know-how', is receiving long-overdue critical attention" (p. 2). His contribution to the literature on embodied learning in adult education is important because he focuses on the hitherto neglected area of the whole person or embodied learning at work (Beckett & Hager 2002; Beckett & Morris 2003; Beckett 2008). In *The Reflective Practitioner*, Schön (1983) argues that the Western educational focus on reason and cognition denies an understanding of the whole person in learning. In contemporary adult learning theory it is sometimes called deeper rather than surface learning, but is more broadly connected to critical pedagogy (Darder, Baltadano, & Torres 2003). Educators need to move away from a cognitive focus of "knowing why" to an embodied focus of "knowing how" (Gonczi 2004). Merleau-Ponty upholds the view that the experience of being "mind-in-action" in the world contributes to how we make meaning and that this meaning is not an internal or isolated act of cognition:

> At the root of all our experiences and all of our reflections, we find then, a being which immediately recognizes itself, because it is its knowledge

both of itself and of all things and which knows its own existence, not by observation and as a given fact, not by inference from any idea of itself, but through direct contact with existence. Self-consciousness is the very being of mind-in-action (Merleau-Ponty 1962, p, 331).

The holistic practices of activists include using the physical body to develop greater skill and expertise. Indeed, the body is an important element in these activists' learning. For example, being a part of a picket line or a public protest, or scaling a large building in order to write a sign of protest are examples of skillful use of the body; it requires balance, coordination, and artistry. The act of physically climbing a tree as a part of a forest blockade is another example of how activists use their bodies in protest; they also develop physical skills in music, dance, and performance. Similarly, the use of humor in protest likewise contributes to the color, culture, and movement of activism (Branagan 2007). The use of the body by activists in a crowd in the midst of action and protest is a social and strategic aspect to activists' pedagogy. It is a part of the theater, color, and movement of protest—the culture of activism—promoted by using the body (Couch 2004). Merleau-Ponty argues the performance of movements in a space are not unrelated to us; we do not think "I will now climb a tree in a protest," we act, we do, we experience and we cannot place everything we do or perceive under the banner of "I think." As he says, "movement is not thought about movement" (Merleau-Ponty 1962, p. 159). Activists use the body in action in protest, their whole body inhabits this space in time, in action, and the experience of being there in that action is a part of embodiment and being in the world:

> Experience discloses beneath objective space, in which the body eventually finds its place, a primitive spatiality of which experience is merely the outer covering and which merges with the bodies very being. To be a body, is tied to a certain world, as we have seen; our body is not primarily in space: it is of it (Merleau-Ponty 1962p. 171).

Tim said he used his skill as an engineer to build a pole illustrating rising sea levels and climate change. He believed going out in public with his prop on the foreshore in a beautiful part of bayside Melbourne would arouse some curiosity from the public. He would then be able to promote climate change. Cam climbed trees as a part of the blockade of the Franklin River protest. *Jonathan* used his body in a human blockade on the border of Israel and Gaza; he was there to assist

Palestinians to move between Gaza and Israel. *Catherine* was a part of a protest along with thousands of activists for the rights of refugees. In the middle of the desert in central Australia, the razor wire and fences of the detention centre in Woomera were torn down and the refugees released into the desert. The corporeality of activism is learning in action and the pinnacle of experiential learning (Dewey 1922). The feeling and emotions that would undoubtedly be present in these dangerous forms of direct action could never possibly be accounted for in dualist notions of learning. These learning practices are embodied as well as conceptual (Hunter, 2004).

When Terry Hicks stood in a cage in a set of orange overalls like those worn by the prisoners at Guantanamo Bay, his action symbolized the harshness of the conditions that the prisoners were living under. He stood in an iron cage, a powerful metaphor for his son's prison in Cuba, in the middle of New York City.

Terry's embodied presence in the cage, including his bodily knowhow, his dispositions, his habits, his practical skill *qua* practical knowledge (Maddison & Scalmer 2006) (both acquired and acquiring through this action), displayed the holistic and dialectical processes of learning in action. He interacted with the crowd, inviting them to come in and experience what it was like to be held in such a small prison. Terry's embodied action alerted the international media about the horrors of Guantanamo Bay. His corporeal learning in that time and space was practically inscribed on the whole body, for all to see and experience. He was learning and teaching in that space, because his embodied protest portrayed his son's incarceration and that of many other prisoners. Terry was teaching the world about the horrors of Guantanamo Bay.

Terry, like some of the other circumstantial activists, had never participated in activism before. They had not learned theories of social change, nor sociology, politics, or philosophy. Terry said the process was "eerie and scary." He had never been overseas before, nor ever performed a public action in the middle of a city and, in doing so, challenged a nation's foreign policy. He learned a lot from experiencing the processes of being there—present in that social space, with crowds around him and the media attending. Terry was learning how activists communicate to present an idea, to persuade an argument for social change. By doing this, he was learning about himself and developing his own corporeal schema and this embodied action was educating the world about an issue of injustice. This is Merleau-Ponty's (1962) mind-in-action. At that time and space, there was no reflective conscious thought or metalearning for Terry (although this came later)—there was only doing and action. This "really useful knowledge" is learning with a social purpose (Crowther & Galloway 2005): Terry was acting in the world in order to change it.

Emotions and Activism

The activists' stories outlined in this research demonstrate the significance and importance of emotions in activists' developing epistemology. The emotions are a significant part of all social life, they permeate the very essence of our being and are displayed in all areas of the social world. As Jasper (1998) states, "emotions do not merely accompany our deepest desires and satisfactions, they constitute them permeating our ideas, identities and interests" (p. 399). This research has found the emotions play an important role in activists' pedagogy. The emotions are often the driver for activists' purposive and intentional pursuit of learning in order to change the world. Yet, little attention is given to the emotions in understanding learning and they are rarely analysed, and often underestimated, in the epistemology of adult education (Hunter 2004). Yet, recent research has connected mind, thought, and the emotions; they are entwined and are dependent on one another. Damasio (2005), a neurosurgeon and sociologist, claims that the emotions are not peripheral to reason and cognition, they are, in fact, crucially connected to rational thinking processes. Damasio argues normal social behavior challenges the scientific rationalism initially familiar to him, claiming that when he "thought about the brain behind the mind, I envisioned a separate neural system for reason and emotion" (2005, p. xv). In Damasio's research of patients with neurological disturbances he found:

> Emotions and feelings may not be intruders in the bastion of reason at all: they may be enmeshed in its networks for worse and for better. The strategies of human reason probably did not develop, in either evolution or any single individual, without the guiding force of the mechanism of biological regulation, of which emotion and feelings are notable expressions.

Gonczi (2004) claims this research has important implications for adult education theorizing and pedagogy and claims Damasio's link between the emotions and the neural underpinnings of reason is important:

> One of the major findings of this research is that reasoning and the emotions are vitally connected. Investigators of patients with particular types of brain damage, which take away their capacity to experience emotions but leave intact cognitive processes, demonstrate that while they can discuss things and seemingly are functioning cognitively, they are unable to plan for their personal futures: that is they lose their capacity for successful action in the world. It is true that emotion can have a negative impact on a person's capacity to reason, but in its absence humans cannot reason well at all (Gonczi 2004, pp. 25–6).

Notwithstanding this, Damasio's claims affirm what some adult educators have long suspected: that there is intrinsic connection between the emotions and learning (O'Loughlin 2006). They know that if learners make an emotional connection to the curriculum, their learning is much richer and deeper (Freire & Freire 1997; Beckett & Hager 2002; Beckett & Morris 2003; Hunter 2004). Hunter (2004) has questioned why there is an absence of the body and emotions in education, and has adapted her preservice teacher training to include embodied and emotional ways of knowing, in order to encourage new teachers to understand their own constitutive pedagogical experiences that education does to them and others. Hunter (2004) is imagining what an embodied pedagogy might look like:

> Can we imagine pedagogy that more consciously recognizes our intelligent bodies, is more deliberate in working with bodily dispositions and effects? With learning redefined as pleasure, play and embodied? Where we can feel the emotions of learning, joy, anxiety, vulnerability, power and risk (p. 7).

O' Loughlin (2006) believes the historical tie of the emotions, their association with irrationality and women's expressive role, has hindered our understanding of their importance in promoting learning:

> The characterization of emotion as irrational because of its supposedly compulsive and disruptive nature, but also because of its historical association with women and "the feminine," is contested; likewise its depiction as threat to the functioning of cognition and rationality. The philosophers of the body, Nietzsche, Dewey and Merleau-Ponty, placed emotion at the very root of all intersubjective encounters (p. 126).

Merleau-Ponty (1962) argues that perception and action bring us into the world and any inner psychological understanding of emotions will inevitably lead us back to being-in-the-world with others. Similarly, Crossley (2001) believes the emotions are embodied, putting forward the view that "the corporeal dimension of emotion is not a third person physiological process, but engaged and expressive practice" (p. 24). Eyerman (2005) argues the emotions are a source of motivation in social movements and emotions such as anger can actually drive activism. He goes on to state, "even the experience of fear and anxiety, not uncommon in the midst of protest, can be a strong force in collective actions" (p. 43). Brown and Pickeral (2009) claim we need to understand the place of emotions and their ability to build and sustain long term resistance in social movements. They argue for a need to build a place for emotional reflexivity and emotional sustainability. Central to this argument is "the need to pay attention to different spaces of activism in order to better understand the complexities of the relationship between emotions and activism" (p. 2). However, as Jasper (1998) has revealed, limited attention is paid to emotions in social movement theory, because the focus is again on rationalism and cognition. This book draws attention to the corporeal and social aspects of activists' learning that includes using the emotions (Eyerman 2005; Maddison & Scalmer 2006; Brown & Pickerill 2009). Emotions are the antithesis of our understanding of the rational detached scientific mind that demands truth and objectivity in knowledge (Williams & Bendelow 1998). Even the place of emotions in teaching and education seem to be denied (Hooks 2003b). For many educators who love the practice and art of teaching, teaching as an act of love (bell et al., 2003) is rarely explored in the literature on adult learning, notwithstanding, of course, Freire's humanistic pedagogy that imparted the importance of love and using our common humanity for utilitarianism (Freire 1972). Yet, with the renewed focus on critical pedagogy, there may well be grounds for hope that the emotions will be given the prominence they deserve in understanding how we learn and, more particularly, understanding learning in radical adult education.

This book demonstrates that learning in social action is frequently preceded by an emotional connection to an issue. Feelings and emotions such as intuition, "gut reactions" and a sense that change is possible, fuel determination and a drive towards a goal or outcome that rarely changes. A desire or longing for knowledge propels these activists forward to learn through social action. These embodied feelings contribute to activists' agency and their motivation to learn and acquire new knowledge. The environmental activists in Kovan and Dirkx's (2003) study similarly revealed that their primary motivation for activism was both intellectual and emotional, and they frequently referred to "being motivated by head, heart and spirit" (p. 109). The activists in this study frequently described emotions such as passion, frustration and anger contributing to their purpose, drive, and agency as activists. As *Catherine* states, "it's really easy to get enraged at government after eleven years of neo-liberalism; we've experienced some pretty tough stuff." Jorge's deep seated anger stemming from his family's persecution under the Pinochet regime was a key driver for his lifelong activism. *Eva* felt "enraged and betrayed" that local government had not adhered to their promise of responsible urban development. *Bahar* claimed you needed to have passion to be involved in social change. *Grace* said it was her "passion" that motivated her to be involved in her campaign. Kerry spoke about the importance of her passion for Indigenous issues and how, through connecting the issues that she was working on with her passion and heart, her mind, feelings and emotions in action helped other people to understand the issues of concern to her. These emotions underpin their desire for change; they precipitate and focus their motivation to act and to change it. This emotional agency of activists, feelings such as passion, anger, rage, and frustration have been frequently referred to by the activists in this study and form the foundation of all intersubjective encounters. Jasper (2009) argues, in recent times emotions have become lost in the sociology of social movements:

> When crowds and collective behavior, not the study of social movements and collective action, was the lens for studying protest, emotions were central. Frustration, anger, alienation, anomie were not merely incidental characteristic but the motivation and explanation of protest (p. 175).

Similarly, emotions such as love, desire, and hope can contribute to the sense of solidarity in a group or movement (Eyerman 2005). Thus, activists may consciously know that an issue or a piece of legislation needs changing but this knowing is embedded in the whole self, in consciousness and in unconsciousness.

Understanding the importance of the emotions in learning is not just useful in knowing how activists make meaning. It can assist and contribute to an understanding of how all learners gain knowledge. By drawing on passion and making a connection between learners' internal "selves" a key can be provided to understanding how adults learn. Learning processes, practices and classroom pedagogy can be altered to foster emotionality in learning (Hunter 2004). Yet the problematic relationship between education and the emotions remains the same (O'Loughlin 2006). Educators tend to steer away from the perceived danger of the epistemology of the body. Bodies are messy and fleshy things, and educators are uncomfortable with emotionality and the agency that emotions can give a learner. They can challenge and shift the authority of the educator in the learning process and in their management of the classroom. Yet, critical pedagogy teaches us that some of the most significant and poignant learning can occur through an open confrontation with feelings in the space of learning (hooks 2003a, 2003b). Perceived and long-held prejudices can be held up to view; they can be reflected on and learned from if a space is opened up for these emotions to be displayed. Perhaps the focus on disembodied learning in western society is threatening; to be emotional is viewed by some as being out of control. Yet, the emotions create purpose and intentionality in learning. My own experience of teaching refugees and migrant community development has shown the deep learning that is possible when emotions are allowed to be present and worked with in the classroom. When students are able to reflect on their own feelings and experiences of being-in-the-world in the classroom, their knowledge is much deeper, and it can be transformative (Mezirow 1991). Of course we know through andragogy, that adults do not learn from behaviorist approaches to pedagogy because, central to adult education theory, the learner needs to be "self-directing" (Knowles 1984, p. 9). Didactic delivery of lectures is what Freire dubbed the banking system of education (Freire 1972b) while Beckett and Hager (2002) call it the "front-loading" model of education. Knowledge is deposited or imparted by academics and learners are passive recipients of it, not active agents constructing their own learning. Yet andragogy (Knowles 1984) has taught us that adults do not learn in this way. Instead, we need to view adult learners as sites of knowledge and allow them to bring this existing knowledge into their learning.

This research has found that, for activists, this is important as their own subjective experiences are often central to their activism. Certainly, for some of the circumstantial activists in this study their embodied emotional experiences precipitate and contribute to their motivation to act. Freire's (1972b) materialistic humanism, similarly, connected mind and emotions. He encouraged the oppressed to open up to their own humanity; in doing so they would have to act to challenge the oppressor.

Freire, a Brazilian educationalist who spent much of his life in exile in Europe, and elsewhere in the world, frequently spoke about his love of humanity, but also the importance of love in teaching (Darder 2003). Teaching, according to Freire, is an act of love:

> It is impossible to teach without the courage to try a thousand times before giving up. In short, it is impossible to teach without a forged, invented, and well-thought-out capacity to love (Freire, Freire, & Macedo 1998, p. 3).

Yet desire and love seem to have escaped educational discourse especially in these neoliberal times where the focus remains on performativity and managerialism. There is measurement of education, outcomes, benchmarking students' performance against one another, and so on (Anderson, Brown, & Rushbrook 2004). These discourses in education impede creative teaching and learning.

It is argued in this book that the emotional agency of activists is important and necessary. Feelings such as passion and anger are disruptive and explosive—they propel the activists to act. This is why *Catherine* said it was impossible to feel the emotional trauma and pain of the asylum seekers and not be moved. *Bahar* is driven by her subjective experience of oppression under the patriarchal representations of Islam in the Turkish community. She is passionate about social change for women in her community. She urges other activists to not see this work as "a job": "You've got to have passion" she claims. Her own experience of oppression and the reification of her experience of oppression with other Turkish women gives her agency; she must act because she does not want other women to suffer in this way. Similarly, Garry's life changed when he went to south-east Asia and lived in and with the experiences of those affected by the war in Vietnam. He could no longer intellectualize about the war in Vietnam being about processes of imperialism. He believed "seeing that kind of human suffering changed him forever." In essence, he had learned to empathize with the victims of a war gone wrong. He was teary expressing this in the interview and claimed reflecting on this made him "feel emotional."

O'Loughlin's (2006) analysis of the emotions, sociality, and embodiment is useful as she claims that we can understand the way that individuals gain empathy and understanding about disadvantage and the action we sometimes take "in the interests of the welfare of others" (p. 131). O'Loughlin (2006) also reminds us that we need to be wary of "othering" social disadvantage through the creation of "passive empathy." The Western lens is often turned outward in the vicarious objectification of disadvantage. It is easy to talk about a crisis happening "over there," rather than here within our own privileged subjectivity. Yet, the development of empathy has been important for the activists in this study, and it will be described as empathy with agency. We know that many people feel disillusioned with society, politics, inequality, and disadvantage in the social world, but not all individuals act to change it. Why was it then that these individuals had to act on an issue rather than remain concerned observers? *Catherine* says it was her anger that motivated her. Cam says it was about striving for an ethical world and not "burning the planet off" in the meantime. Felicity's own embodied sexuality, that is, being a lesbian woman with partner and child, gave her agency and purpose. Her activism was at the very core of her "self" ascribed through her own corporeal sexuality.

Activists have agency and purpose—they cannot observe inequality and not be moved by it. This is what Cam referred to as the "thinking and complaining and not acting" of the cynic, who observes and rails against inequality among various social groups and does nothing. Perhaps it is our commonness of humanity that develops empathy—as O'Loughlin, (2006) reminds us, we are talking about other human bodies when we are speaking about disadvantage:

> We need to be reminded of the corporeal realities of our existence, and that ultimately it is human bodies which make claims of the compassion of their embodied fellows. (p. 133)

Emotional Work

The data revealed that there are some differences in the way lifelong activists utilize the emotions in their activism. Lifelong activists, at times, make careful use of their emotions for the theater of protest (Jasper 1998; Crossley 2002; Maddison & Scalmer 2006). The sociology of social movements has shown that emotions are a crucial aspect of successful protest (Jasper & Goodwin 2004; Jasper 2009). It is not just about the emotions that activists display during protest but also the emotions that are purposefully expressed to create an environment of resistance and solidarity (Jasper 1998; Crossley 2002; Maddison & Scalmer 2006; Brown & Pickerill 2009). However, as we have seen, many protesters are outside of organized movements yet still participate in social action (Jasper

1998). Therefore, there are different spaces and places of activism and it is those protesters outside of formal social movements that really require further empirical research (Ollis 2008a; Brown & Pickerill 2009). The question, therefore, is how might the emotional agency of these protestors be harnessed to enhance and create more powerful social movements?

Hochschild's (1979) development of the concept of "emotional management" is useful here, because her writing on emotions shows that in many areas of our lives we are playing a role for a particular audience. We may be feeling deep and distressing emotions, but they are managed in a certain setting or particular environment. As this study has found, some of the lifelong activists use emotions as part of the theater of organizing (Eyerman 2005; Brown & Pickerill 2009). Emotional displays such as the use of anger towards the opposition is deliberately deployed to undermine their arguments and negotiations (Jasper 2009). As Brown and Pickerel (2009) note, "there is a long history of popular political mobilizations, as responses to expressions of rage, anger and fear at the actions of others" (p. 3). Sometimes, emotions are used in social movements to motivate activists to maintain their ongoing commitment and participation (Brown & Pickerill 2009). In contrast, emotional feelings can be managed and put into the background as activists pursue a particular goal. Some activists in this study who have dealt with the media disassociated themselves from their feelings of rage or anger. They believed if they displayed strong emotions it would be used inappropriately by the media and could ultimately be an impediment to their campaign or the long-term objectives of the social movement.

Hochschild's (1997) theory on emotional management shows how emotions can be managed to create an effect: "an act of emotion management, ... is an effort by any means, conscious or not to change one's feeling or emotions" (p. 9). Similarly, Jasper in (Brown & Pickerill 2009) believes emotions are used strategically by organizers to maintain, promote and sustain activism (p. 3).

Goffman (1959), a microsociologist, developed a theory of the emotions that he called "dramaturgy." Goffman believes the world in that we inhabit is a performance, what we do in front of others is often a presentation of the self in everyday life. We do this as workers, parents, sisters, brothers, sons, and daughters or even as activists. Goffman claims we are often required to put on a performance in certain social settings. We perform and play a particular role in effect to fit into that setting (Goffman 1959). Social life is full of certain roles that we produce to portray ourselves in different ways in different settings. Like an actor playing a particular role or part for a play, some activists put on a performance to display emotions that they skillfully manage to produce a desired outcome. For example, *Max* says he needed to put his "emotions in the background" in his union negotiations. If any emotion is shown, it "is a bit of theatre" in the form of an angry thump on the table or a calculated walk out. The research has shown that emotional management is engaged in increasingly as activists develop greater expertise.

However, the experience of *Grace, Eva,* and *Bahar* suggest that they have not learned to manage their emotions and are still very intensely expressive of their feelings towards government and institutions in society. Goffman (1959) believes we construct a performance in order to convince others and ourselves that what we are doing reflects appropriate cultural standards. Terry says he would "never get angry" in public. He would be frustrated and emotional but was mindful of the impact his emotional expression might have on his portrayal in the media. *Catherine* says it's really easy to be enraged at governments, but you have to "be strategic" because once you have the attention of governments, the time comes to sit down and negotiate. Activists may, of course, purposely use musical performance, humor and theater as distinct and powerful forms of protest (Branagan 2007; Brown & Pickerill 2009) from rumba bands (Brown & Pickerill 2009) to satirical interactions with effigies. Or the Zapatistas's use of the balaclava to mask their identity vis-a-vis their activism, now an iconic symbol of "Zapatismo"[2] a representation of resistance to the dominance of globalization and now firmly placed as an artifact in popular culture and the theater of protest (Couch 2004). As Branagan and Boughton (2003) argue:

> Amidst the seriousness of civil disobedience, theatre's humor has tactical advantages and averts hostility, while flamboyance engages the media. The arts generally are invaluable in gaining the attention of the media, but in marked contrast to violent protests, much of this attention is positive. The creation of a spectacle rather than an angry mob helps the non-violent process of conversion of opponents and third parties; the more spectacular the action, the more widespread it is often broadcast by the media. (Branagan & Boughton 2003)

Thus, communicative performance, feelings and emotions in activism are often staged as the performance and theatre of protest; they are sometimes used powerfully as a strategy in protest. Emotions can also be disruptive and a motivator for why people become engaged in activism in the first place, and they assist in maintaining a commitment to an issue or a cause over the longer term.

Emotional Reflexivity in Intelligent Bodies

Activists need a high level of knowledge to equip them in their practice. To be challenging as a practitioner and to be open to challenge can often push the learner out of their "comfort zone." Yet, it is in these edgy moments of tension that occur through praxis that the greatest learning can happen. It is through reflection, after what Beckett and Hager (2002) refer to as the "hot action" of practice, that real meaning is produced. Once you leave the dynamics of the social space, you are left with the resonance of what actually occurred. Freire (1972b) argues critical reflection is all important to the process of learning; he believed, through reflection critical awareness is raised. Through careful reflection activists revise and remake their practices. Schön (1983) claims, through reflection educators improve their practice. Activists often ask themselves questions such as: What worked well? What did not work? How can I better engage this individual? They reflect on moments of difficulty as well as moments of triumph. They revise and review judgments made in the heat of action. Beckett (2008) and Beckett and Hager (2002), believe judgment is central to practice. If we are really serious about understanding what we do in the workplace, we cannot discount that people make judgments every day.

Jorge's reflexivity is careful reflection on his own practices as an activist (Edwards, Ranson, & Strain 2002). His frequent reflexivity even keeps him awake at night:

> You have probably caught me at a time when I am particularly reflective about this in fact; I'm waking up at night sometimes thinking about this.... I remember when first reading Descartes at least this guy's got one thing right if you keep asking questions you will get there.

Jorge's reflexivity or metacognition is skillful reflection on his own practices as an activist, through which he revises and renews his practice. Freire knew the learning associated with critical reflection very well and referred to it as "conscientization" (Freire 1972, p.81). Through critical reflection, individuals would understand their own and others' oppression and seek to change it. Freire warned about what he termed fatalistic or naive consciousness and argues for a critical consciousness, a self-awareness that would encourage people to act to change their circumstances (Jesson & Newman 2004). *Kerry* says she might leave a meeting feeling angry that she wasn't being heard. She would then reflect on what went wrong and might decide to "write the paper in a different way" or discuss the issue in a different manner. She is remaking her practice through reflection in order to be successful. In doing this, she is honing her craft, mastering the skills of policy development, and lobbying. This often makes her uncomfortable—as she says, sometimes she leaves a meeting that has been undermined by powerful people and thinks "those bastards!" Yet her anger drives her to be more reflective about her practice and to regroup and strategize about what to do next. Through using the reflective act of making judgments about her practice, she is becoming expert (Beckett & Hager 2002).

Critical Thinking in Intelligent Bodies

Critical thinking is an important part of activists' learning. They learn to think critically about the world around them (Branagan & Boughton 2003; Jesson & Newman 2004). They also learn about current political, economic and social discourses in society that create inequality and learn to deconstruct and reconstruct these discourses (Foley 1999, 2001; Branagan & Boughton 2003; Jesson & Newman 2004). Jorge believes that learning to ask critical questions and critique ideas about society and the world around him has been important. He raised the significance of questioning and critique when he reflected:

> Definitely the asking questions thing is probably the main thing; tenacity, courage; but they tend to come with circumstance.... Yet I'm a great believer that even the greatest coward will be courageous in certain circumstances; passion is probably the main thing, and you need to be self-conscious of what you are doing.

Jorge's statement synthesizes critical thinking (both rational and emotional) and the experiential aspects of activists' knowing. Both emotionality and rationality are mutually reinforcing his criticality and are of equal value. Jorge thinks the ability to think critically about systems and structures and how they connect to inequality in the world is essential, and he links this view with what he refers to as being "anti-systemic." This conscious "awareness" (Freire 1972, p. 81) or learning to question or critique in order to understand circumstances that create oppression is what Jorge refers to as "being anti-systemic." Jorge has learned through his activism about politics and international systems of government and that this has occurred through his direct action:

> I very much think ideas, what I would believe to be about structures and world systems, I learned through my direct action; it's not like I was going to seminars or anything, sometimes maybe. But it did embed for life the spirit of questioning for me, if nothing else you would never be happy with the first answer, and you know I am amazed just with my own teaching and stuff how many people are happy with the first answer or if they are not happy do nothing.

The ability to question situations and circumstances is a specific skill that activists develop in their practice (Branagan & Boughton 2003; Jesson & Newman 2004). Being able to reflect on the discourses of inequality and to be able to reframe or reconstruct these discourses assists activists to make meaning (Foley 2001). As a young child, *Max* questioned the teachings of love in Christianity, recognizing that biblical teachings might not always be practiced by those who had authority in the church. His first action of resistance was to claim he no longer wanted to be an altar boy. *Max* claims this action was central to developing a critical ontology (Lave & Wenger 1991). While critical thinking may require the use of reason, Brookfield (2000; 2005) argues critical thinking needs the power of theory and he argues critical reflection without an analysis of systemic oppression is a form of self-indulgent aggrandizement. Cam made an active decision at 17 to become an activist, he was a keen bushwalker and skier, who had seen a lot of beautiful places become destroyed through logging. He was able to make connections between the need for environmental sustainability and the conflicts of maintaining a sustainable ecological system within the constraints of capitalism. A critical schema was developing in early adolescence about the environment, and he found himself becoming committed to working with other likeminded people through social action. *Catherine*, a passionate advocate for refugees, was frequently enraged at government policy that was discriminatory and instinctively knew her campaign had to move from the direct action phase to one that was "strategic." She needed to steer support within government and the wider community to get legislative reform for asylum seekers.

Spirituality

It appears from the research that spirituality is embedded in these activists' corporeal schema. Most of the lifelong activists and some of the circumstantial activists in this study were influenced by their religious upbringing. Cam, Felicity, *Rose, Max,* and Jorge, and the circumstantial activists, *Catherine, Eva,* and Tricia, were influenced in some way by Christianity, while Garry's parents were Zionist Jews, *Bahar* was Muslim, and *Kerry* described a spiritual connection to her land and country as an Indigenous women. The influence of spirituality and formal religion on their motivation for these activists to take action cannot be discounted. The activists influenced by Catholicism found the symbolism of the church highly influential in their developing sense of social justice at an early age. Both *Eva* and Felicity found the work of missionaries fascinating. *Max* believes the Marist brothers laid the foundation of his social justice values.

Other studies have similarly shown that people are more likely to become involved in social movements if they have attended a church or been involved in some form of formal religion (McAdam 1986; Jasper 1998). Studies of environmental activists have also confirmed that a number of activists view their activism as a calling that is beyond themselves, not necessarily originating from a deity, but from a spiritual connection with the environment and the desire to preserve the planet (Kovan & Dirkx 2003). More interestingly, however, most of the activists interviewed for this study, with the exception of *Bahar*, no longer observed their original faiths. Garry, for example, has become a practising Buddhist; Jonathan and Cam have a spiritual connection to the environment but do not follow any formal religion, while *Catherine* indicated that her Christian values were now reconstructed as a form of humanism. It appears from the data that the role and symbolism of religion in people's upbringings remained an influence on activists' perception of the world around them and, in particular, played a key role in their ability to identify and understand constructs of privilege and disadvantage. It had initiated a sense of responsibility to act for others and discouraged individualism. The sense of care for others translated, in several cases, into a concern for the planet and society that was reframed as a humanist approach. As Tricia stated, "I have rejected God and all things religious and all things god and godliness since then. In reality I am a humanist, which is about people thinking and doing the right thing by others."

Conclusion

This chapter on embodied learning has uncovered the embodied practices of activists as they develop their corporeal schema through being in the world of activism. It outlines the significant role of the emotions in motivating and sustaining activists' participation in social movements and in social issues over the longer term, for some, often over a lifetime. Hochschild's (1979) "emotional management" is outlined to reveal more experienced activists' use of emotions to persuade an outcome or argument or ultimately be successful in their activist work. Merleau-Ponty's (1962) existential phenomenology provides insight into activists' developing epistemology as they participate in the world of activism and in doing so develop considerable expertise and knowledge. Activists use highly developed critical thinking skills in their intelligent bodies. They are reflective about their practices and they use reflection to renew and remake their practices and, in doing so, they develop a critically reflective ontology.

The next chapter explores the social and informal learning dimensions to activists' pedagogy. It follows activists' learning in the sites and social spaces of communities of practice represented by student unions and social organizations. It outlines the rapid learning on the job of activism for circumstantial activists, as they are taken out of their comfort zones and compelled to develop new knowledge and skills.

7
Informal and Social Learning

Introduction

This second discussion chapter draws on adult education theory, particularly that from the social learning tradition, known as "Situated Learning" (Lave & Wenger 1991). The chapter contextualizes social learning by introducing the concept of "communities of practice" and the theory's relationship to activists' pedagogy (Lave & Wenger 1991). It is argued that Lave's writing is highly relevant to embodied learning; even though this is not explicitly stated, she argues for learning that goes beyond cognition, and draws on the experience of learning with others in a social space (Lave 1991, 1996). The chapter posits the site of the neighborhood as a place of struggle and resistance, and draws on similarities in activists' practices to argue that the local neighborhood, local campaign, or social movement becomes a site where significant knowledge and skill is produced. The development of activist "apprenticeships" is examined in relation to "newcomer / old-timer" constructs and the typology of circumstantial and lifelong activists (Lave 1991, p. 68). The concept of "rapid learning" by circumstantial activists is also explored in relation to the "hot action" of practice described by Beckett and Hager (2002). Activists' learning is examined in light of Bourdieu's analysis of self learning and the autodidact. Knowledge constructed in this way is neither legitimated nor recognized as a real way of knowing because cultural capital is given to formal modalities of knowledge. Finally, learning to be and become an activist is considered as a project of identity work that can occur in communities of practice represented by activist networks and social organizations.

Social Learning: Communities of Practice

Over the past 20 years, no tradition of learning has dominated adult education discourse in the same way as Lave and Wenger's (1991) theory of situated leaning. Their development of a theory of adult learning, which situates learning in social and community sites, has contributed to understanding knowledge formation through informal learning. Lave and Wenger's work is a sociocultural interpretation of learning that positions and locates learning within the social environment of work or communities. Lave (1991) argues that this learning

> is neither wholly subjective, nor fully encompassed in social interaction, and it is not constituted separately from the social world (with its own structures and meanings) of which it is part. This recommends a de-centered view of the locus and meaning of learning, in which learning is recognized as a social phenomenon constituted in the experienced, lived-in-world, through legitimate peripheral participation in and ongoing social practice. (p. 64)

Most epistemologies of learning are based on assumptions about people, the world and their relations to it. We internalize knowledge or we receive it in a variety of ways, and we learn to absorb this information and assimilate it (Lave & Wenger 1991). However, many adults bring to their learning a level of existing knowledge through having lived a long life full of complexity, with the result that some learning may not transfer, but rather synthesize with existing knowledge. Lave (1996) analyses the learning that takes place between the newcomer / old-timer in the processes of apprenticeship. Her study of apprentices learning the craft of tailoring in the early 1970s in Liberia is useful for understanding the way circumstantial (newcomer) activists develop their craft and become masterful. In this site of learning, Lave observed the work of 250 masters and apprentices in the space called "Tailors Alley" (p. 151). The research examined how the processes of apprenticeship allowed young tailors to become more masterful at their craft. Lave (1996) critiques rational learning in formal education and the "narrow" focus of informal learning, which exemplifies the development of skill, but ignores many of the moral discourses that constitute and impact on our learning. What Lave is chiefly concerned about, however, is whether teaching and the transmission of knowledge is a necessary condition for learning (p. 151). She is critical of the dualist approaches to pedagogy central to most traditions of learning because of their relativist focus on cognition, as this approach to pedagogy often alienates people who are the most marginalized. She points out that there needs to be a theory of learning that does not entrench "social inequality in our society" (p. 149). Lave is referring to our reliance on cognition for understanding ways of knowing, and in a sense, her work is similar to Merleau-Ponty's (1962) existential examination of somatic knowledge developed though perception and being in the world. Although Lave (1991) does not explicitly argue for embodied learning per se, she does argue for rethinking the rationalist ontology of learning in favor of an epistemology of education that is holistic:

> Such a view invites a rethinking of the notion of learning, treating it as an emerging property of the whole persons' legitimate peripheral participation in communities of practice. Such a view sees mind, culture, history and the social world as interrelated processes that constitute each other, and, intentionally blurs social scientists' divisions among component parts of persons, their activities, and the world (pp. 63–64).

What Lave and Wenger (1991) are arguing for is a view of learning that goes beyond a mere transfer of knowledge. They claim the focus on transition models of education do not account for the nature of the learner in the social world, and are largely "cerebral" (p. 47). As Lave (1996) observed in the Liberian apprentices' daily work, they were learning about the social and cultural worlds around them. They were learning about class distinctions and the "divisions in Liberian society" which were being played out in the daily "business of dressing" (p. 151). They were learning about their craft, learning to live, learning to make an income; in essence, they were learning to become master tailors. They were learning about the status they would receive when they eventually became masters of their trade. In effect, the apprentices were learning about the historical and cultural world around them (Lave 1996).

The epistemology of popular education has revealed, mainly through the writing of humanist educators such as Freire (1972b), that in the site of struggle learning will always occur. Neighborhoods and communities are often sites of education where we learn to acculturate hegemony and resist hegemonic practices in society (Gramsci 1971; Gramsci & Forgacs 1988). A recent site of study was that of the San Bernano Elders, whose communal living arrangements over many generations were threatened by urban development (Lucio-Villegas, Garcia, & Cowe 2008). Here, the neighborhood site becomes a place of resistance and struggle. The neighborhood effectively becomes a classroom, in which the San Bernado Elders learned the skills of campaigning and resistance, including community education, using the media and how to physically blockade their building. They developed knowledge about the capitalist practices of the developers and their collusion with local government; in effect, they were learning to resist the empire (Lucio-Villegas, Garcia, & Cowe 2008). More recently, in Melbourne, the St. Kilda foreshore became the site of struggle, as we have seen through *Eva's* account of activism triggered by developers' proposal for a high-density shopping complex. *Eva's* activism exemplifies learning in the site of struggle through her involvement in a local community campaign to resist the developers. She claims her biggest area of learning has been in understanding group dynamics and understanding processes of local government. She was learning about resistance, and her own agency to act through resistance, as well as learning about the politics of local and state governments.

The practices of activism are usually closely connected to communities, community development, and social movements. Sites of community and social movements are the spaces and places where activists learn through socialization with one another, by learning in "communities of practice" (Lave & Wenger 1991, p. 31). Learning in activism is a naturally social process; through time, and the opportunity to observe and interact with others, activists become more expert at what they do. Like the tailors in Liberia, activists learn a range of skills through working with one another, although this is not always recognized as learning or knowledge by the activists themselves (Newman 1994, 2006; Foley 1999). They learn about the world around them, they learn about systems of government, key advisors, and key politicians, they learn to hone their communication skills, to speak in public, and they learn to engage with, and use, the media (Branagan & Boughton 2003; Jesson & Newman 2004). More experienced activists learn to become event managers; by learning how to plan a large rally, they deal with planners, police, local government, traders, and large crowds of protesters, and they effectively navigate and negotiate these events in the same way that any major events planner would do. Like the Liberian apprentice tailors, activists learn through the daily practice of everyday activities, many of which develop their foundational community development skills (Kenny 1994, 2006; Mayo 2005), including skills for networking, group work, planning and facilitation, social policy, and research.

Apprenticeship Learning: The Role of Mentors

Activists learn from other activists all of the time, particularly though the support and guidance of mentors, and the theory of social learning highlights this relationship between the "old-timers and the newcomers" (Lave & Wenger 1991; Lave 1996). As indicated in Chapters 4 and 5, the role that more experienced activists play involves assisting newcomer activists to develop their initial skills and become masterful or more expert in turn. Almost all the activists had at least one mentor. According to Lave and Wenger (1991), newcomers start out on the periphery of practice and, as they develop more experience, they become more masterful at their practice, and, through socialization, pass on their skills to others (Wenger 1998). For example, Garry practiced his newly developing skills with the mentor who assisted him with his media skills. They would meet in her office and role play some of the potential questions he would be asked about poverty and the financial issues of his clients. They used visualization processes to quell his anxiety about speaking to the media and role-played interviews. *Grace* also had a significant mentor in her early days of activism. There was a person whose skillful handling of meetings she would observe in order to learn how to steer the agenda and discussion to get a desirable outcome. Similarly, *Rose* had a number of skillful mentors who encouraged her to become involved in a lot of community groups and policy processes, thereby developing her skills through socialization. This sharing of expertise opened up to her a whole network of activists, community development workers, and educators, and, through this process, *Rose* was becoming immersed in the pedagogy of activism. Both *Catherine* and *Bahar* learned their early skills on fieldwork placements where they were "apprenticed" to different but highly skillful women who had been involved in campaigning for many years. *Max*, too, had a mentor who was highly skilled and taught him about neighborhood development. Cam had several mentors in the early days of his activism, from whom he learned, but it was the community of practice in FOE where he was really challenged by the feminist women to develop his self-awareness, a process that he found "really useful." *Kerry's* mentors were especially significant because they fostered her developing sense of Indigenous identity. They connected her not just to knowledge about activism but to a deeper sense of cultural identity—of belonging to ancient peoples and to an ancient place. It was this "bonding" with cultural identity that gave *Kerry's* politics purpose and drive. Like the mentor experiences of the other activists, there was also a common set of values that developed through the growing sense of respect and admiration of the apprentice to the master practitioner, which has enhanced their acquisition of knowledge and skill.

Community of Practice in Student Unions

Most of the lifelong activists had some involvement in student politics and it appears from the research that the situated site of student unions represented a community of practice for activists. These activists found that the student unions replicated the workings of the Australian political system. They learned about conservative and progressive politics and the role of factions in political parties. They learned to be strategic to caucus and compromise on decisions. They developed knowledge about the constraints and benefits of a two-party system of government and also learned how to collectively resist a policy by taking a strong and firm position on an issue. Jorge, *Max, Rose*, Felicity, and Garry were all involved in the student union movement as undergraduate students; all apart from Garry took on elected senior roles on the Victorian or National Student Union. They learned community development skills in advocacy and networking. They learned communication skills such as how to develop an argument, how to persuade others, how to speak in public, and how to use the media. They developed a reified (Lave & Wenger 1991; Wenger 1998) practice, through observing and interacting with other student activists in the union. Jorge says he learned about pickets and protests and all of the tenacity that goes with direct action. Felicity says she learned everything she needed to know about politics from the student union ("it's all about factions!").

For most of the lifelong activists this social space of learning marked the commencement of a long journey of political understanding and apprenticeship in activism. This experience differed to that of the circumstantial activists who learnt rapidly and in more diverse communities. The student unions allowed individuals to test and rehearse their values, beliefs and ideology. These activists had the opportunity to incrementally develop their values, beliefs, and ideology, they were learning about politics and protest in this community of practice (Lave & Wenger 1991; Wenger 1998), and in doing so were creating a habitus of activism (Bourdieu 1977).

Learning Community

When Marx and Engels called for the "workers of the world" to unite in order to change their collective oppression, it was a call to collective action, a call to educate the community of workers that unity would enable social change to occur (Marx & Engels 1967). They knew that if workers united they would be a force to be reckoned with and could alter the course of capitalist exploitation and, thus, the course of history. Marx's writing has been influential in the history of revolutionary struggle in both the nineteenth and twentieth centuries (Marx 1853). Merleau-Ponty (1962) argues that the revolutionary can intellectualize a practice but the revolution will not occur unless the worker finds other people to experience and practice the revolution with. He makes the point that, as people begin to view themselves in relation to others, a "social space begins to acquire a magnetic field and a region or the exploited is seen to appear" (pp. 396–97). Merleau-Ponty is committed to the view that the experience of oppression allows the oppressed to gain insight into their exploitation, creating the social space for the revolution to occur. The social space fosters intent and purpose among the workers; it reifies their exploitation and emboldens them to act (Merleau-Ponty 1962). The social space develops commonality and solidarity among the working classes. Unless the relationships between self and others becomes reified or are "finally experienced in perception as a common obstacle to existence of each and everyone" change will not occur (Merleau-Ponty 1962, p. 397). Thus, Cam went looking for other activists with whom he could work. *Jonathan* socialized with other activists through his involvement in FOE and other activist groups. Jeannie found a group of mothers who were equally concerned about the war in Vietnam and they socialized with and learned from one another. *Kerry* finds sitting around with her Indigenous community, friends, colleagues, and elders allows her to reflect, debrief about difficult events, and regroup about Indigenous issues she is working on. Felicity and *Rose* both have a firm social network and community of practice through their involvement in Rainbow Families.

This learning community is in contradiction to the idealist project of Plato, which posits that through objective thought we understand and make judgments. Yet objectivist modes of knowledge tend to reproduce themselves through their "structured dispositions" within the world (Bourdieu 1977, p. 3). For example, if we take as our focus the notion of structural materialism, and argue that it has no relationship to the subject, the individual is outside of these systems rather than taking on any of these representations whatsoever. This would lead us to believe that understanding forces of oppression through systems is an objective intellectual pursuit, rather than discourses we experience. Merleau-Ponty (1962) challenges this proposition by arguing that we carry systems and structures with us through and because of our experiences of dealing with them "What makes me proletarian," he says,

> is not the economic system or society considered as systems of impersonal forces, but these institutions as I carry them within me and experience them; nor is it an intellectual operation devoid of motive, but my way of being in the world within the institutional framework. (p. 515)

These systems and structures, and the discourses that are associated with them, we take on through our experience. Thus, activists, learners and educators take on the discourses of the life world through being-in-the-world of practice.

The Importance of Practice

This research has found that activists develop practical and experiential knowledge. What this research demonstrates is that activists need to practice their techniques and strategies in order to obtain the required dispositions needed to be successful activists. However there are impediments to this practice. Bourdieu (1977) claims we are "trapped" in the social sciences between dualist constructions of objectivity/subjectivity, that a theory of practice can incorporate practical knowledge taken through both our experience of the world as well as objective knowledge (pp. 4–5). He argues this should not be viewed as a humanist project of "scientific objectification" in the name of "lived experience" and the rights of "subjectivity," but argues for a theory of practice that "puts objectivist knowledge back on its feet by posing the question of the (theoretical and also social) conditions which make knowledge possible" (Bourdieu 1977, p. 4). What Bourdieu highlights is the tendency of the social sciences to consign either/or constructions of knowledge. What he is claiming is by rejecting objectivism we create a form of dualism in itself, one which privileges subjectivity and relegates objective thought to the margins:

> The shift from the practical scheme to the theoretical schema, constructed after the event, from practical sense to the theoretical model, which can be either read as a project, plan or method, or as a mechanical program, a mysterious ordering mysteriously reconstructed by the analyst, lets slip everything that makes temporal reality of practice in process. Practice unfolds in time and it has all the correlative property, such as irreversibility, that synchronization destroys. Its temporal structure that is, its rhythm, its tempo, and above all its directionality, is constitutive of its meaning. (p. 81)

But what Bourdieu is really arguing for is a reflexive practice, one that includes objective as well as subjective ways of knowing, an integrated practice that does not privilege rationalism but recognizes the value of the practical knowledge of the autodidact as being just as important as formal scholarly knowledge produced through the authoritative dispositions of formal universities and educational institutions (Bourdieu 1977, 1984, 1998). Unfortunately cultural capital tends to lie with the latter rather than the former. What this research has demonstrated is that for the conditions of learning to occur, activists need a praxis, which is an integration of theory and practice (Freire 1972b). Marx and Engels (1967) knew this when they called for direct action by workers of the world in the *Communist Manifesto*. They knew workers had to act to change the exploitation of their labor power being used in the means of production (Marx 1848, p. 393). This was an embodied call for both mindful and experiential action, in essence for praxis. This call, of course, set the foundation for a future union movement, which has dominated social movement theorizing up until the 1970s. Prior to this the prevailing belief was that only labor movements had the "capacity to transform societies" (Burgmann 2003). Nevertheless, with the advent of new social movements such as those concerned with issues of gender and sexuality, it was revealed there were other areas of society where change was required (Burgmann 2003).

This research has found activists use mentors and older, more experienced, activists to learn from; they work in and with communities and social movements to develop their skill. The majority of their skill develops through situating themselves with other activists in a learning community of practice. This is why Cam "went in search of all sorts environmental groups that he could work with;" he needed a social space where other activists congregated, for him to learn his trade. He needed to know that there were other people out there who had a commitment to social change and the environment so that he could commune, socialize, and take action with them. Jorge states that he "loves learning in collectives," he loves to "impart and share other people's knowledge." *Grace* who is a self-described intellectual and thinker knew she had to leave behind her intellectualism and share her skills with her colleagues so that she could bring the group along with her in their pursuit of a goal. *Grace* had to learn to be more social because she was used to being in charge and "just getting on with it." *Eva* similarly needed to develop her skills in group work; she was not used to group processes and knew that she had to learn how to build relationships with other people in the group, to allocate workloads and tasks and to be a part of a developing sense of purpose and solidarity. For activists, the social space of activism, and the sociality that occurs within this field of practice, creates an agency and urgency to act. Through the use of the social space activists' practices are reified and experience is gained; there is a communality that develops and a commonality of practice that occurs within the social space (Lave & Wenger 1991). Activists are becoming acculturated into a practice by experiencing that practice with others.

Self Learning—The Autodidact

As shown in chapter 5, most of the activists in this study are self learners and widely read. Bourdieu (1984) in *Distinction* uncovers cultures of knowledge that preference particular knowledges and delegitimize less formal ways of knowing. Formal knowledge resulting in credentials from education institutions such as universities is given greater esteem than the knowledge acquired informally by the autodidact (Bourdieu 1984). The activist who reads widely and is interested in a range of political, social, and philosophical ideas, and is involved with various groups and organizations, has gained knowledge that is wide-ranging. The extent of their knowledge is not dissimilar to knowledge acquired through formal structured systems of education.

Yet, informal knowledge is not legitimated as real knowledge, because cultural capital is placed on formal modalities of knowledge and less esteem is given to knowledge that is acquired through practice (Bourdieu 1984).

Jonathan and Cam, for example, have read a great deal of nonviolence theory, and are committed to nonviolent practice in activism. Both have read and studied feminist theory, which has formed their understanding of the politics of patriarchy and masculinity and has led them to identify as being profeminist. Jorge has read the works of ancient philosophers such as Plato and Aristotle, and the classical philosophers such as Hegel, Descartes, and Marx. The informal schemata acquired through these activists' own self-learning, therefore, has much in common with knowledge acquired through formal education systems. Jorge, for example, is able to speak on many of the key tenets of these philosophies. Cam and *Jonathan* both have highly developed knowledge of feminism and patriarchy, while Jeannie absorbed knowledge about socialism and communism from her parents. *Jonathan* and *Grace* have degrees in science, and have both read widely and have demonstrated the ability to obtain and interpret complex information from the internet and other sources. It is interesting to note that, even before the recent onset of discourses around competence and competency in learning and education systems, Bourdieu (1984) recognized that two people may have the same ability and perform the same job but have different qualifications, yet deference is given to the individual with the higher qualification,

> the justification for this being the idea that only the competence certified by the higher qualifications can guarantee possession of the basic knowledge which underlies all practical know-how. (Bourdieu 1984, p. 147)

Bourdieu speaks about the "scholastic mode of production" and knowledge of the autodidact being:

> A collection of unstrung pearls, accumulated in the course of unchartered exploration, unchecked by the institutionalized, standardized obstacles, the curricula and progressions which make scholastic culture a ranked and ranking set of independent levels and forms of knowledge. (p. 328)

Activists' knowledge, like the unstrung pearls, is not always perceived by the world as such because knowledge acquired through a hierarchical education system, with its exams, essays, and performance measures, is perceived to have met certain benchmarks. Sanctioned and legitimized by the state, knowledge associated with qualifications is held in greater esteem than the knowledge of the autodidact

(Bourdieu 1977, 1998). Formal knowledge is legitimated and reproduced through credentials and converts to educational capital for the holder of these qualifications, because they have gone through an authorized process, and are perceived as having acquired the necessary knowledge to perform in a designated profession (Bourdieu 1984). Bourdieu's research alludes to the intellectual and educational capital "allocated" to certain professions and institutions when he writes:

> The qualifications awarded by the French grandes ecoles guarantee, without any other guarantee, a competence extending far beyond what they are supposed to guarantee. This is by virtue of a clause which, though tacit, is firstly binding on the qualification holders themselves, who are called upon really to procure the attributes assigned to them by their status. (p. 24)

This research supports an alternative view of the activist autodidact, whose connection to community and practice provides a frame of reference to inform and validate the knowledge and understanding generated through noninstitutional reading and reflection. The practical way of knowing of the autodidact, not sanctioned by traditional learning processes yet knowledge nonetheless, is reminiscent of Aristotle's phronesis or practical knowledge, common sense, or wisdom. In ancient Greece, Aristotle resolved the importance of practical knowledge, this way of knowing theorized about in "Plato's Republic"; one of the four cardinal virtues was informal knowledge—wisdom, prudence, or phronesis (Plato & Davis).

Rapid Learning "on the Job" of Activism

Lave and Wenger's (Lave 1991) theory of situated learning has subsequently been expanded and developed by other theorists to include understandings of how individuals learn at work (Boud & Garrick 1999; Foley 2000; Beckett & Hager 2002; Soloman 2003; Billett 2004). It is widely understood that adults learn all of their lives and that a majority of this learning occurs in the workplace (Hodkinson & James 2003). The empirical research has shown that learning of a similar nature takes place in the unpaid work of activists (Ollis 2008a). As demonstrated in the literature review, there are many variations of workplace learning, from learning that is transmitted didactically in the workplace, with a focus on knowledge transfer, to learning through networks (Engeström, Miettinen, & Punamäki-Gitai 1999; Engeström 2007). More recently, Beckett and Hager's Australian model of workplace learning has focused on a holistic approach to developing competence (Beckett & Hager 2000; Beckett 2008). Educators are now more aware of the implications of learning and knowledge development in the workplace (Soloman 2003). In the present era of lifelong learning, and in the context of contemporary conditions of work, we are now entering the phase of the "new worker" a socially constructed identity (Gee, Hull, & Lankshear 1996):

> In our view the new work order is largely about trying to create new social identities or new kinds of people: new leaders, new workers, new students, new teachers, new citizens, new communities, even new private people, who are supposed to dissolve the separation between their lives outside work and their lives inside of it. (p. xiv)

Workers are expected to work harder, smarter, longer, and faster than ever before. Critics of workplace learning and lifelong learning are concerned that learning through work can potentially be hijacked by the discourses of neoliberalism, whereby workers are expected to learn in order to increase their level of productivity in the workplace (Anderson, Brown, & Rushbrook 2004). Workers are now expected to simultaneously be learners and workers (Soloman 2003). Work has become increasingly commoditized, to be bought and sold in the labor market. In the process, commoditization has increased the potential for workers' alienation from their product and potentially, as Marx (1959) outlined, from themselves (Marx 1959; Hodkinson et al., 2004). Furthermore, theories of social learning and learning in the workplace are not all harmonious (Hodges 1998) and this will be dealt with later in this chapter by exploring issues of power and the social learning model. Lave and Wenger's theory of situated learning is, however, very useful for explaining the social nature of learning through work. Certainly, learning of a similar nature takes place in the unpaid work of social activists; that is, social learning or learning in a "community of practice" (Lave & Wenger 1991; Wenger 1998). The best way to prepare people for professional practice and for learning in life in general is through some type of social learning, apprenticeship, or community of practice (Gonczi 2004). Thus, learning is an inherently social process situated in our daily interactions with one another. Beckett and Hager (2002) argue professional workers develop expertise in the "hot action" of practice. By learners practising what they do in the workplace they become more expert at what they do (Beckett & Hager 2002). In the hot action of activism, in the rapid learning of activism, activists, too, develop greater expertise. In the art of making judgments in the hot action of practice, workers incorporate their know-how into practice. Individuals are able to develop their skills through participation in a community of practice; they develop with one another a shared repertoire of skillful practice (Lave & Wenger 1991). They may start as a newcomer on the periphery of practice, and through time, observation, and practice, move to full participation and engagement in learning (Wenger 1998):

> Legitimate peripherality is a complex notion, implicated in social structures involving relations of power. It is a place in which one moves toward more-intensive participation, peripherality is an empowering position. A place in which one is kept from participating more fully – often legitimately, from the broader perspective of society at large – it is a disempowering position. (Lave & Wenger 1991, pp. 35–36).

As this research has demonstrated, learning occurs through activists immersing themselves into a practice with other organizers, confirming Lave and Wenger's (1991) supposition "that engaging in practice, rather than being its object, may well be a condition for effective learning" (p. 93). Learning occurs by having the opportunity to practice and to perfect what they are doing as activists and by situating themselves in the "hot action" of activism (Beckett & Hager 2000, p. 302).

Learning on the job is often based on our social interaction in the workplace and is often informal (Boud & Garrick 1999; Beckett & Hager 2002).The dynamics of social interaction and conversation in the workplace of activism can lead to fruitful learning. Every day, activists connect through discussing their desires, needs, wants, and aspirations. This is sometimes done unconsciously, but also done most purposefully, while looking for a solution to a particular issue or problem. Those passing conversations about political processes, impending legislation, or organizing campaigns are all potential learning experiences. As they swap stories of practice, they are also revealing their concern for the future of this knowledge and being able to pass it on to future generations of activists (Maddison & Scalmer 2006).

At times, they learn accidentally through their everyday experiences, sometimes through what may seem trivial activities:

> Under these circumstances, the initial "circumferential" perspective absorbed in partial, peripheral, apparently trivial activities—running errands, delivering messages, or accompanying others—takes on a new significance: it provides a first approximation to the armature of the structure of community of practice. Things learned, and various and changing viewpoints, can be arranged and interrelated in some ways that gradually transform that skeletal understanding. (Lave & Wenger, 1991, p. 96)

As Whelan (2005a) reminds us, there is a great deal to be learned in social action, even when a campaign fails. Both Cam and *Jonathan* believe they learned most of their skill and knowledge on the job of activism. They learned how to manage large scale events, to stage thousands of protesters to be able to march through city streets. They learned how to brief police, stage musical and theatrical events in the midst of protest. *Jonathan* learned how to be a part of a human blockade in Palestine on the border with Israel. He learned about danger in protest, but also about the solidarity that comes from social action, and being with other activists who were committed to a long journey of resistance. Similarly, Cam learned about the long haul from his action in the Franklin River blockade. Felicity learned a great deal of her skill through being involved in numerous protests, through her involvement in the student union and the DSP, but more recently through her lobbying for social change in parental rights for lesbians. Terry's learning is experiential, he argues he has always been someone who would master a skill through doing it rather than reading instructions, he says that way you get a better perspective. *Bahar's* and *Catherine's* on the job training in community development allowed them to practice their actual skills by being present and involved in a campaign. This knowledge contributes to their skillful practice, and through time, and the opportunity to practice and experience activism, they become expert in what they do.

Rapid Learning and Circumstantial Activists

It is important here to explore the rapid learning of circumstantial activists as they go about their everyday practices with an agency to learn that is sometimes urgent. Terry, with no experience whatsoever in public speaking or dealing with the media, walks out into the hot action of practice and holds a media conference. He said he was lucky that through his experiences of using the media, he learned early on in the campaign to get his message out short and simple and, most importantly, to not claim that he had more knowledge than he did, or that he was an expert in international law or terrorism. This skill, learned in action, contributes to his toolkit of practice. These skills developed on the job are being synthesized with other skills and knowledge and are contributing to a developing epistemology of practice. *Eva* attends a public meeting about the proposed development at her local government chambers with hundreds of residents, activists, politicians, and media attending. The meeting is tense, it is disruptive, some people are angry, and some people wanted a resolution. The meeting erupts with people yelling, it is explosive, and the council members threaten to walk out and start to do so. *Eva*, who describes herself as someone who is uncomfortable putting herself in this type of situation, stands on a chair in the middle of the meeting and calls for the protesters to settle down, to calm down so that the meeting could recommence. She claims in this situation she was anxious, her action was something that she did that was "completely spontaneous," she is out of her comfort zone as a learner, and she is developing skill, through trusting her judgment in this social space. *Bahar*, frustrated with the subjugation of the women around her, speaks to the Imam about male violence in the Turkish Muslim community. She challenges him to offer teachings about women's freedom and equality. She says it's not good enough to only have a 15-minute lesson once a year about the role of women; there needed to be more education about women's rights for the men who attended the mosque. This action is empowering and transformative for her, a Muslim woman whose identity, ascribed to her body by wearing the veil, symbolizes oppression to the Western world (Mezirow 1991, 2000). It is a powerful action because *Bahar* is challenging the patriarchal systems in her community and, by doing so, is promoting change to the customary gender roles. Beckett and Hager (2002) claim we need to take more seriously judgments made in the heat of practice; instinctive feelings such as gut reactions and intuition help learners to make judgments and assist them to develop expertise. *Bahar's* social action at her mosque is learning in action by making judgments within a context of conflict. Aristotle's phronesis includes making conscious and unconscious judgments in practice, and *Bahar*, through her action, is developing practical wisdom (Aristotle 1962, p.395). *Eva* is learning about how to engage with the crowd and speak in public; she is learning about the emotional environment of protest, in the hot action of activism she is learning how to make judgments amidst the environment of protest, in doing this she develops further skill and expertise (Beckett & Hager 2000; Beckett 2008). Terry's "hot action" in holding a media conference was risky, yet he made judgments in action. These judgments in practice would lead him to develop considerable expertise in his future use of the media.

Power and the Social Learning Model

Learning in a community of practice cannot be considered without understanding the contested nature of the term "community." Community is a contentious term often described as social closeness or a close knit community in a geographic location. Wenger's (1998) view of community is often harmonious, yet human relationships are complex, especially in the workplace where specific roles are constructed, produced, and reproduced through hierarchical subjectivities of being a worker, team-leader, coordinator, or a manager. Conflict occurs in the workplace, people are bullied, and their performance is monitored and managed. The epistemology of communities of practice rarely discusses why particular groups may have access to a community of practice or why they may feel excluded from it. An individual's exclusion from a community within the workplace may make them peripheral to the practice. In turn, they may feel marginalized from the practice they are engaging in and therefore learn very little (Hodges 1998). Similarly, workplaces may perpetuate unethical behaviors and values (Hodkinson et al., 2004). Chappell (2003) reminds us that discursive representations in the social world do important political and cultural work on the self:

> The self is not seen as neutral representations, of the subject/person but rather as discursive representations that do important political and cultural work in constructing, maintaining and transforming, both individuals and their social world. (p. 28)

Hodges (1998) argues there are times when the person feels marginalized in such a way as "other," where the normative identification with a practice is challenged by difference:

> Non-participation constitutes an identificatory moment when a person is accommodating in participation and yet is experiencing an exclusion

from any "normative," or unproblematic identification with practice. Quite crucially, non-participation describes conflict in the space between activity and identification, where there is a moment of multiplicitous identifications or identificatory possibilities. (p. 1)

This is no different to the social environment of the workplace or community. Mentors and masters can pass on poor practice to newcomers and thwart their ability to learn, or their learning can be closed off by existing power relations (Foucault 1980). Bourdieu's (1977) habitus is a useful guide here for understanding the enculturation of activists' practices. Certain dispositions, certain practices are expected and passed down in communities. That is, certain approaches to a social issue are embedded in the practices of activism that occur through the creation of habitus.

Lifelong activists such as *Kerry* are already a part of an existing habitus of Indigenous politics; tied to a history of dispossession and imperialism. The creation of a habitus of connecting "country" to culture and educating Australian society about this reifies her practices within the habitus. In the habitus of Indigenous activism there are certain discourses, actions, practices, and processes that are expected and adopted through social action and are ready to be passed on. While these dispositions may vary from community to community or from social movement to social movement, there are nevertheless certain habitus that are unique to this social field of practice (Bourdieu 1998).

Newcomers to the practices, such as circumstantial activists like *Kerry, Grace,* and Tim, are often outside of the social space, but need to quickly find their way in to learn the skill of activism. As Lave and Wenger (1991) believe, newcomers to a practice are often on periphery of practice. Habitus can maintain a practice or alternatively can constrain or inhibit it. *Kerry*'s initial awakening about her culture and Indigenous politics was empowering because she was told to learn about her history and this gave her motivation to become actively involved in Indigenous politics. Felicity's learning, however, was constrained by the gendered practices of the DSP, which compelled her to reject specific aspects of the practices she observed. Likewise, both Cam and *Jonathan* found the dogma of Marxism within the DSP excluded other ways of knowing. Terry's perceived concerns about the so-called radical practices of some activists were sufficient for him to distance himself from organized social movements and groups. Tim still finds that some activists are suspicious of his work as an engineer in a corporate organization and this has impeded his complete immersion into the habitus of environmental activism. Although he moves in and out of the community of practice in the environment movement, he is not fully immersed in the movement, and his practice is not completely reified because of this (Wenger 1998). Arguably, the movement loses a most talented activist who has learned rapidly, developed new skills and knowledge to add to his existing level of knowledge and creativity. Tim has much to contribute to the pedagogy of activism, if he is given the opportunity.

Learning to "Become" an Activist

One of the central questions to this research has been the stages and processes of learning and identity formation that occur through social action. In particular, this research sought to find out if there were any significant differences in identity formation of the newcomers to activism, in this study the circumstantial activists. If a changing identity is a necessary condition for learning (Chappell et al., 2003) then what does that mean for understanding activists, their pedagogy, and their motivation to be involved in protest? Fundamentally, learning is a process of becoming; learning, it has been argued, does important identity work on the learner (Beckett & Hager 2002; Chappell et al., 2003; Soloman 2003). As Chappell et al. claim,

> Power resides in all discourses including those economic, social and political theories that attempt to explain identity. Put simply, our conception of who we are, our identity, is constituted by the power of all the discursive practices in which we speak and which, in turn, "speak" to us. (Chappell 2003, p. 41)

For most of the lifelong activists in this study, the processes and practice of activism involves their daily life, their identity, their formation of politics and ideology, and their relationships with others. Being an activist is an important part of their identity, although some do have reservations about their role. *Kerry* views herself more as a role model for other Indigenous people because she doesn't like some of the "harsh messages" she associates with some activists. Garry dislikes labeling himself as an activist and equivocates on whether he identifies as an activist or not, although in the interview he does come to claim and name his identity. *Max* is reluctant to take on the identity of an activist, as he says he is not doing anything special. He is also cautious in claiming this identity because it may affect his future professional opportunities in the union movement. Nevertheless, all three are still actively involved in social change on a daily basis. One of the prominent features of communities of practice is the identification of a work practice with self and other workers around you (Lave & Wenger 1991). Newcomers are not yet completely immersed into a culture of identification practices of the community; they are still often outside of the practice on the periphery and need time and opportunity to fully immerse them into the community of practice. The processes of political and cultural work in constructing an identity is an ongoing project (Chappell et al., 2003). Cam, *Jonathan*, Felicity, *Rose,* Jeanie, and Jorge are all fully immersed in their identity; there is no equivocation about whether they are activists, although Felicity notes her present role is more of a lobbyist than someone who is engaged in direct action. Jeannie, now in her seventies, says she will still take to the streets if the issue is important to her. *Jonathan* says that his purpose and meaning in life is very much driven by his identification of being an activist.

Some of the lifelong activists had shifts in their identification with specific practices within activist communities over time. Felicity, as we have seen, disliked the practices of the DSP and she felt some members who were vulnerable were treated harshly. She argued most social and political movements attract some vulnerable individuals and she believed there should have been greater care taken with some of these members. Jorge became disillusioned with the ALP and the union movement because he could no longer reconcile their shifting stance with his own ideology. The expected dispositions that were a part of the habitus of practice within the movement were alienating him and making him question the movement (Bourdieu 1977). Self-regulatory moments, or reconstructing discourses in specific times of practice, are moments when the lifelong activist may separate from a practice, disillusioned with the collective identity of the group or practice, and needing to change in order to maintain their involvement (Foucault 1980, 1983). There are moments in a practice where the shift in self is so dramatic that the individual is outside of a practice because he/she is alienated from the normative practices of the group (Hodges 1998). The expected dispositions, practices, ideas, dress, and image of the group are not in sync with the individual member (Bourdieu 1977). It seems the practices of activists need to be inclusive by embracing the diversity of people in the movement or else learning may be impeded rather than advanced. Activist groups, organizations, and social movements need to ensure that they are being inclusive and not exclusive, and there needs to be an awareness of power and power relations taking place in the movement's analyses of worker/activist identities (Foucault 1980). Bourdieu's notion of "practice" provides us with a way forward (Bourdieu 1977, 2000). We need to move away from restrictive either/ or notions of conservative and progressive activism, subjective or objectivist knowledge, critical or noncritical activism and use the concept of "practice." We need to ask ourselves what practices are effective in achieving broader social change (Bourdieu 1977, 2000).

Circumstantial activists, on the other hand, are often reluctant to identify as activists or with particular social movements because of representations of activists as radical or feral. Alternatively, they may cordon off an aspect of the identity associated with activist activities, like Tim who is willing to consider himself an activist for climate change but not a "Greenie." *Grace*, *Bahar*, and Terry do not identify as activists at all and do not feel comfortable with the term. *Andrew* says if you had asked if he was an activist five years ago, he probably would have said yes. But he now identifies as a person involved in promoting leadership within the disability community. Terry identifies as a concerned parent and someone who is now interested in human rights, whereas he never was before. He may not completely identify as an activist, but he has acquired new knowledge and says that he will pass on this knowledge to others.

Conclusion

This chapter on the informal and social learning dimensions of activists has revealed the broad range of places and spaces where activists learn from one another through socialization. Drawing on Lave and Wenger's theory of situated learning in "communities of practice" we uncover the knowing and skill development that occurs as activists learn from one another on the job. Rapid learning in the case of circumstantial activists is outlined in detail. Activists frequently have to learn new knowledge in a very short period of time in order for them to be effective activists. Circumstantial activists protest but do not necessarily identify themselves as activists. On the other hand, lifelong activists develop an activist ontology very early on in life as adolescents. Identity change appears to be a common element across all of the respondents in the research. Some are prepared to self-identify as an activist and others only acknowledge the change in their identity by being involved in a particular social or political issue.

8

A Critical Pedagogy of Embodied Education

Introduction

This research has presented the rich and complex modes of learning that occur through the processes of social action. Current research and practice in adult education in Australia has largely underemphasized social action and radical adult education as fields of inquiry, ensuring this epistemology of learning remains in its infancy (Branagan & Boughton 2003). This research has demonstrated that the learning of activists is holistic and situated in practice. It provides insight into how all adults learn not only in activism, but also through the daily business of developing knowledge and skill by being in the world. This chapter summarizes the key findings of the research, referring back to the central research question: "What are the stages and processes of learning and identity formation for activists engaged in social action?"

A summary of the research findings is provided and with a particular focus on the holistic, embodied, and social nature of activists' learning and acquisition of knowledge. The typology of circumstantial and lifelong activists is revisited to show the similarities and differences in learning in these two groups of activists. This concluding chapter explores the implications for future practice by outlining the facilitating conditions that are necessary for activists to learn effectively. I analyze the contribution to knowledge that this study makes by demonstrating the critical ontology of activists, revealing that their learning is both mindful and embodied. This research is, in itself, a process of social change. It outlines the extraordinary learning of activists and contributes to knowledge in the epistemology of radical adult education, and social movement learning. I argue strongly that the epistemology of radical adult education should no longer remain on the margins of adult education. If we have insight to understand the facilitating conditions for activists' learning, we will be able to build stronger social movements, community groups, solidarity networks and popular education movements.

The Typology of Lifelong and Circumstantial Activists

This research sought to find out the differences and similarities in learning for two groups of activists. It described the newcomers to practice—the circumstantial activists—who were protesters but not always aligned with social and political movements. Their learning was contrasted with the learning of the lifelong activists—those activists who commenced practice from an early age, usually in adolescence. As Jasper (2009) reminds us, there are protesters who are situated outside the learning practices of social movements, and further research is required in order to fully understand these protesters, and their motivations for taking action. This research has demonstrated that, while there are similarities in the two groups' knowledge and skill development, there are also distinct differences. For example, both groups' learning is mindful and embodied; they learn to think critically about the world around them, but their learning is significantly driven by the emotions. Early socialization and identity formation tend to occur incrementally for the lifelong activists in the social space of student unions. These activists are very much a part of social movements in their area of social change, and participate and identify as movement members. In contrast, circumstantial activists' learning practices are rapid. They often participate in activism following a significant life event, a personal crisis, an illness, their disability, a divorce, or a space in midlife that has been the impetus for them to participate in protest. Generally, there is a sense of moral obligation to act, which has led them to become involved in activism. These activists do not always identify with social movements and many remain on the periphery of social movements and activist groups. There are, however, some exceptions to the typology and some activists, like *Catherine*, have now been involved in activism for some time, taking on some of the characteristics of practice and dispositions associated with lifelong activists.

Activists' Stages and Phases of Learning (Both Groups)

As this research has demonstrated, the daily business of activism in all of its complexity proved a fertile space and place for learning to occur. For activists engaged in social activism, the social dimension of learning is important. By socializing with other activists and observing others in their practice they develop a critical ontological praxis. This framework is often then passed on through mentoring newcomers to activism. The study has revealed that both lifelong and circumstantial activists can be mentored by more experienced activists who have practiced over a longer period of time, sometimes over a lifetime.

Early Learning, Religion, Values and Ethics

As this research has outlined, lifelong activists are able to develop their skill and knowledge over a long period of time. For many of the lifelong activists, exposure to religious teachings, often those of the Catholic Church, provided an introduction to discourses of benevolence, charity, and helping the poor. These discourses of morality, alleviating poverty, being a good person, and helping others were constructions of an identity of "doing good." For many of the lifelong activists such as Cam, *Max*, Felicity, and *Rose*, the religious discourse of Catholicism were embedded in their childhood. Others were also influenced by religious contexts; Jorge went to a Catholic school; Garry's parents were orthodox Jews. Differently, Jeannie claims her father was a humanist. Most of those who recounted the teachings and experiences of a religious upbringing are, however, now no longer religious. Yet, the influences of these religious discourses cannot be discounted in understanding the construction of a corporeal schema of benevolence and charity, and the development of a sense of social justice in most of these activists. Even though religion may have been rejected by most of the lifelong activists, those early lessons still resonated with them. Older research by McAdam (1986) also revealed that those who had some form of exposure to religion were more likely to participate in activism and social change and this study confirms those findings.

Similarly, many of the circumstantial activists had exposure to religious teachings and frameworks of understanding. Like the lifelong activists, few of the circumstantial activists continue to actively practice the faith taught to them in childhood. *Eva, Catherine, Grace,* and Tricia, were all exposed to the Catholic Church at an early age, although none of these women remain practising Catholics. Like the lifelong activists in this study, they have reconstructed their religious discourses into humanistic beliefs and a commitment to social justice. It appears from the research that knowledge about values and ethics are influential in the formation of activists' ontology, especially their motivations and desire to act for social change. Others such as Cam, *Jonathan,* and *Kerry,* described their spirituality in terms of a connection to the land, place, or the natural environment. *Jonathan* and Cam spoke about the importance of living an ethical life; they are both committed to the philosophy of nonviolence. *Kerry,* in particular, has a spiritual connection to land and place, because of her belongingness to ancient peoples, the Australian Aborigines. The research has demonstrated that theological values have been important in the early learning of these organizers. Philosophical ideas such as ethics and humanism have also been important in forming the early foundation of learning for activists. There is also a spiritual dimension to some of the activists' early learning. Reflecting back in terms of the stages and phases of learning and identity formation for activists, it is clear from this research that philosophical, spiritual, and religious values form the foundations of activists' epistemology.

Learning Community Development Practice

Activists learn foundation skills in community development. These are sometimes learned formally through community development studies, but more often learned on the job and through socialization with other activists in practice. Informally acquired knowledge and skill are nevertheless similar to those gained through formal community development courses and study. Activists learn foundational community development skills such as interpersonal communication, both verbal and written. Some activists, including Garry, Terry, Cam, *Catherine, Eva, Rose,* and Felicity, learned to speak publicly and became highly skilled in using the media,. Most activists learned about politics and systems of government. Some learned case and systems advocacy and about legal systems that are useful for legislative reform and change (Ife & Tesoriero 2006).

Most of the activists learned communication skills through the hard work of learning in groups. They developed awareness of and understanding about group dynamics, leadership skills, conflict resolution, organizational dynamics, and governance. All activists had had some involvement in small community groups, community-based organizations, or larger NGOs and peak organizations. Some of the circumstantial activists such as Tim, *Andrew,* and *Grace* had never been associated with community groups until midlife when they became deeply involved in protest. Their learning therefore entailed some experience of frustration as they learned for the first time about the democratic and undemocratic processes that may occur in any community context.

Through the job of activism, many of the more seasoned lifelong activists also acquired sophisticated event management skills, such as how to manage a huge crowd, how to run a large scale public rally, how to deal with police, manage the campaign speakers, entertainment, food, drink stalls, and so on. The skills associated with the management of these large-scale events are primarily learned on the job of activism, by being involved in numerous public rallies and campaigns, sometimes over many years.

Embodied Practice

A key finding of this research is the embodied nature of activists' learning. Activists are mindful and embodied learners, their corporeality developed through socializing with other activists or simply through being in the life world of practice (Merleau-Ponty 1962). This book has critiqued the history of rationalism and the dominance of this way of knowing in the epistemology of education and adult education more particularly. The focus on the mind, cognition and intelligence in the way adults learn has historically denied the embodied and corporeal learning of activists. Both groups of activists have demonstrated that they are knowledgeable and experiential learners. They bring their constituted experiences of education, both positive and negative, to their learning. We need to remember that adult learners are rich sites of knowledge, insightful about their learning needs, and their capacity to take on new knowledge is dynamic because they are agentic. Activists act with agency and purpose, demonstrating intentionality in their learning. The research has found that the literature and analysis of learning in radical adult education has focused primarily on a rationalist ontology—the mind, the intelligence, and the thinking process of adult activists—often at the cost of understanding their experiential, practical, and constructivist knowledge developed through practice.

The Symbolic Use of the Body

Underrepresented in the theorizing on radical adult education is the symbolic use of the body in protest. Activists use their intelligent bodies purposefully in protest. They use music, performance, song, dance, poetry, and humor in their social change work, sometimes forming a complex repertoire of skills that go beyond verbal communication and speech associated actions. The body can be used to portray a particular narrative or role relating to social issues. The symbolic protest of climbing a tree in an environmental blockade, or participating in a picket line or blockade with hundreds of other activists, linking arms to prevent the police from breaking the protest, is skillful use of the body. It requires a physical presence and emotional agency to be successful; mind, body and emotions in action (Crossley 2001, 2002). Terry Hicks's protest in New York offered perhaps the most powerful example of the body's symbolic use in protest, although a number of activists, including Tim and *Catherine*, made notable and effective use of bodies on a mass scale. Activists developed skills through the symbolic use of the body, and in doing so, they gained a feel for the mastery of the game of activism, its dispositions and practices (Bourdieu 1977, 2000). This, again, is Merleau-Ponty's (1962) mind in action and confirms Crossley's (2001) observation of humans being both mindful and embodied agents.

Mentors

One of the important findings of this research is the role that mentors play in passing on knowledge and skill to the novice activists. Almost all of the activists have been mentored by other more experienced activists. Mentors encourage activists to reflect on their practice, suggesting strategies and tactics that can be used in a campaign. The activists who were mentored expressed their admiration for the skillful practice of the more experienced activist. Having access to their knowledge assisted them in honing existing skills and encouraged them to learn more. The research has demonstrated that both groups of activists have benefited from mentoring processes and, as a consequence, mentoring processes should certainly be encouraged in activist learning contexts.

Critically Reflexive Ontology

This research has shown that activists learn to think critically about the world around them, employing reason and high order cognition.

They learn to develop a framework of resistance, including the capacity to understand systemic oppression, government systems, financial, political, economic, and social policy processes. They learn about machinations of government and the complexity of the political system. Yet, as in Merleau-Ponty's (1962) mind in action, they think critically in their intelligent bodies. They are reflexive about their practices and this reflexivity is intrinsically connected to how they feel about an issue, hence the emotions are crucial to their reflexivity. The activists in this study have demonstrated the ability to be reflective about their practices and, through reflection, they are able to change, alter or remake their practice in order to be more effective and successful. This critical reflexivity is not some form of self-indulgent superficial reflection, but a deeper level of learning that comes through restless and impatient attention to the detail of their practice and that of others (Schön 1983; Brookfield 2005). This metalearning is a skill that is frequently used by all of the activists.

Situated Learning in the Site of Activism

All of the activists learned through socialization with other activists in practice, through the situated site of activism in community groups, students unions, NGOs, or by being involved with solidarity networks, direct action protest, and large social movements. Activists need other activists to socialize with so that they can learn through observation and practice. Significant friendships were formed and powerful and useful networks made as activists socialized and worked with one another. Lave and Wenger's (1991) "community of practice" reminds us of the importance and significance of the social site as a space and a place for learning to occur. It is now known that a majority of the knowledge and skills that we acquire comes from going about our daily work. This development of skills and expertise in the social space of activism is no different for activists and is vital in understanding their learning. Some NGOs and community groups encouraged reflective and evaluative practices that allowed activists such as Cam, *Jonathan*, *Rose,* and Felicity to really develop the dispositions of reflexivity. Activists rarely act alone. They need to practice with others in order to be effective in bringing about social change. Activists, through practicing with one another, develop an intrinsic feel for the game of activism, its strategies, dispositions and techniques, and its habits and practices (Bourdieu 1984).

Differences between Lifelong and Circumstantial Activists

Lifelong Activists' Emotional Management

Humans are emotional beings, and the emotions are central to any learning process.

Embodied feelings and emotions such as passion, desire, and anger are all present in activists' learning and are sometimes the motivation for acting in the first place. Lifelong activists learned how to manage these emotions (Hochschild 1979, 1997) to sustain their motivation, and also learned how to use the emotions as a part of the theatre of protest. Emotions were deliberately evoked at times, to create an environment of solidarity and resistance in the midst of protest. In addition, emotional management was used intentionally to undermine the tactics and strategies of the opposition.

Circumstantial Activists and the Emotions

The emotions that drove circumstantial activists were, however, more disruptive and explosive, and included feelings of anger, disappointment, or betrayal. They also referred frequently to feeling passionate or committed to an issue, but it has been revealed in the research that it was the intense and unfamiliar outburst of emotions that gave circumstantial activists the agency and the desire to act when they may not have acted before. These initially disruptive emotions drove the circumstantial activists to develop, very rapidly, the new knowledge needed to practice effectively. Some of the circumstantial activists subsequently learned to put their feelings into the background during later negotiations for change.

Circumstantial Activists' Reflexivity

This research found that circumstantial activists are frequently reflexive because their learning is so rapid. They are frequently on a learning edge, experiencing anxiety about what they do not know and, more importantly, what they need to know in order to be successful. Activists' reflexivity, fostered through discussion with other activists, through reading and writing, and through observing other activists' poor and skillful practice, allows them to hone their knowledge and skill, creating an environment of constant renewal of praxis. However, this critical thinking in intelligent bodies, connecting mind, body, and emotions in learning, results in a highly skilled practice. This has implications for adult education pedagogy and this finding of the research draws attention to the importance of reflexivity to revise, renew, and remake the practices of adult learners.

Lifelong Activists' Apprenticeship in Student Unions, Organizations and Societies

The situated site of the student union, clubs, political associations, and societies was a space and place for early learning of lifelong activists, of which circumstantial activists had no experience. The student union, its social environment, discourses, meetings, strategy groups, campaigning, and action groups formed a central experiential learning ground where lifelong activists could develop their practice. The only lifelong activist who was not involved in student politics, clubs, or associations of some form at university was Jeannie, yet she nevertheless socialized with many students through SOS and the campaigns against the Vietnam War and conscription.

In the student union, a microcosm of Australian politics, with its factions of "left" and "right" groups, political processes were played out in the daily business of student activism. This apprenticeship learning in activism within this social space of the student unions was crucial in the development of an activist epistemology. Exposure over some years to an activist culture within the student union and to activists' groups outside the student union allowed master practitioners to pass on their knowledge, skills, and expertise to the newcomers to activism. The early exposure to activism laid the foundation of a critical activist ontology in lifelong activists' early years of practice. They were able to develop a habitus of practice, which developed incrementally through participating in this social space (Bourdieu 1977, 2000). In recent years, there have been significant changes to the political environment of student unions, arguably resulting in rather less politicized student associations that may have implications for the development of future generations of activists.

Circumstantial Activists' Rapid Learning in "Hot Action"

Circumstantial activists' early stages of learning are fundamentally different to the slow building of a corporeal schema among lifelong activists. Most of the circumstantial activists developed an emotional connection to an issue, which precipitated their motivation to act and become involved in activism. For some, it was an important and significant event that exposed them to the necessity for taking action, for others a space became available in midlife after a divorce or a troubled marriage. For some others, their physical disability was the impetus for them to become involved in disability activism. The learning edge for these activists is enormous, they must develop knowledge rapidly in order to be on top of the issue or, as some claim, in order to get back into their comfort zone. This has enormous implications for adult education and, in particular, the harnessing and cultivation of passion and desire in promoting learning.

Early knowledge development for the circumstantial activists is often done through self-reading and learning. Circumstantial activists such as *Grace* and Tim found the new technology of the internet an important source of information. Circumstantial activists' immersion into community groups, action groups, and strategy meetings was also an important site for learning. They, like the lifelong activists, learn foundational community development skills such as personal development skills, communication skills in public speaking, group work skills, and advocacy skills. These skills are primarily learned "on the job" of activism.

Lifelong Activists, Learning to "Become" an Activist

The research has demonstrated that learning is a process of identity change. Identity change was a common element across both groups of activists; they were changed in some way because of their learning. Most of the lifelong activists identified themselves as activists; others acknowledged a change in their identity following their involvement in a social or political issue. Some activists lamented their identity change from "activist" to "lobbyist" or "advocate" although they continued to identify with the practices of activists. Some of the activists disassociated from some of the perceived negative dispositions of other activists' undemocratic organizing and discrimination toward some activists. There was a perception that some movements did not have a duty of care to other movement members. Sexist behaviors that excluded women activists from being active in social movements were alienating to some. Nevertheless, it appears from the research that lifelong activists are more likely to be immersed in the identification processes of being an activist, and this identification is formed early in adolescence. They generally identify themselves as members of social movements.

Circumstantial Activists' Identity and Peripherality

Circumstantial activists do not always identify themselves as activists, and they rarely identify as members of social movements, although they may have other identificatory expressions of why they are involved in protest. For example, some identify as a concerned parent or a concerned resident. While some circumstantial activists participate in social movements, it is piecemeal and not always ongoing. For example, *Eva, Bahar,* and *Grace* have little to do with social movements and they equivocate about being "activists" because of what they perceive as the radical practices of social movements. Tim participates in the climate change movement, but does not identify as a "greenie" and is not involved in other social movements. Terry remains on the periphery of social movements, preferring to acknowledge other groups who assisted his campaign as support groups, rather than acknowledging the connections they may have had to wider movements for civil liberties or human rights. *Andrew* is involved with disability rights in NGOs. Only *Catherine* and Tricia have immersed themselves into the practices of social movements and are involved in a range of different groups and social movements. For some activists, the identificatory dispositions of the group are alienating to them and thwart their full immersion in the movement. They remain on the periphery of the practice and never fully become engaged in social movements. If learning is a process of becoming, then social movements need to be more inclusive to the newcomers to protest, especially if they want to engage new movement members.

Facilitating a Critical Pedagogy of Activism: A Way Forward

How can we develop a critical pedagogy that engages explicitly with relations of power and gives prominence to the collective learning in popular education and social movements for progressive social change? This research has shown that critical pedagogies' broad premise of education for social change must be aligned with social and popular education movements, for social justice.

This book has demonstrated that learning in activism is both mindful and embodied. Philosophers, for centuries, have sought to explore what are the necessary conditions for learning to occur. How do we gain knowledge and what conditions lay the foundations for learning?

As this research has observed, activists' pedagogy has previously been viewed through a prism of rationalism, a Cartesian exploration of the mindful cognition and critical intelligence of activists (Foley 1999; Branagan & Boughton 2003). This research has demonstrated activists' learning is multidimensional; there is much to be learned from their mindful and embodied practice.

We look to Bourdieu's (1977, 2000) notion of "practice" to provide a way forward in facilitating activists' important pedagogy. Bourdieu (1984), who has written about the development of dispositions, practices, cultures, and habitus, has outlined the cultural and intellectual capital derived through our positioning in the world. He encourages sociologists and social scientists to move away from dualist constructions of knowledge, from either/or ways of knowing to merely talk about practice (Bourdieu 1977, 2000). He claims we are trapped in the social sciences with discussion about subjectivity versus objectivism and objectivist knowledge versus practical knowledge (Bourdieu 1977). This is particularly interesting when we consider Bourdieu's earlier work, which very much focused on objectivist modes of knowledge (Bourdieu & Passeron 1977). Yet, Bourdieu's reflexivity changed him; there was a fundamental change to his own scholarship, a turn took place in his theorizing. The shift led him to move from his structuralism to contemplate practice. In *Outline of a Theory of Practice,* he writes about the shift that took place in his work when he could no longer write as a "blissful structuralist" (Bourdieu 1977, p. 9). This turn in his own theorization came when he started to observe through his anthropological studies of peasant practices in Algeria that his objectivist research could no longer account for the practices that he saw taking place:

> For it was becoming apparent to me that to account for the quasi miraculous and therefore somewhat incredible necessity, without any organizing intention, that was revealed by analysis, one had to look at the dispositions, or more precisely the body schema to find the ordering principles capable of orienting practices in a way that is unconscious and systematic (Bourdieu 1977, p. 10).

He found that objectivist modes of knowledge excluded a feel for the social game, the mastery of a practice in all its complexity, the "body schema" of the practice (Bourdieu 1990). His own empirical research began to record and reflect the daily practices of people being in the world. They were no longer subjects but living people, going about their daily practices. This was affirmed in his later research in his book *Weight of the World*, where his research spoke about the experiences of individuals he was working with and the sensitivity with which sociologists must practice themselves. These lived experiences of people in impoverished social situations led Bourdieu to become immersed in the narratives of their lives (Bourdieu 1999). Perhaps, he became concerned with their empirical expressiveness of being. He told the narratives of their lives exposed to poverty, homelessness, mental illness, with a grace and tone that remind us that we are dealing as philosophers and sociologists with the corporeality of the human experience. O'Loughlin (2006) reminds us that the empathy that we develop for others is often created through the corporeal nature of our own existence. We are embodied humans after all, speaking about our other fellow embodied human beings. This leads me to reflect on the importance of writing this research, and the significance of promoting activists' pedagogy, because it is inherently about a broader project of progressing their social change work. It is through activists' complexity of practice, their resistance within and against the state that ultimately this project of social change occurs. Could there possibly be a more important pedagogy than this act of doing and being in the world for social change? Like Bourdieu's move from objectivist modes of knowledge to outline a theory of practice, the activists in this study remind us of the importance of moving away from the prism of rationalism to move towards an embodied radical adult education.

This leads me to discuss practice, and how activists can pass on their embodied knowledge to other activists. Facilitating learning is necessary, but it does not have to be in a formal training environment. Perhaps this is why Whelan (2002) has found that formal training and education in activist organizations is rare. If a social space is developed and provided for activists to learn socially from one another, knowledge will be acquired and passed down from one activist to another. Lave and Wenger's model of situated learning in a community of practice provides a useful model for learning, particularly if power relations that can thwart learning are observed. I have outlined in chapter 7 a community of practice model that can be strengthened using Bourdieu's theory of habitus.

The development of a formal and strategic mentoring process may well promote activists' learning rather more than the current, ad hoc processes that depend upon activists managing to find someone to observe and watch. NGOs, organizations, and community groups should encourage reflexivity and evaluation practices, because this metalearning assists activists to develop expertise. Activists' groups may well benefit from training in community development skills such as group communication processes, advocacy, and social policy.

There is a need for further research investigating why some of the circumstantial activists do not identify with or completely immerse themselves into social movements; they remain on the periphery of these organizations because they are alienated from some of their dispositions, practices and habitus.

The Intelligent Body

What this research reminds us, is the importance of bringing a focus on the body back into learning, that, as Crossley claims, humans are both mindful and embodied human beings. Merleau-Ponty affirmed this in his book *Phenomenology of Perception*—we develop knowledge through being in the world and this is not only a cognitive act. Learners are both mindful and feeling human beings. Dewey knew this when he wrote about experiential learning, he knew that learners' constituted experiences influenced further educational experiences— learning was inherently experiential, it was about doing and being done to. The activists in this research remind us of the importance of agency in learning—when we are passionate about an issue, a story, an idea, a philosophy, a theory, or a case study, we engage in education and our learning is much deeper and richer because of this. Marx knew this when he spoke about thinking dialectically—he reminded us that in looking back on history we could understand and interpret the present, by doing this we could also act to change the future.

Freire's Legacy

In pedagogy of the oppressed, Freire revolutionized our understanding of education by drawing attention to rationalism and behaviorism, the foundations of a system of education where the teacher was the keeper of knowledge, a powerful player in a banking system of education that largely ignored the agency of learners and saw them as passive recipients of knowledge. My undergraduate social action students know this when they are first introduced to his writing and are shocked that their own learning thus far has represented a banking system of education. They frequently speak to me about how they do not learn in this way, and are surprised that a large amount of their educational experiences, so far, have been based on a model of learning that has little regard for their own embodied knowledge, for their own constituted experiences that they bring to learning through being-in-the-world. What Freire has encouraged us to do is to engage in dialogue, that learning must be a dialogical process with one another and not an isolated act. He believed that learning was a collective process, learner to teacher, teacher to learner. As Antonia Darder (2009) has claimed, for Freire teaching and learning is an "act of love,"

> For Freire, a liberatory education could never be conceived without a profound commitment to humanity.... I must point out that his notion of humanity was not merely some simplistic or psychologized notion of "having positive self-esteem," but rather a deeply reflective interpretation of the dialectical relationship between our cultural existence as individuals and our political and economic existence as social beings. (pp. 567–68)

Freire believed that education had the power to transform ordinary people's lives. That is, as people became aware of their own circumstances of disadvantage and inequality, they would become able to act collectively to change it. As Freire (1970) so notably claimed,

> Knowledge emerges only through invention and re-invention, through the restless, impatient, continuing, hopeful inquiry human beings pursue in the world, with the world, and with each other. (p.29)

In *Pedagogy of the Oppressed,* Freire introduced a discourse that focused on the agency of the learner, called "conscientization"—he was working among the poor in Brazil, and he argued that if learners opened up to their own and others' humanity, they would have to act collectively to change their own oppression. Of course, this was a threatening proposition for those in power at the time, and Freire was exiled because of it. This term of conscientization, and its contemporary corollary now known as "empowerment," formed the foundation of Frere's pedagogy and has influenced the practices of professions that deal with disadvantaged and marginalized people such as critical community development work, social work, youth work, international development work, human rights work, and the practices of social movements and popular education struggles around the globe. Freire also warned against what he perceived as "naive activism," activism that was entirely associated with theorization or without acting to change the world. Freire, like Marx before him, believed activism must be entwined with action, that theory without practice or action was self-indulgent. The point of progressive activism, of course, as Marx believed was to change the world. Freire used the term "praxis" to define an activism that is inherently embodied and actively engaged in education for social change. We can see his philosophy of education at work in Chiapas in Mexico with the Indigenous Zapatistas, in the reconciliation movements with Indigenous Australians, in the recent student protest movements in Britain and Chile, in the "Arab Spring" uprisings in the Middle East, and in the workers protests in Wisconsin, where the collective struggle for social change is flourishing.

More recently, we see his ideas being practiced pedagogically in the activism of the protesters of the Occupy Movements, who have challenged the dominance of neoliberal economic fiscal policy, now so dominant in both the developed and developing world. The mobilizations of these movements around the globe are embodying a praxis grounded in problem-posing dialogue so resonant of Freire's call for an activism that puts theory into practice.

A Final Word

The significance of the learning practices of activists engaged in social change has been outlined in this book. In an environment of lifelong learning in education, which focuses on core graduate attributes in students, like the development of communication skills and problem-solving and critical-thinking skills, there is much to learn from these activists' important pedagogy. The issues these activists have been involved with are wide and varied. Their activism has included the areas of corporate globalization, the environment, climate change, asylum seekers and refugees, civil liberties, urban development, and discrimination on issues relating to gender, disability, and sexuality. They also include Indigenous politics and the rights of refugees, some of the most important social and political issues in Australia and around the world. This research has demonstrated that activists learn from one another through socialization and it has shown that activists' learning is not rational but embodied. It has also demonstrated the differences in learning and identity formation between the circumstantial and lifelong activists.

The importance of the research cannot be underestimated, particularly as it gives insight into the skill and knowledge that activists need, to practice effectively. This research has implications for campaign groups, community organizations, NGOs, and social movements. The significance of activists' work must be recognized in a world where social and political action will be needed more than ever before, especially if we take seriously our custodian role for a world and a planet that will need to sustain future generations.

It is little wonder in the present environment of adult education that the richness of activists' learning should provide us with insight into their holistic work as practitioners. I have argued the practices of these activists are not only social but embedded in the everyday interactions of practice, whereby learning is inherently connected to the emotions and is driven by passion, a desire to change the world, and a need to promote social justice. It is difficult to comprehend that an epistemology of learning such as this is so often neglected by educators as a legitimate form of knowing, particularly when the practices of activism are educationally so rich. It is hoped this book assists in further promoting their learning.

Notes

1 A Critical Pedagogy of Activism

1. "Ontology" is a term used to refer to philosophy or the study of theory of being.
2. This website from Amnesty International outlines some of the key concerns of the Van Nguyen campaign: http://action.amnesty.org.au/news/comments/261/.
3. Heather Osland was released from prison in 2005 after serving more than nine years in jail for the murder of her husband. For more information on the "Release Heather Osland" campaign see http://home.vicnet.net.au/~rhog/.
4. "Really useful knowledge" is commonly used by educators as description for education that has social change purposes (see, for example, Johnson, 1988).
5. Kenny (2006) identifies social movements "as forms of collective action aimed at social reorganization and/or social change." They are organized "around social, cultural and environmental concerns that have become central issues in contemporary political life" (p. 50).
6. The role of the monarch's representative, the governor general of Australia, was viewed as that of a figurehead of government until the "dismissal" of the Whitlam Government in 1975. Sir John Kerr's actions called into question the exercise of power by the head of state.

2 Case Study Research

1. See the case study of Terry Hicks in chapter 7.

3 The Politics of Adult Education

1. Postmodern refers to an approach to sociology that critiques the nature and history of the enlightenment project. The postmodern concept of pastiche of ideas is relevant and pertinent to postmodern writing in education.

2. Reification as used by Lave and Wenger (1991) and Wenger (1998) relating "reification" to identity formation in a community of practice. They claim participants, (in a community of practice), often negotiated a shared repertoire of practice with one another, as they immerse themselves into a social practice. Identity in practice is defined socially not merely because it is reified in a social discourse of the self and of social categories, but also because it produces a lived experience of participation in specific communities. What narratives, categories, roles, and positions come to mean as an experience of participation is something that must be worked out in practice (Wenger 1998, p. 151). This is different to sociological interpretations of reification associated with historical materialism and popularized by Lukak's use of the term that reification is a process of making something thing-like, particularly in capitalist societies and with regard to the exchange of goods. Reification thus is seen as a natural process rather than a process of exploitation, lacking examination of social relations (Abercrombie, Hill, & Turner, 2006).

4 The Lifelong Activists

1. The ALP, led by Bob Hawke, was in power from 1983–1991.
2. St. Vincent de Paul Society is a charitable organization in Australia and a large Catholic NGO.
3. Bob Santamaria led a split of the Australian Labour Party (ALP) by forming the Democratic Labor Party (DLP) and taking a majority of Catholic ALP members with him. The DLP was opposed to the labor movement's stand on communism. Consequently, the DLP had a preference for conservative parties for many years, preventing the ALP from forming government.
4. Joh Bjelke-Peterson was the leader of the Conservative National Party in Queensland, holding office from 1968 to 1987.
5. ALP politician and premier of Victoria since 2007.
6. "Culture jamming" describes tactics that aim to subvert, thwart, or disrupt dominant cultural practices and discourses. This may include, for example, refiguring logos, advertisements, or product images to produce ironic or satirical political commentaries.
7. A protest action undertaken by Rainbow Families Victoria.
8. The Democratic Socialist Party, now known as the Democratic Socialist Perspective, is a political organisation. Its purpose is to promote revolutionary change to capitalist systems in society (see http://www.dsp.org.au/).
9. The ALP campaigned against the damming of the Franklin River.
10. The World Economic Forum was held in Melbourne on September 11, 2000.
11. Bioregionalism is a political, environmental, and cultural system that promotes sustainability of consumption and use of local goods, services, and produce. One of the first writers to use the term was Peter Berg (1996).

12. The missions were often controlled by religious organizations. The movement of Aborigines at this time was restricted and monitored. Permits were required for them to leave the reserves.
13. HSC was the highest secondary school qualification students could complete before going on to university; it has now been replaced by the Victorian Certificate of Education (VCE).

5 The Circumstantial Activists

1. TAFE—Tertiary and Further Education is the name for publicly provided colleges that provide apprenticeships, certificate, and diploma-level courses.
2. Formerly vice president of the United States, Al Gore has become well known for his climate change action campaign and narration of the documentary, *An Inconvenient Truth*, which outlined the processes of climate change and their impact on the world.
3. Mamoud Habib was another Australian citizen imprisoned by the United States at Guantanamo Bay.
4. The documentary was produced by Curtis Levy. A synopsis of the film is available at: http://www.documentaryaustralia.com.au/da/caseStudies/details.php?recordID=16
5. In 2003, the Howard government introduced a policy of mandatory detention for refugees and asylum seekers. Men, women, and children were held in detention centers while their applications for refuge or asylum were being processed.

6 Embodied Learning

1. The sociology of the body is an important site of study for sociologists around the world. While I draw on some theory and literature from this area on sociology and the body, the literature is chosen because it has some relationship to social movements and activism or adult education. For more detailed examination of the sociology of the body see Crossley, N. (2002). *Making Sense of Social Movements* (Buckingham, UK: Open University Press).
2. "Zapatismo" is the term used for the culture of the social movement of the Zapatistas, the people formerly of Chiapas (see Couch 2004, for example).

Bibliography

Adorno, T. W. 1969, *The Authoritarian Personality*. New York: Norton.
Adorno, T. W., R. Tiedemann, & ebrary Inc. 2001, *Kant's Critique of Pure Reason (1959)*. Stanford, CA: Stanford University Press.
Alinsky, S. 1971, *Rules for Radicals: A Pragmatic Primer for Realistic Radicals*. New York: Vintage Books.
Allan, B. & K. Shields, 1998, "Activist Empowerment and Learning: Strategic Questioning, a Tool for Creating Change and for Reflection," *The Bulletin of Good Practice in Adult & Continuing Education*, vol. 4, 36–42.
Allman, P. 1999, "Revolutionary Social Transformation—Democratic Hopes, Political Possibilities and Critical Education," *Critical Studies in Education and Culture Series*. London: Bergin & Garvey.
Allman, P. & J. Wallis, 1995, "Challenging the Postmodern Condition: Radical Adult Education for Critical Intelligence," in M. Mayo & J. Thompson (eds), *Adult Learning, Critical Intelligence and Social Change*. Leicester, UK: National Institute of Adult Continuing Education.
Althusser, L. 1969, *For Marx*. Hammondsworth, UK: Penguin.
Anderson, D. M. Brown, & P. Rushbrook, 2004, "Vocational Education and Training," in G. Foley (ed.), *Dimensions of Adult Learning: Adult Education and Training in a Global Era*. Corws Nest, NSW: Allen & Unwin, pp. 234–50.
Armstrong, P. & N. Miller, 2006, "Whatever Happened to Social Purpose? Adult Educators' Stories of Political Commitment and Change," *International Journal of Lifelong Education*, vol. 25, no. 3, 291–305.
Baxter, S. S., J. Williams, & Ebooks Corporation, 1997, *Emotions in Social Life: Critical Themes and Contemporary Issues*, Routledge, (http://w2.vu.edu.au/library/EBookSearch/files/EBL.pdf).
Beckett, D. 2008, "Holistic Competence: Putting Judgements First," *Asian Pacific Educational Review*, vol. 9, no. 1, 21–30.
Beckett, D. & P. Hager, 2000, "Making Judgements as the Basis for Workplace Learning: Towards an Epistemology of Practice," *International Journal of Lifelong Education,*, vol. 19, no. 4 (July–August 2000) 300–11.
——— 2002, *Life, Work, and Learning: Practice and Postmodernity*. London; New York: Routledge.

Beckett, D. & G. Morris, 2003, "Performing Identities: The New Focus on Embodied Adult Learning," in P. Kell, M. Singh & S.S. (eds), *Adult Education @ 21st Century*. New York: Lang pp. xxv–299.

———2004, "Learning for/at Work: Somali Women 'Doing it for Themselves,'" *Journal of Workplace Learning*, vol. 16, no. 1/2, 75–82.

Bell, L. A., S. Washington, G. Weinsteing, & B. Love, 2003, "Knowing Ourselves as Instructors," in A. Darder, M. Baltadano & R. Torres (eds), *The Critical Pedagogy Reader*. New York: RoutledgeFalmer pp. 464–78.

Billett, S. (ed.) 2004, "Learning Through Work, Workplace Participatory Practices" in *Workplace Learning in Context*. London: Routledge.

Boud, D. & J. Garrick, 1999, *Understanding Learning at Work*. London: Routledge.

Boughton, B. 2005, "The Worker's University: Australia's Marx Schools," in J. Crowther, V. Galloway & I. Martin (eds), *Popular Education: Engaging the Academy: International Perspectives*. Leicester, UK: NIACE, pp. 100–109.

Boughton, B., T. Taksa, & M. Welton, 2004, "Histories of Adult Education and Training," in G. Foley (ed.), *Dimensions of Adult Learning: Adult Education & Training in a Global Era*. Sydney: Allen & Unwin.

Bourdieu, P. 1977, "Outline of a Theory of Practice," *Cambridge Studies in Social Anthropology*. Vol. 16, Cambridge, UK; New York: Cambridge University Press.

———1984, *Distinction: A Social Critique of the Judgement of Taste*. Harvard, MA: Harvard University Press.

———1990, *In Other Words: Essays Towards a Reflexive Sociology*. Cambridge, UK: Polity Press in association with Basil Blackwell.

———1998, *Practical Reason*. Stanford, CA: Stanford University Press.

———1999, *The Weight of the World: Social Suffering in Contemporary Society*. Oxford, UK: Polity.

———2000, *The Logic of Practice*. Stanford, CA: Stanford University Press.

Bourdieu, P. & J-C Passeron, 1977, *Reproduction in Education, Society and Culture*. London; Beverly Hills, CA: Sage Publications.

Branagan, M. 2007, "The Last Laugh: Humour in Community Activism," *Community Development Journal*, vol. 42, no. 4, 470–81.

Branagan, M. & B. Boughton, 2003, "How Do You Learn to Change the World? Learning and Teaching in Australian Protest Movements." *Australian Journal of Adult Learning*, vol. 43, no. 3, 346–60.

Brookfield, S. 1987, *Developing Critical Thinkers: Challenging Adults to Explore Alternative Ways of Thinking and Acting*. Milton Keynes, UK: Open University Press.

——— 2005, *The Power of Critical Theory for Adult Learning and Teaching*. Maidenhead, UK: Open University Press.

Brookfield, S. 2000, "Transformative Learning as Ideology Critique," in J. Mezirow & Associates (eds), *Learning as Transformation*. San Francisco, CA: Jossey-Bass, pp. 125–47.

Brown, G. & Pickerill, J. 2009, "Space for Emotion in the Spaces of Activism," *Emotion, Space and Society*, vol. 2, no. 1, 24–35.

Burgmann, V. 2003, *Power, Profit and Protest, Australian Social Movements and Globalisation*. Crows Nest, NSW: Allen & Unwin.

Chappell, C., C. Rhodes, N. Solomon, M.Tennant, & L. Yates, 2003, *Reconstructing the Lifelong Learner—Pedagogy and Identity in Individual, Organisational and Social Change*. London; New York: RoutledgeFalmer.

Charmaz, K. 2000, "Grounded Theory: Objectivists and Constructivist Methods," in N. Denkin & Y. Lincoln (eds), *Handbook of Qualitative Research*,, 2nd edn. Thousand Oaks, CA: Sage Publications, pp. 509–36.

Chase, S. 2000, *The Education and Training Needs of Environmental Activists and Organizers*. New York: University of New England.

Clough, P. & C. Nutbrown, 2002, *A Students Guide to Methodology*. London: Sage Publications.

Colley, H., D. James, M. Tedder, & K. Dement, 2003, "Learning as Becoming in Vocational Education and Training: Class, Gender and the Role of Vocational Habitus," *Journal of Vocational Education and Training*, vol. 55, no. 4, 389–406.

Couch, J. 2004, "This Is What Democracy Looks Like: The Genesis, Culture and Possibilities of Anti-Corporate Activism," PhD thesis, Victoria University of Technology, 2004.

—— 2009, "From the Salt Marches to Seattle," Lecture Notes, Australian Catholic University.

Cranton, P. 1996, *Professional Development as Transformative Learning: New Perspectives for Teachers of Adults*. San Francisco, CA: Jossey-Bass.

Crossley, N. 2001, *The Social Body: Habit, Identity and Desire*. London; Thousand Oaks, CA: Sage Publications.

—— 2002, *Making Sense of Social Movements*. Buckingham, UK: Open University Press.

—— 2008, "Social Networks and Student Activism: On the Politicising Effect of Campus Connections," *The Sociological Review*, vol. 56, no. 1, 18–38.

Crowther, J., I. Martin, & V. Galloway, 2005, *Popular Education: Engaging the Academy: International Perspectives*. Leicester, UK: NIACE.

Daloz, L. 2000, "Transformative Learning for the Common Good," in J. Mezirow (ed.), *Learning As Transformation*. San Francisco, CA: Jossey-Bass.

Damasio, A. 1999, *The Feeling of What Happens: Body and Emotion in the Making of Consciousness*, 1st edn. New York: Harcourt Brace.

—— 2005, *Descartes' Error: Emotion, Reason, and the Human Brain*. London: Penguin.

Darder, A. and R. D. Torres, 2003, *After Race: Racism after Multiculturalism*. New York: New York University Press.

Darder, A. 2003, "Teaching As an Act of Love: Reflections on Paulo Freire and his Contributions to Our Lives and Our Work," in A. Darder, M. Baltadano & R. Torres (eds), *The Critical Pedagogy Reader*. New York: RoutledgeFalmer, Taylor and Francis Group, pp. 497–510.

Darder, A, M. Baltadano, & R. Torres, 2003 (eds) 2003, *The Critical Pedagogy Reader*. London: RoutledgeFalmer.

Darder, A.,M. Baltadano, & R. Torres, 2009 (eds), *The Critical Pedagogy Reader*, 2nd edn. London; New York: RoutledgeFalmer.
Debelle, P. 2003, "How Long Can Terry Hicks Keep Going?" *The Age*, August 3, 2003.
Denzin, N.K. & Y.S. Lincoln, 2000, "The Discipline and Practice of Qualitative Research," in N.K. Denzin & Y.S. Lincoln (eds.), *Handbook of Qualitative Research*, 2nd edn. Thousand Oaks, CA: Sage Publications.
Descartes, R. 1983, *Principles of Philosophy*. Boston; Hingham, MA: Reidel. Distributed by Kluwer BostonDordrecht, Holland.
Dewey, J. 1922, *Human Nature & Conduct*. New York: Henry Holt.
—— 1930, *Democracy and Education: An Introduction to the Philosophy of Education*. New York: The Macmillan Company.
—— 1937, *How We Think*. Boston: Heath.
—— 1938, 1998 ed, *Experience and Education*, The 60th anniversary edn. West Lafayette, IN: Kappa Delta Pi.
Edwards, R., S. Ranson, & M. Strain, 2002, "Reflexivity: Towards a Theory of Lifelong Learning," *International Journal of Lifelong Education*, vol. 21, no. 6, 525–36.
Engeström, Y. 2007, "Activity Theory and Workplace Learning" *Journal of Workplace Learning— Issue 6*. Bradford, UK :Emerald Group Publishing.
Engeström, Y., R. Miettinen, & R-L Punamäki-Gitai, 1999, *Perspectives on Activity Theory (Learning in Doing: Social, Cognitive and Computational Perspectives)*. Cambridge, UK; New York: Cambridge University Press.
Engeström, Y. & T. Tuomi-Gröhn, 2003, "Between School and Work: New Perspectives on Transfer and Boundary-Crossing," *Advances in Learning and Instruction Series*. Amsterdam; Boston: Pergamon.
Eraut, M. 2000, "Non-Formal Learning and Tacit Knowledge in Professional Work," *British Journal of Educational Psychology*, vol. 70, 113–36.
Eyerman, R. 2005, "How Social Movements Move—Emotions and Social Movements," in H. Flam & D. King (eds.), *Emotions and Social Movements*. Abingdon, UK: Routledge, Taylor and Francis Group, pp. 41–56.
Foley, G. 1999, *"Learning in Social Action: A Contribution to Understanding Informal Education", Global Perspectives on Adult Education and Training*. New York: Zed Books.
—— 2000, "Politicising Learning in the Workplace," *Education Links*, vol. 61–62, 12.
—— 2001, "Radical Adult Education and Learning," *International Journal of Lifelong Education*, vol. 20, no.1–2, 71–88.
—— (ed.) 2004, *Dimensions of Adult Learning: Adult Education and Training in a Global Era*. Crows Nest, NSW: Allen & Unwin.
Foley, G. 2001, *Strategic Learning: Understanding and Facilitating Organisational Change*. Sydney: Centre for Popular Education.
Foucault, M. 1977, *Language, Counter—Memory, Practice: Selected Essays and Interviews*. Ithaca, NY: Cornell University Press.
—— 1980, "Truth and Power," *Power/Knowledge: Selected Interviews and Other Writings 1972–1977*. New York: Pantheon Books.

―――― 1983, "The Subject and Power," in *Michel Foucault: Beyond Structuralism and Hermeneutics*, 2nd edn. Chicago: University of Chicago Press.
―――― 1988, "Truth, Power, Self: An Interview with Michel Foucault," in *Technologies of the Self, A Seminar with Michel Foucault*. Amherst: University of Massachusetts Press.
Friere, P. 1972a, *Cultural Action for Freedom*. Harmondsworth, UK: Penguin.
―――― 1972b, *Pedagogy of the Oppressed*. Harmondsworth, UK: Penguin.
―――― 1974, *Education for Critical Consciousness*. London: Sheed and Ward.
―――― 2005, *Education for Critical Consciousness*. New York; London: Continuum.
Freire, P. & A. M. A. Freire, 1997, *Pedagogy of the Heart*. New York: Continuum.
Freire, P., A. M. A. Freire, & D. P. Macedo, 1998, *The Paulo Freire Reader*. New York: Continuum.
Freire, P. & P. Freire, 1973, *Education for Critical Consciousness*, 1st American edn. New York: Seabury Press.
Freire, P. & I. Shor, 1987, *A Pedagogy for Liberation: Dialogues on Transforming Education*. South Hadley, MA: Basingstoke, UK: Bergin & Garvey; Macmillan.
Gee, J. P., G. Hull, & C. Lankshear, 1996, *The New Work Order, behind the Language of the New Capitalism*. Boulder, CO: Westview Press.
Ginieniewicz, J. & D. Schugurensky, 2006, *Ruptures, Continuities and Re-learning: The Political Participation of Latin Americans in Canada*. Toronto, Canada: Transformative Learning Centre, University of Toronto.
Goffman, E. 1959, *The Presentation of Self in Everyday Life*. Garden City, NY: Doubleday.
Gonczi, A. 2004, "The New Professional and Vocational Education and Training," in G. Foley (ed.), *Dimensions of Adult Learning: Adult Education and Training in a Global Era*. Crows Nest, NSW: Allen & Unwin, pp. 19–34.
Goodwin, J. & J. M. Jasper, 2009, "The Social Movements Reader: Cases and Concepts," 2nd edn., *Blackwell Readers in Sociology*. Oxford: Wiley-Blackwell.
Gore, J. 2003, "What We Can Do for You! What Can We Do for You? Struggling over Empowerment in Critical and Feminist Pedagogy,'" in A. Darder, M. Baltadano & R. Torres, 2003 (eds.), *The Critical Pedagogy Reader*. London: RoutledgeFalmer.
Gould, D. 2004, "Passionate Political Processes: Bringing Emotions Back into the Study of Social Movements," in J. M. Jasper & J. Goodwin (eds.), *Rethinking Social Movements: Structure, Meaning, and Emotion*. Lanham, MD; Oxford: Rowman & Littlefield Publishers, pp. 155–72.
Gramsci, A. 1971, *Selections From the Prison Notebooks*. New York: International Publishers.
―――― 1988, *A Gramsci Reader: Selected Writings 1916–1935*. London: Lawrence and Wishart.
Gramsci, A., D. Boothman, & ebrary Inc., 2001, *Further Selections from the Prison Notebooks*. London: Electric Book Co.
Gramsci, A. & D. Forgacs, 1988, *A Gramsci Reader: Selected Writings 1916–1935*. London: Lawrence and Wishart.

Habermas, J. 1984, *The Theory of Communicative Action: Reason and the Rationalization of Society*, vol. 1. Boston: Beacon Press.

Hager, P. 2000, "Know-How and Workplace Practical Judgement," *Journal of Philosophy of Education*, vol. 34, no. 281–296, 14.

Hochschild, A. 1979, "Emotion Work, Feeling Rules and Social Structure," *The American Journal of Sociology*, vol. 85, no. 3, 551–75.

——— 1997, "The Sociology of Emotion as a Way of Seeing," in S. Baxter & S. Williams (eds.), *Emotions in Social Life: Critical Themes and Contemporary Issues*. London: Routledge.

Hodges, D. 1998, "Participation as Dis-Identification Within a Community of Practice," *Mind, Culture and Activity*, vol. 5, no. 4, pp. 272–90.

Hodkinson, P., H. Hodkinson, K. Evans, N. Kersh, A. Fuller, L. Unwin, & P. Senker, 2004, "The Significance of Individual Biography in Workplace Learning," *Studies in the Education of Adults*, vol. Spring 2004, no. 36, Issue 1, 6–24.

Hodkinson, P. & D. James, 2003, "Transforming Leaning Cultures in Further Education," *Journal of Vocational Education and Training*, vol. 55, no. 4, 389–406.

Hollingworth, D. 2006, *Race and Racism in Australia*, 3rd edn. Melbourne: Thompson-Social Science Press.

hooks, b. 1994, *Teaching to Transgress: Education as the Practice of Freedom*. New York: Routledge.

——— 2003a, "Confronting Class in the Classroom," in A Darder, M Baltadano & R Torres, 2003 (eds.), *The Critical Pedagogy Reader*. London: RoutledgeFalmer.

——— 2003b, *Teaching Community—A Pedagogy of Hope*. New York: Routledge.

Horkheimer, M. 1974, *Eclipse of Reason*. New York: Seabury Press.

Horton, M. & P. Freire, 1990, *We Make the Road by Walking: Conversations on Education and Social Change*. Philadelphia, PA: Temple University Press.

Hunter, L. 2004, "Bringing the Body Back into Education?," *Redress*, vol. September, 2004, 2–10.

Ife, J. 2002, *Community Development: Creating Community Alternatives in an Age of Globalisation*, 2nd edn. Sydney: Pearson Education.

Ife, J. & L. Fiske, 2006, "Human Rights and Community Work, Complimentary Theories and Practices," *International Social Work*, vol. 49, no. 3, 297–308.

Ife, J. & F. Tesoriero, 2006, *Community Development—Community-Based Alternatives in an Age of Globalisation*, 3rd edn. Crows Nest, NSW: Pearson Education.

Jasper, J. 1998, "The Emotions of Protest: Affective and Reactive Emotions In and Around Social Movements," *Sociological Forum*, vol. 13, no. 3, 397–424.

——— 2009, "The Emotions of Protest," in *The Social Movements Reader Cases and Concepts*, 2nd edn. West Sussex, UK: Wiley Blackwell.

Jasper, J. & J. Goodwin, 2004, *Rethinking Social Movements: Structure, Meaning, and Emotion, People, Passions, and Power*. Lanham, MD; Oxford: Rowman & Littlefield Publishers.

Jesson, J. & M. Newman, 2004, "Radical Adult Education and Learning," in G. Foley (ed.), *Dimensions of Adult Learning: Adult Education and Training in a Global Era*. Crows Nest, NSW: Allen & Unwin.

Johnson, R. 1988, "Really Useful Knowlege, 1790–1850, Memories for Education in the 1980's," in T. Lovett (ed.), *Radical Approaches to Adult Education*. London: Routledge.

Keniston, K. 1968, *Young Radicals: Notes on Committed Youth*, 1st edn. New York: Harcourt, Brace & World.

Kenny, S. 1994, *Developing Communities for the Future– Community Development in Australia*, 1st edn. Melbourne: Nelson ITP.

—— 1999, *Developing Communities for the Future-Community Development in Australia*. Melbourne: Nelson Publishers.

—— 2006, *Developing Communities for the Future*, 3rd edn. Melbourne: Nelson Thompson.

Kincheloe, J. 2004, "Critical Pedagogy Primer," *Peter Lang Primer*. New York: P. Lang.

Kincheloe, J. & P. McLaren, 2000, "Rethinking Critical Theory and Qualitative Research," in N.K. Denzin & Y. S. Lincoln (eds.), *Handbook of Qualitative Research*, 2nd edn. Thousand Oaks, CA: Sage Publications.

Kincheloe, J. L. 2005, "Critical Constructivism Primer," *Peter Lang Primer*. New York: P. Lang.

Knowles, M. S. 1984, *Andragogy in Action*, 1st edn. San Francisco, CA: Jossey-Bass Management Series, Jossey-Bass.

Kovan, J. & J. Dirkx, 2003, "Being Called Awake: The Role of Transformative Learning In The Lives of Environmental Activists," *Adult Education Quarterly*, vol. 53, no.2, 99–118.

Lave, J. 1991, "Situated Learning In Communities of Practice," in L. Resnick, J. Levene & S. Teasley (eds), *Perspectives on Socially Shared Cognition*. Washington, DC: American Psychological Association, pp. 63–82.

—— 1996, "Teaching, as Learning, in Practice," *Mind, Culture, and Activity*, vol. 3, no. 3, 149–64.

Lave, J. & E. Wenger, 1991, *Situated Learning, Legitimate Peripheral Participation*. New York: Cambridge University Press.

Liamputtong, P. & D. Ezzy, 2005, *Qualitative Research Methods*, 2nd edn. South Melbourne: Oxford University Press.

Loughlin, K. 1996, "Learning to Change: New Dimensions," *Australian Journal of Adult & Community Education*, vol. 36, no. 1, 54–62.

Lovett, T. 1975, *Adult Education, Community Development and the Working Class*. London: Ward Lock.

Lucio-Villegas, E., D. Garcia, & L. Cowe, 2008, "Adult Education as Cultural Struggle," paper presented to SCUTREA 2008, 38th Annual Conference—Whither Adult Education in the Learning Paradigm? University of Edinburgh, United Kingdom, July 2–4, 2008.

Macionis, J. J. & K. Plummer, 2008, *Sociology: A Global Introduction*, 3rd edn. Harlow, UK: Pearson Prentice Hall.

Macy, J. 1991, *World as Lover, World as Self*. Berkeley, CA: Parallax Press.

Maddison, S. & S. Scalmer, 2006, *Activist Wisdom: Practical Knowledge and Creative Tension in Social Movements*. Sydney: University of New South Wales Press.

Maddison, S. 2009, *Black Politics: Inside the Complexity of Aboriginal Political Culture*. Crows Nest, NSW: Allen and Unwin.

Manne, R. 2004, "Sending Them Home, Refugees and the New Politics of Indifference," *Quarterly Essay*, no. 13, 2004, 1–77

Marcuse, H. 1964, *One Dimensional Man*. Boston: Beacon.

Marx, K. 1987, "Revelations Concerning the the Communist Trial in Cologne," in K. Marx & F. Engels (eds.), *Collected Works*, Vol 39: Letters 1852–55, United Kingdom, Lawrence and Wishart.

────── 1959, "The Process of Capitalist Production as a Whole," *Capital—A Critque of the Political Economy*, 1978 edn. Book three, vol. 111. Moscow: Progress Publishers

Marx, K. & F. Engels, 1967, *The Communist Manifesto*. Harmondsworth, UK: Penguin.

Mayo, M. 2005, *Global Citizens: Social Movements and the Challenge of Globalization*. London; Toronto: Zed Books; Canadian Scholars' Press Inc.

Mayo, M. & J. Thompson, (eds.) 1995, *Adult Learning, Critical Intelligence and Social Change*. Leceister, UK: The National Organisation for Adult learning.

Mayo, P. 1999, *Gramsci, Freire & Adult Education, Possibilities for Transformative Action*. London; New York: Zed Books.

────── 2006, *Learning and Social Difference. Challenges for Public Education and Critical Pedagogy* (co-authored with C. Borg). Boulder, CO: Paradigm.

McAdam, D. 1986, "Recruitment to High Risk Activism: The Case of Freedom Summer," *The American Journal of Sociology*, vol. 92, no. 1, 64–90.

McLaren, P. & J. L. Kincheloe, 2007, "Critical Pedagogy: Where Are We Now?" *Counterpoints: Studies in the Postmodern Theory of Education*, vol. 299, New York: Peter Lang.

Merleau-Ponty, M. 1962, "Phenomenology of Perception," in *International Library of Philosophy and Scientific Method*. London: Routledge.

Merleau-Ponty, M. & J. O'Neill, 1974, *Phenomenology, Language and Sociology: Selected Essays of Maurice Merleau-Ponty*. London: Heinemann Educational.

Merriam, S. 1998, *Qualitative Research and Case Study Application in Education*, Revised and expanded from Case Study Research in Education. San Francisco, CA: Josey-Bass Publishers.

Mezirow, J. 1991, *Transformative Dimensions of Adult Learning*. San Francisco, CA: Josey-Bass Publishers.

Mezirow, J. & Associates. 2000, *Learning as Transformation: Critical Perspectives on a Theory in Progress*. San Francisco, CA: Josey-Bass.

Miles, M. & A. Huberman, 1994, *Qualitative Data Analysis: An Expanded Sourcebook*, 2nd edn. Thousand Oaks, CA: Sage Publications.

Newman, M. 1994, *Defining the Enemy: Adult Education and Social Action*. Sydney, Australia: Stewart Victor Publishing.

—— 2006, *Teaching Defiance—Stories and Strategies for Activist Educators, a Book Written in Wartime*. San Francisco, CA: John Wiley & Sons Inc.

O'Loughlin, M. 2006, *Embodiment and Education*, Springer on Line Service (http://0-dx.doi.org.library.vu.edu.au/10.1007/1-4020-4588-3). http://w2.vu.edu.au/library/EBookSearch/files/Springer_E-Books_Online.pdf>.

Ollis, T. 2001, *Volunteers, Ideology and Practice—Towards A New Century of Volunteerism*. Carlton, Melbourne: Victorian Association of Social Studies Teachers, VASST.

—— 2008a, "The 'Accidental Activist': Learning, Embodiment and Action," *Australian Journal of Adult Learning*, vol. 48, no. 2, pp. 316–35.

—— 2008b, "The 'Circumstantial' Activist: Holistic Practice, Learning and Social Activism. Paper presented to SCUTREA Edinburgh, Scotland, July 2–4, 2008.

Pink, B. 2007, *Adult Learning in Australia*, edn. 42290. Canberra, Australia: Australian Bureau of Statistics (ABS), December 3, 2009, Data/statistics.

Plato & H. Davis, *Plato's Republic*. New York: Leon Amiel.

Price, J. 2000, *Philosophy Through the Ages*. Belmont, CA: Wadsworth Thompson Learning.

Puigvert, L. & R. Valls, 2005, "Dialogic Learning in Popular Education Movements in Spain," in J. Crowther, V. Galloway & I. Martin (eds.), *Popular Education: Engaging the Academy: International Perspectives*. Leicester, UK: National Institute of Adult Continuing Education (England and Wales) (NIACE).

Said, E. (1978), *Orientalism*. New York: Random House.

Schön, D. 1983, *The Reflective Practitioner: How Professionals Think in Action*. New York: Basic Books.

Schön, D. A. 1987, *Educating the Reflective Practitioner*. San Fransisco, CA: Jossey-Bass Higher Education Series, Jossey-Bass.

Silverman, D. 2001, *Interpreting Qualitative Data: Methods for Analysing Talk, Text, and Interaction*, 2nd edn. London; Thousand Oaks, CA: Sage Publications.

Soloman, N. 2003, *Changing Pedagogy: The New Learner-Worker*. Sydney: The Australian Centre for Organisational, Vocational and Adult Learning, University of Technology.

Stage, F. & K. Manning, 2003, *Research in the College Context, Approaches and Methods*. New York: Brunner-Routledge Publishers.

Stake, R. 1995, *The Art of Case Study Research*. Thousand Oaks, CA: Sage Publications,.

—— 2003, " 'Case Studies," in NK Denzin & YS Lincoln (eds), *Strategies of Qualitative Inquiry*, 2nd edn.Thousand Oaks, CA: Sage Publications.

—— 2006, *Multiple Case Study Analysis*. New York: The Guilford Press.

Thomas, H., R. Maddison, & Victoria. Dept. of Labour, 1986, *Things Past, Things to Come: IYY and Beyond*. Melbourne: Dept. of Labour.

Vygotskii, L. S. & M. Cole, 1978, *Mind in Society: The Development of Higher Psychological Processes*. Cambridge, MA: Harvard University Press.

Wadsworth, Y. 1997, *Do It Yourself Social Research*, 2nd ed. St. Leonards, NSW: Allen & Unwin.

Weeks, W., L. Hoatson, & J. Dixon, 2003, *Community Practices in Australia*. Frenchs Forest, NSW: Pearson Education.
Wenger, E. 1998, *Communities of Practice, Learning Meaning and Identity: Learning in Doing, Social Cognitive and Computational Perspectives*. New York: Cambridge University Press.
Whelan, J. 2002, *Education and Training for Effective Environmental Advocacy*. PhD thesis, Griffith University.
—— 2005a, "A Hard Road: Learning in Failed Social Action," in J. Crowther, V. Galloway & I. Martin (eds.), *Popular Education Enagaging the Academy— International Perspectives*. Leicester, UK: NIACE, pp. 157–68.
—— 2005b, Popular Education for the Environment: Building Interest in the Educational Dimension of Social Action, *Australian Journal of Environmental Education*, vol. 21, 117–28.
Williams, R. & J. Higgins, 2001, *The Raymond Williams Reader*. Malden, MA: Blackwell Publishers.
Williams, S. & G. Bendelow, 1998, *Lived Body : Sociological Themes, Embodied Issues*. London: Routledge, (http://w2.vu.edu.au/library/EBookSearch/files/EBL.pdf).

Websites

Bring David Hicks home, official website accessed August 11, 2008.
http://www.bringdavidhickshome.org/
Release Heather Osland Group, official website accessed August 11, 2008.
http://home.vicnet.net.au/~rhog/
Amnesty international briefing of the Van Nugyen case
http://action.amnesty.org.au/news/comments/261/ accessed August 12, 2008.
Same Same 25: The 25 Most Influential Gay and Lesbian Australians, 2008. http://www.samesame.com.au/25/2008/FelicityMarlowe, accessed November 2, 2009.

Index

accidental activist, 6
activism
  accidental, 117, 136–142, 201
  and environment, 3, 24, 29, 39, 40, 45, 49, 74, 148, 161, 176, 186, *see also* case studies: Tim Forcey; Walker, Cam
  human rights, 9, 28, 39, 58, 66, 78, 84, 93, 111, 131, 136
  non-violence, 96–98
activist
  pedagogy, 1–2, 37, 38–39, 163, 191, 219
  as researcher, 24–27

Beckett, David, 12, 18, 49–51, 182–183, 198–203
  and Morris, Gayle, 160–170
behaviourism, 7, 17, 19, 164, 170, 222
Bourdieu, Pierre, 11, 18, 31–32, 187, 194–198, 204–207, 220–221

case studies
  Catherine, 143–148
  Grace, 111, 153–159
  Hicks, Terry, 136–143
  Jorquera, Jorge, 60, 82–90
  Kerry, 60, 102–107
  Marlowe, Felicity, 59, 90–95
  Tim Forcey, 110, 148–159
  Walker, Cam, 58–59, 95–101

circumstantial activists, 2, 4, 10–15, 17–18, 27, 29, 62
  case studies, 135–161
  data, 109–135
communities of practice, 14, 16, 37, 50, 55, 186–207
critical pedagogy, 2, 13, 23–24, 42, 169–170, 175, 177, 209, 219

Darder, Antonia, 223

education, 1–8, 12–13, 37, 39, 42, 166–167, 169–178, 189, 197–198
  adult, 2, 5, 7–13, 37–54, 163–175, 182–188, 210–225
  popular education, 3, 10, 37–40, 47, 169, 189, 219, 223
  radical adult education, 5–10, 12, 16, 18, 37–46, 54, 164–165, 175, 209–213, 221
embodiment, 37, 55, 171, 178
  and learning, 51–52, 163–166
emotions, 131, 158
  and activism, 173–175
  and learning, 77–80, 131–132, 168, 174

Foley, Griff, 10–11, 29, 38, 40–42, 47, 49, 164–166, 220
Freire, Paulo, 39–40, 41, 164–165, 169, 175, 177–178, 182–184, 189, 195
  Legacy, 183, 198–203, 222–224

Hicks, Terry, 6, 10, 110, 114, 136–143
Hochschild, Arlie, 180, 186, 216
hooks, bell, 9, 177
human rights, 2–3, 28, 39, 58, 66, 78, 84, 93, 129, *see also* case studies: Catherine; Hicks, Terry; Jorquera, Jorge; Kerry; Marlowe, Felicity

Knowledge, 2, 12, 164–165, 189
  activists, 8, 10–12, 16–23, 40–44, 82, 134, 164, 192, 207
  autodidact, 187, 196–198
  embodied, 170, 221, 233
  junk category, 11, 18, 169–170
  objectivist, 194, 207
  postcolonial, 54
  practical, 29, 40, 51–52, 168–173, 175–177, 194–196, 220–222

Lave, Jean, 48–50, 55, 187–196, 198–201, 204, 207, 215, 221
learning
  apprenticeship, 199
  edge, 132, 135, 159, 216, 218
  identity, 14, 33, 35, 53, 55, 57, 134, 136, 205, 209, 210, 212
  on the job, 12, 32, 48, 106, 117, 186, 200
  social action, 7, 37–54, 120, 164–165, 175, 201, 204–205, 209
  stages and phases, 13, 57, 62, 112, 211–212
  transformative, 43–45, 177, 202
life-long activists, 12–17, 35, 179–180, 192, 205–206, 210–217
  case studies, 82–108
  data, 57–82
  definition, 2, 6

Marx, Karl, 223–224
Marxist schools, 46–47
Merleau-Ponty, 51–52, 164, 167–186, 189, 193–194, 214–215, 222
Methodology, 21–36

phenomenology, 21, 23, 167, 222

rationalism, 16, 17, 52, 165–167, 173, 175, 195, 213, 220–222
religion, 14, 16, 80, 113, 133, 144, 185, 211, *see also* social justice; spirituality
research
  case study, 21–36
  insider/outsider, 24–25
  method, 21–22
  methodology, 21–36
  objectivist, 24
  qualitative, 21–36
  questions, 13–15, 30, 33

Schon, Donald, 18, 170, 182, 215
social justice, 1–3, 24, 28, 62, 80–81, 133–134, 185, 211–212, *see also* religion; spirituality
social learning, 7, 14, 16, 32, 46–50, 69, 187–207
social movements, 3–19, 28–30, 39, 46, 52, 167–169, 175–180, 190, 195, 204, 207
  learning, 5, 11, 28–29, 210
spirituality, 18, 80, 133, 185, 212, *see also* religion; social justice
student politics, 6, 9, 10, 12, 16, 35, 57–61, 64–65, 192, 217

Wenger, Etienne, 203–207, 215, 221

GPSR Compliance
The European Union's (EU) General Product Safety Regulation (GPSR) is a set of rules that requires consumer products to be safe and our obligations to ensure this.

If you have any concerns about our products, you can contact us on

ProductSafety@springernature.com

In case Publisher is established outside the EU, the EU authorized representative is:

Springer Nature Customer Service Center GmbH
Europaplatz 3
69115 Heidelberg, Germany